GABRIEL KOLKO received his B.A. from Kent State University, M.S. from the University of Wisconsin, and Ph.D. from Harvard. From 1964 to 1968 he was Associate Professor of History at the University of Pennsylvania, and since 1968 he has been Professor of History at the State University of New York at Buffalo. His other publications include *Wealth and Power in America* (1962); *The Triumph of Conservatism, 1900-1916* (1963); and *The Politics of War, 1943-45* (1968).

RAILROADS
AND REGULATION
1877-1916

Railroads
and Regulation

1877-1916

By

GABRIEL KOLKO

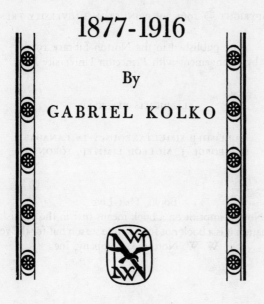

The Norton Library
W · W · NORTON & COMPANY · INC ·
NEW YORK

Books That Live
The Norton imprint on a book means that in the publisher's
estimation it is a book not for a single season but for the years.
W. W. Norton & Company, Inc.

SBN 393 00531 3

ACKNOWLEDGMENTS

THIS study was awarded the Transportation History Prize of the Mississippi Valley Historical Association, which has also helped to support its publication. I am indebted to Raymond C. Miller and the members of the prize committee of the M.V.H.A. for their decision, and to Frank Freidel for his later aid and advice on the details of publication.

An earlier draft of the manuscript was submitted as my doctoral thesis to the History Department of Harvard University, and I benefited from the critical advice and insights of Frank Freidel and Arthur M. Schlesinger, Jr., advisers and readers, and Oscar Handlin. I am most grateful for the indispensable assistance given by members of the staffs of the National Archives, the Manuscript Division, Library of Congress, the Harvard University Libraries, the West Virginia University Library, and the Bureau of Railway Economics Library, Washington, D.C. I especially appreciate the fact that the Interstate Commerce Commission opened its hitherto closed vaults and archives.

It goes without saying that I assume all responsibility for the interpretation of materials in the possession of these libraries and the I.C.C., and that neither the Interstate Commerce Commission, the Mississippi Valley Historical Association, nor my advisers necessarily agree or disagree with the thesis of this book, much less assume responsibility for possible errors of judgment or fact.

I conceived of this volume as part of a larger study of the relationship of the state to the American economy during the crucial period of industrial change and development at the end of the 19th and beginning of the 20th centuries; but it was written to stand alone, and can be read as such. The theoretical generalizations in

ACKNOWLEDGMENTS

my *The Triumph of Conservatism: A Reinterpretation of American History, 1900-1916* (New York, 1963), are largely applicable to the railroad experience as well as to the broader economic and political events described in that volume. In this work I have deliberately restricted certain theoretical analyses, in part to avoid redundancy, but also because the railroad experience alone did not necessarily justify more extensive conclusions relevant to the substantially longer period of 1877-1916.

GABRIEL KOLKO

CONTENTS

CONTENTS

INTRODUCTION

FROM the end of the Civil War until the beginning of
the First World War, the railroad was a central, if not
the major, element in the political, economic, and social
development of the United States. In addition, the railroads have captured the imagination of American historians. The "Robber Barons," for the most part,
consisted of railroad speculators such as Jim Fisk, Jay
Gould, and Dan Drew. The Compromise of 1877, ending the political divisions created by the Civil War,
was due to the intrigues of railroad men in pursuit of
government aid. Until the rise of big business in steel,
agricultural machinery, and oil, the epic villains in
American history in the period from 1870 to 1900
were, John D. Rockefeller excepted, railroad men.

The traditional interpretation has seen the epic
struggles for a resurgent democracy as primarily, and
at times exclusively, struggles against the overwhelming
economic power of the railroads and their political hire-
lings. The Granger Revolt, the Great Strike of 1877,
and the major labor conflicts of the period, and in large
measure Populism, are portrayed as part of a larger
effort to obtain justice from the rulers of the railroads.
The goal of this effort, historians commonly supposed,
was regulation primarily by the federal government. In
their interpretation of the federal regulation of the railroads until 1916, the writers of specialized as well as
general history have traditionally assumed that the
villainous railroads, with very few exceptions, strongly
and consistently opposed the extension of federal control over their industry. "The entire period of almost two
decades," I. L. Sharfman has concluded, "discloses a
basic struggle for supremacy between the government
and the railroads. . . ."[1]

[1] I. L. Sharfman, *The Interstate Commerce Commission* (New
York, 1931-1937), I, 39.

Historians, as a result of their comprehensive assumption about the general nature of federal regulation and Progessivism, naturally assumed the railroads opposed federal regulation. They have regarded the federal government in the Progressive Era as a neutral, impartial force attempting, in a period of rising social consciousness, to redirect the balance of economic power on behalf of the public and to eliminate the evils accompanying rapid industrial development. And, based on such an analysis, the prevalent history of the federal regulation of railroads has reinforced the larger view of the nature of Progressivism as a general movement, and has become its single most important verification. Such a view, in this writer's opinion, orients the historian toward the theory that federal regulation and Progressivism were "a counterpoise to the power of private business" and "the complaint of the unorganized against the consequences of organization."[2]

The suggestion that the railroads opposed federal regulation has had important consequences for the general theory of Progressivism from the era of Theodore Roosevelt until the beginning of the First World War. It has encouraged a too facile polarization of political, economic, and social forces—the railroads allegedly opposed federal regulation, and it seemed only natural that other industries, growing to power and maturity in this period, also opposed efforts to extend federal regulation over them as well. This polarization, I believe, has led to serious neglect of the origin and purpose of federal regulation as a whole, and has inspired the notion that advocates of federal regulation were progressive in the generic as well as the political sense—progressive in their fundamental desire to redress

[2] Richard Hofstadter, *The Age of Reform: From Bryan to F. D. R.* (New York, 1955), pp. 214, 231.

the balance of economic, social, and political power in favor of the average citizen.

In the following pages I shall attempt critically to reexamine the relation of the railroads to federal regulation and the assumption that the national government consciously or in fact always acted in a manner that the majority of important railroad men considered fundamentally inimical to their interests. Rather, I will suggest that the intervention of the federal government not only failed to damage the interests of the railroads, but was positively welcomed by them since the railroads never really had the power over the economy, and their own industry, often ascribed to them. Indeed, the railroads, not the farmers and shippers, were the most important single advocates of federal regulation from 1877 to 1916. Even when they frequently disagreed with the details of specific legislation, they always supported the principle of federal regulation as such. And as the period advances, this commitment to regulation grew ever stronger.

From the 1870's until the end of the century American railroad history moved in a crude cycle of voluntary or, alternately, political attempts to solve economic problems. Contrary to the common view, railroad freight rates, taken as a whole, declined almost continuously over the period, and although the consolidation of railroads proceeded apace, this phenomenon never affected the long-term decline of rates or the ultimately competitive nature of much of the industry.[3] In their desire to establish stability and control over rates and competition, the railroad executives often resorted to voluntary, cooperative efforts involving rate agreements and the division of traffic. When these efforts failed, as they

[3] An excellent source of detailed rate data supporting this conclusion is Interstate Commerce Commission, *Railways in the United States in 1902: A Forty-Year Review of Changes in Freight Tariffs* (Washington, 1903), *passim*.

inevitably did, the railroad men turned to political solutions to rationalize their increasingly chaotic industry. They advocated measures designed to bring under control those railroads within their own ranks that refused to conform to voluntary compacts. When political measures failed or proved inadequate, the railroads returned to voluntary efforts, mergers and the absorption of competitors as well as pooling agreements, to eliminate internecine competition. At various times the railroads attempted to implement both the voluntary and political solutions simultaneously, but until the end of the century they were unable to solve their basic problems by either means. However, from the beginning of the 20th century until at least the initiation of World War I, the railroad industry resorted primarily to political alternatives, and gave up the abortive efforts to put its own house in order by relying on voluntary cooperation. Unless the history of the national regulation of the railroads is approached in the context of the broader efforts of the railroads to attain stability and solve their problems by whatever means seemed most opportune, the history of railroad regulation will fall into one or another simple, and false, category.

In formulating a program designed to cope with the unpredictable threat of control by the various states, and to protect themselves from their competitors or large shippers demanding expensive rebates, most railroad men approached the issue of regulation with purely opportunistic motives. The doctrine of laissez-faire or the conservative interpretation of the social implications of Darwinism inhibited very few practical executives; most ignored intellectual issues and concentrated on meeting immediate problems in the most expeditious manner possible. Insofar as railroad men did think about the larger theoretical implications of centralized federal regulation, they rejected the validity and relevance of the Darwinian analogies and the entire notion of laissez faire. Consciously or operationally, most railroad leaders increasingly relied on a Hamiltonian conception of the national government. They saw in certain forms of federal regulation of railroads the solution to their many economic problems as well as the redirection of public reform sentiments toward safer outlets. If their motives were usually opportunistic, the functional consequences of their actions were identical to those of a growing number of railroad leaders who explicitly rejected the laissez-faire assumptions of contemporary American conservatism by suggesting that their economic interests, and genuine conservatism, would be served best by certain types of federal regulation. By 1914, in common with most Americans, the railroads overwhelmingly supported the basic premises of what is known as "Progressivism."

It is not my contention, of course, that railroad leaders were the only group favoring the federal regulation of transportation. The mere fact that they did not always get their specific legislative demands indicates that not only were the railroads divided among themselves as to precisely what legislative measures they wanted passed, but that they faced opposition on many points from shipping groups who had their own goals and demands. Railroad interests differed from line to line, and the disagreements among the railroads were frequently as strong as the disagreements between the bulk of the railroads and many shippers. The crucial point is that the railroads, for the most part, consistently accepted the basic premises of federal regulation since only through the positive intervention of the national political structure could the destabilizing, costly effects of cutthroat competition, predatory speculators, and greedy shippers be overcome. Moreover, the railroads were a much more constant force for federal regulation than the shippers, and the deeper divisions within the ranks of shippers often meant that their agitation for regulation contributed to the interests of the railroads. Legislative proposals, to be successful, usually needed the support of both the railroads and important shipping groups, and throughout the period from 1877 to 1916 neither could obtain legislation without the support of the other for some general form of legislation.

Virtually all histories of railroad regulation have focused on the views and actions of politicians, farmers, or shippers. And while these groups played a crucial part, and I discuss them in detail in the following pages, the role of the railroads and the railroad men in the movement for federal regulation has largely been ignored, beyond the automatic assumption that they naturally opposed regulation. Such a perspective, in this writer's opinion, is like ignoring the role of the Confederates in the Battle of Gettysburg. What were the railroad journals writing while their industry was being legislated in certain directions? What were the problems of the railroad industry and their relevance to the regulatory movement? What were railroad leaders saying, writing, and doing? What did the federal regulatory mechanism consist of, what was its role in the period, and what interaction existed between the Interstate Commerce Commission and the railroads?

In an attempt to answer these and related questions, I shall lean heavily on entirely new materials, such as the hitherto unexploited railroad journals, the speeches and letters of railroad leaders, and the general files of the Interstate Commerce Commission until 1900. If the traditional view of the federal regulatory process and the nature of Progressivism is found to be inadequate in the light of such sources, our conventional understanding of the period as a whole can also be submitted to a critical review. The federal regulation of the railroads, after all, is the first example of national Progressivism, and possibly its most important single illustration throughout the period of 1877 to 1916.

CHAPTER I

IN QUEST OF STABILITY

1877-1883

THE railroad industry throughout the 1870's was intensely competitive and most railroads tried ceaselessly to bring about conditions of greater stability. The instability was caused not only by the fact that railroad mileage increased by 50 per cent from 1870 to 1876— and much more slowly until 1880—but by the inherently competitive nature of the industry in most parts of the nation. Shippers in St. Louis and Atlanta, to illustrate the extreme, had the option of twenty competitive routes between the two cities, ranging in distance from 526 to 1,855 miles. Virtually any shipper in a coastal city might send his goods westward by any number of routes merely by transporting them by water to a city with more favorable railroad rates.[1] In light of the major shipper's power to choose alternate routes for his goods, the railroads could maintain rates only by negotiating workable rate agreements with potential competitors. Their failure is reflected in the consistent decline in freight revenue per ton mile throughout this period, from 1.88 cents in 1870, to 1.22 cents in 1880, 0.94 cents in 1890, and 0.73 cents in 1900.[2] Under these circumstances, the bankruptcies which characterized most major railroads

[1] For railroad mileage, see U.S. Bureau of the Census, *Historical Statistics of the United States, Colonial Times to 1957* (Washington, 1960), pp. 427, 429; for competitive routes, see U.S. Industrial Commission, *Final Report*, House Doc. No. 380, 57th Cong., 2d Sess. (Washington, 1902), XIX, 356.

[2] Industrial Commission, *Report*, XIX, 280; *Historical Statistics of the U.S.*, pp. 428, 431.

at one point or another in their careers are entirely explicable. Only the growth of the total volume of freight prevented an even greater number of insolvencies.

In this context of declining income, fixed costs, growing competition, and imminent bankruptcy, the leaders of American railroads naturally attempted to stop the secret rebates, rate cutting, and over-expansion that threatened them all. The outcome was a continuous effort, from 1874 on, voluntarily and cooperatively to maintain rates, preserve existing market divisions, and end internecine competition by use of the pool.

Numerous pools were organized throughout the period —there were at least eight in operation in 1879 alone— but with only one exception they all rapidly failed.[3] Although there are records of rate agreements as far back as 1856, the first genuine pool was organized in 1870, to stabilize rates in the Iowa area and exclude new competitors, by the Rock Island Railroad, the Chicago and Northwestern, the Michigan Central, the Chicago, Burlington and Quincy, plus several smaller lines. The result was a most uneasy alliance with constant infractions and rate cutting, especially by aggressive officers. In 1872, outside shorter lines, and in 1873 the Union Pacific, began attacking the pool's domain and destroyed it by 1874—although it revived and lingered on as a formal structure until 1885.[4]

The first serious pooling effort in the East came in August 1874, when William H. Vanderbilt of the New York Central took the initiative to end the decline of rates that followed in the wake of the Depression of

[3] U.S. Treasury Department, *Report on the Internal Commerce of the United States, December 1, 1879* (Washington, 1879), pp. 164-183.

[4] Julius Grodinsky, *The Iowa Pool: A Study in Railroad Competition, 1870-84* (Chicago, 1950), is the definitive work on the topic. Also see Grodinsky, *Transcontinental Railway Strategy, 1869-1893* (Philadelphia, 1962), chap. IV.

1873. He invited the major lines east of St. Louis to send representatives to his home at Saratoga—the first of many similar meetings at that place—to establish rate agreements and two regional commissions to enforce them. The New York Central, Erie, and Pennsylvania lines were represented, but the Baltimore & Ohio, under the presidency of John W. Garrett, decided to remain aloof. Despite Vanderbilt's attempt to get him to join, Garrett stayed outside the pool in the hope of obtaining a larger share of freight traffic. The pool lasted about six months, when rebates and violations by freight and ticket agents forced the railroads to abandon it. Intense rate wars followed, especially between the Pennsylvania and the B. & O., and were to persist for years.[5]

The second major pool effort came in the South in 1875, where the large number of small lines and the constant competition of river and ocean-going boats made the possibility of bankrupting competition ever-present. The Southern pool was based not merely on rate agreements, but on an informal division of traffic arranged in late 1873. Under the initiative of Albert Fink, then vice-president of the Louisville and Nashville Railroad and the nation's chief advocate and director of the pool structure until 1886, a number of Southern lines created a formal organization at a series of meetings in Atlanta in late 1875. Thirty-two lines joined the agreement, each with one vote; violations were to be penalized by expulsion. The pool appointed Fink general commissioner of the agreement, and members could appeal his decisions to a special board of three arbitrators. Rates and a division of markets were bind-

[5] "The Saratoga Agreement," *Railroad Gazette*, VI (August 15, 1874), 317; Chauncey M. Depew, *My Memories of Eighty Years* (New York, 1922), pp. 231-234; statement of Isaac H. Sturgeon in U.S. Senate, Select Committee on Interstate Commerce, *Report*, Sen. Report No. 46, 49th Cong., 1st Sess., January 18, 1886 (Washington, 1886), p. 161.

ing on all members; they were revised at the end of each year. The Southern Railway & Steamship Association was the sole pool to operate successfully throughout 1876-1886, if only because Southern railways were too weak and fragmented to survive extensive rate warfare.[6]

In September 1876, the Southwestern Railway Association was formed by seven major lines. "Notwithstanding it is to the immediate interest of a road when it becomes party to a pool to adhere strictly to the agreement, such is the weakness of human nature, under the blandishments of shippers, that few are the number who firmly resist," concluded J. W. Midgley, the commissioner of the Association. "This has been the mortifying experience of all compacts, thus compelling the admission that *no* means have yet been devised whereby an *absolute maintenance* of established rates can be assured."[7] After a brief and precarious history, the pool collapsed in early 1878.

During March through May of 1877, the major Eastern trunk lines reconvened after three years of furious competition to make another major effort at forming a pool. The meetings were an almost immediate failure insofar as the maintenance of rates on eastbound traffic was concerned, and the lines terminated the agreement after three or four months. Violations by the Grand Trunk Line of Canada soon left the entire agreement in shambles. Given the failure of voluntary pools to create some semblance of reason and stability in the railroad system, despite successive attempts too numerous to

6 Details of the agreement are found in Southern Railway and Steamship Association, *Agreement and Rules Adopted in Convention at Atlanta, Ga.* (Atlanta, 1875); Southern Railway and Steamship Association, *Proceedings of the Convention* (Atlanta, 1875-1876), I. The best secondary account is Henry Hudson, "The Southern Railway & Steamship Association," *Quarterly Journal of Economics*, V (October, 1890), 70-94, who concluded that the pool was successful.

7 In Senate Select Committee on Interstate Commerce, *Report*, (1886), p. 230.

itemize here, railroad men then turned to the government for possible salvation.

The one item that the railroads managed to agree upon, however, was an understanding that in June and July 1877 the wages of railroad workers would be cut by 10 per cent. The result was the most important and extensive strike in American history, certainly until 1877 and probably since that time as well, and a frightened period of reflection by men of wealth on the problem of their economic security in a democracy.[8]

The Great Strike of June and July 1877, not surprisingly, was quite unexpected by railroad leaders and conventional opinion makers after four years of the deepest depression in American history and extensive wage cuts. The strike involved all of the major roads east of St. Louis, and spread to most of the major cities. It "seemed to threaten the chief strongholds of society and came like a thunderbolt out of a clear sky, startling us rudely," wrote banker-turned-historian James Ford Rhodes in 1909.[9] His widely shared shock over the many riots and scores of deaths was natural—after all, it had never happened before. For the Great Strike focused attention on the new problems of an economy susceptible to intensive depressions, and especially on the growth of a working class capable of subverting and destroying by political, or even more direct means, the existing power structure.

During this first industrial conflict in the United States the presumably democratic commitments of the dominant economic classes were strained to the breaking

[8] For the wage cut, see the testimony of Thomas Scott in Pennsylvania Senate and House of Representatives, *Report of the Committee Appointed to Investigate the Railroad Riots of July, 1877*, May 23, 1878 (Harrisburg, 1878), pp. 928-929. See also *Railway World*, XXI (October, 6, 1877), 950-951; Robert V. Bruce, *1877: Year of Violence* (Indianapolis, 1959), pp. 40ff.

[9] James Ford Rhodes, *History of the United States, 1850-1896* (New York, 1920), p. 46.

point. Out of the crisis came a working view of the role of the state in industrial society which was consistently applied during the next three decades: if for some reason the power of various key business interests was endangered, even for causes of their own making, the state was to intervene to preserve their dominant position. This principle, more than a logical extension of the older tenet of exploiting the state for capital accumulation or profitable favors, was almost consistently applied by big business to labor relations and internal business instability from the late 1870's. The pretense that the state was a neutral arbiter between conflicting segments of the population was restricted to theory. The year 1877 is the first in which major American anti-democratic ideologies relevant to an industrial society are articulated. This reconsideration centered on the problem of labor and the franchise, the role of the recent European immigrant, and the militia as a means of social control.

In 1877, Edwin L. Godkin was fairly representative in shifting his concern from the manners of Jay Gould to the "universal suffrage [which gives] an air of menace to many of the things civilized men hold most dear."[10] Another writer, commenting in the *International Review*, declared, "That form of government will wither and die like a girdled tree if the thousands who pay taxes get no protection from the millions who govern."[11] Democracy no longer seemed to hold out that inspiring promise of human and social progress which stirred the imaginations of pre-Civil War orators. "For a long series of years," remarked the *New York Times*, "the better class of our urban population have seen with comparative indifference the control over their affairs pass into the

[10] *The Nation*, XXV (August 2, 1877), 68.
[11] W. M. Grosvenor, "The Communist and the Railway," *The International Review*, IV (September, 1877), 586.

hands of the nominees of the roughs—the nominees of the corner groggeries."[12]

Under these circumstances spokesmen for the upper class applauded the general mobilization of the National Guard for the strike and the first major use of federal troops in a labor dispute, and proposed their continued use in the event of future economic crises. "It is a pity," the *New York Tribune* declared charitably, "that the very first resistance to law was not met by the shooting of every rioter within range of a musket ball."[13] The future course of action was outlined by *Harper's Weekly*: "The time has come in this country when there must be the most ample and ready supply of the organized force necessary to maintain order at all costs."[14]

The National Guard had declined to little more than a fancy-dress parading society after the Civil War. During the strike they proved to be worse than useless in Pennsylvania, where many troops deserted to the strikers, and generally ineffective elsewhere. Immediately after the strike the Guard was reorganized in most states, its officer corps chosen by criteria related to military functions, discipline sharply increased, and street fighting and riot control taught. State appropriations increased sharply, and most Northern cities constructed new armories, usually with public funds, but when the 7th Regiment of New York lacked funds for its new armory, the Vanderbilts, Astors, Lenox', Morgans, and other leading financial figures provided the cash. "The future historian of the National Guard will write of A. D. 1877," commented *The National Guardsman*, " 'In this year began the Era of Appreciation.' "[15]

[12] *New York Times*, July 29, 1877.
[13] *New York Tribune*, July 24, 1877.
[14] *Harper's Weekly*, XXI (August 11, 1877), 618.
[15] *National Guardsman*, I (October 1, 1877), 42, 70.

Railroad spokesmen immediately called for protection by the national government. "A departure must now take place," editorialized the *Railway World* in the midst of the conflict. "The lines of railway[s] are no longer to be considered merely state organizations, and under state control, but national in their character . . . . the Government must be placed, by law, in such a position as to protect, when necessary, the railways, or take control of them, without the interposition of state authority."[16] General federal supervision of the railroads was receiving greater consideration in railroad circles because of the strike, the *Railway World* noted a few weeks later.[17] And in August, John A. Wright, a long-time director of the Pennsylvania Railroad, called for the protection of the federal government against strikers, Granger states, and railroad speculators driving the roads to bankruptcy with their cutthroat rate policies. "The General Government should assume the direct protection of the property of the railways," including not merely control over stocks and bonds or federal charters, but the right to fix rates for various classes of service, to be maintained "under penalty of criminal prosecution."[18] The national government, Wright noted, was far less likely than the states to respond to the people.

In September, Thomas A. Scott, president of the Pennsylvania Railroad, added his weight to the demand for federal intervention by calling for a 75,000-man militia for labor disputes. ". . . with the increasing population of our large cities and business centres . . . the late troubles may be but the prelude to other manifestations of mob violence. . . ."[19] Congress must "take all neces-

16 *Railway World*, XXI (July 28, 1877), 698.
17 *Ibid.*, XXI (August 11, 1877), 747-748.
18 John A. Wright, "Control of Railways by the General Government," *ibid.*, XXI (August 17, 1877), 771-775.
19 Thomas A. Scott, "The Recent Strikes," *North American Review*, CXXV (September, 1877), 357.

sary measures to secure protection to life and property.
. . ."[20] In late September, *The Nation* complained that
railroad men were advocating federal intervention in
every labor dispute.[21]

A laissez-faire attitude on the part of railroads at this
time would have been incongruous. After all, the federal and state governments had intervened during their
ordeal in their behalf and for their protection. Even more
important, the railroads during the 1870's were the products, in large measure, of the financial efforts of the state
and federal governments—about $350 million in state
and federal funds, plus many millions of acres in land-
grants, were pumped into the canal and railroad system
until 1873.[22] And despite this massive government investment, the extent of governmental management within
the various railroads was very slight indeed—railroads
found they could work with the government largely on
their own terms, and to their own profit.[23] More likely
than not, the average railroad president in the 1870's
had a background in politics—over half held some political job before or during their careers as railroad presidents.[24] Surely the ogre of government intervention could
not have appeared too formidable to men with important
political connections themselves and familiar with the
intricacies and possibilities of politics.

The rise of state commissions may have prejudiced
some railroad men against regulation, but more often

20 *Ibid.*, 361.

21 *The Nation*, xxv (September 27, 1877), 193. Evidence supports it; see *Railway World*, xxi (October 13, 1877), 965-966, for
example.

22 Carter Goodrich, *Government Promotion of American Canals
and Railroads, 1800-1890* (New York, 1960), pp. 268-271.

23 *Ib'd.*, p. 290 discusses this problem.

24 Ruth Crandall, "American Railroad Presidents in the 1870's:
Their Backgrounds and Careers," *Explorations in Entrepreneurial
History*, ii (July 15, 1950), 295. Of fifty-three presidents studied,
twenty-eight held political jobs before or during their presidency,
fourteen after—for a total of eighty-five different posts at any time.

than not, as we shall see, these agencies converted them to a belief in federal as opposed to state regulation. State commissions, which existed in one form or another in New England from 1839, were not so ominous as has been commonly supposed—and the railroad leaders undoubtedly appreciated this fact. The New England commissions, for the most part, protected the railroads from the farmers. The Massachusetts commission was reconstituted in 1869 with the power to recommend rates to the Legislature, but the chief architect of the Massachusetts commission, Charles Francis Adams, Jr., surely did not win the antipathy of railroad men—he quickly became a pool arbitrator and ultimately the president of the Union Pacific.[25] The first commission with mandatory rate powers was established in Illinois in 1873, and by 1887, although all but twenty states had commissions, only eight states assigned rate-making powers to their regulatory bodies. But the railroads in these Midwestern "Grange" states discovered the existence of these commissions did not prevent the railroads from being as profitable as those in unregulated states. Significantly, the National Grange soon turned against commissions as the means of regulating railroads.[26] Chaun-

[25] See Edward Chase Kirkland, *Men, Cities, and Transportation: A Study in New England History, 1820-1900* (Cambridge, 1948), II, 232-263, for an excellent history of New England commissions.

[26] John E. Benton, "The State Commissions and the Interstate Commerce Commission," in Interstate Commerce Commission, *Exercises Commemorating the Fifty Years' Service of the Interstate Commerce Commission* (Washington, 1937), pp. 22-36; Solon Justis Buck, *The Granger Movement, 1870-1880* (Cambridge, 1913), pp. 232ff.; Lee Benson, *Merchants, Farmers, and Railroads: Railroad Regulation and New York Politics, 1850-1887* (Cambridge, 1955), p. 201. George H. Miller, "Origins of the Iowa Granger Law," *Mississippi Valley Historical Review*, XL (March, 1954), 657-680; and Benson, *Merchants, Farmers, and Railroads*, pp. 59-61, both illustrate the extent of merchant control of state regulatory movements. Miller suggests that the movement for regulation to prevent discrimination between locations preceded the Granger organization by many years, and was based on the desire of the eastern Iowa grain merchants to hold on to their share of the grain market against the more advantageously placed St. Louis and Chicago merchants.

cey M. Depew, the attorney for the New York Central, after opposing commissions for a few years, admitted that he "became convinced of their necessity . . . for the protection of both the public and the railroads. . . ."[27] And he converted William H. Vanderbilt to this view as well.

In 1877, the main danger posed to the railroad was not from state and federal governments that had provided cash in time of need and troops in time of labor conflicts, but from cutthroat competition, rate wars, and the manipulators of stocks.

But even the Great Strike did not produce sufficient political intervention to bring about stability. The railroads therefore embarked on another effort at self-regulation.

In July 1877, the major Eastern trunk lines met again as the Joint Executive Committee, with Fink as its head, to reconstitute a pooling agreement, hoping for greater effectiveness than had resulted from earlier agreements. By September, it was discovered that the Grand Trunk Line of Canada and the Wabash Railroad were cutting rates, especially on livestock. A minimum of one meeting a month to perfect the organization, and end weaknesses in cotton and grain rates, failed to establish the desired stability.[28] In February 1878, the pool agreed to blacklist all employees secretly granting rebates, but failed to create a contract pool necessary to control the actual rebating going on. By March 1878, the Joint Executive Committee's regulation of the division of freight shipped via Detroit and Milwaukee collapsed because of disagreements among smaller lines, and Toledo,

[27] Depew, *Memories of Eighty Years*, pp. 241-242.
[28] For the roads east of the Mississippi, see Joint Executive Committee, *Proceedings*, September 27, 1877, October 4-6, 1877, November 21, 1877, December 13, 1877 (New York, 1878-1880); *Railway World*, XXI (October 6, 1877), 950-951.

Peoria, Cincinnati, Louisville, Columbus, and other cities soon were outside the pool agreement. In June, N. Guilford, one of the Committee's commissioners, resigned because the pool's plan for "maintaining remunerative freight rates . . . had utterly failed to accomplish that end."[29]

The railroads, however, were not quite ready to throw all caution to the winds, and continued talking as they cut their rates and embarked on vast expansion programs. Most of their time was spent discussing violations, adjusting rates, and reapportioning tonnage quotas. In December 1878, in an effort to end rebates distributed by freight agents, presumably without the knowledge of their superiors, through-rates for the eastern and western branches of the roads were established, Pittsburgh to the Mississippi marking the western territory. The whole structure was brought under the directorship of Fink, and a number of irate lines cajoled back into the agreement.[30]

The railroads, however, failed to take the pool seriously and again prepared for warfare. In 1878 and 1880, the major trunk lines began disputing the existing division of eastbound freight from Chicago. Charges of rate cutting, illegal freight classifications—a favorite

[29] Joint Executive Committee, *Proceedings*, June 11, 1878, p. 5, also see February 6, March 7, March 26, 1878; *Railway World*, XXII (June 15, 1878), 579. D. T. Gilchrist, "Albert Fink and the Pooling System," *Business History Review*, XXXIV (Spring, 1960), 41, maintains that the new pool was a success until mid-1880. The Joint Executive Committee, sometimes called the "Trunk Line Association" east of Pittsburgh, never attained its goal of ending rebating and establishing reasonable market divisions. Only its degree of failure varied.

[30] Joint Executive Committee, *Proceedings*, August 20-24, September 5-6, September 24, October 10-11, November 8-9, December 18-19, 1878 (New York, 1878-1880). See also *Railway World*, XXII (August 24, November 30, December 14, 1878), 813-814, 1153, 1194-1195. At the same time, independent efforts to build pools in the far West were going on. See *Railway World*, XXII (June 8, 1878), 555-556.

form of rebating—and unfair divisions continued. By September 1880, Fink was pleading with the railroads that *"the good faith of the members of this committee is the only guarantee for the continuance and permanency of this organization."*[31] But the good faith of the railroads was insufficient, for in 1879, with the return of prosperity, they embarked on a massive road-building program. Mileage increased from 105,000 miles in 1879 to 141,000 miles in 1882, with no corresponding increase in the volume of business. It was inevitable that existing pool divisions would collapse.

In 1881, as a result of pressure from New York merchants, the New York Central initiated an unprecedentedly severe rate war in the East. The railroad and the merchants correctly claimed that lower rates to Baltimore and Philadelphia were diverting to those cities much of New York's usual traffic.[32] In March 1881, the Joint Executive Committee decided to cut all its rates to the lowest then prevailing, in order to meet the competition. Between July and October 1881, freight rates fell 50 per cent in the East, and to a nearly equivalent degree in the West.[33] The Wabash Railroad and the New England railroads were dangerously weakened.

By January 1882, the Eastern lines were ready to appoint an independent commission to determine the fairness of the existing rate differentials to the major Atlantic ports. Its report, which decided on the pre-rate-war status quo so unsatisfactory to New York, left mat-

[31] *Proceedings of the Joint Executive Committee*, September 16, 1880 (New York, 1880), p. 196. Italics in the original. Also see *Argument Regarding the Division of East Bound Freight from Chicago between the Terminal Roads, Submitted to the Board of Arbitration, August, 1879* (New York, 1879); *Railway World*, XXIV, (September 11, 1880), 875.

[32] Depew, *Memories of Eighty Years*, pp. 240-241.

[33] Joseph Nimmo, Jr., *The Railroad Problem* [reprinted from U.S. Treasury, *Annual Report on the Internal Commerce of the United States*, October, 1881] (Washington, 1881), pp. 22-24.

ters seething. The Joint Executive Committee, after having given up meetings since August of 1881, decided to try to reconstitute the organization in March 1882. For a time competition continued merely at the normal rather than the disastrous level, with rate cutting of the more casual sort being reported regularly for adjustments. But by the end of the year more than usual signs of weaknesses in rates began appearing. The brief respite was to end.[34]

In 1881, Jay Gould began acquiring control over the Wabash and developing the West Shore Line to compete with the New York Central. In early 1883, the two lines embarked on a two-year rate war that was to drag in the entire Eastern railroad system. By this time the Joint Executive Committee was merely an empty piety without real power or meaning. Fink warned the railroad men that they would lose money by their policies—which they very well realized—but he was unable to obtain their cooperation.[35] There were too many parties, too many potential areas of friction, for successful control to come via voluntary agreements.

Businessmen, Grangers, and Regulation

The movement for federal regulation of the railroad system was not, in any strict sense, deliberately initiated by the railroads. The dominant theorists on the origin of regulation claimed, as in the case of Solon J. Buck, that it was the agitation of the Grangers that led to the creation of the Interstate Commerce Commission in 1887, or, as Ida M. Tarbell suggested, the activities of

[34] *Report of Messrs. Thurman, Washburne & Cooley, Constituting an Advisory Commission on Differential Rates by Railroads* (New York, 1882), *passim;* Joint Executive Committee, *Proceedings and Circulars, 1882* (New York, 1882), *passim.*

[35] Joint Executive Committee, *Proceedings and Circulars, 1883* (New York, 1883-1884), *passim;* Joint Executive Committee, Passenger Department, *Proceedings,* June 12-14, 1883 (New York, 1883), pp. 58-78.

the independent Pennsylvania oil producers. These time-honored theses were not challenged until 1955, when Lee Benson proposed "that New York merchants constituted the single most important group behind the passage of the Interstate Commerce Act," although he concedes some importance to the Grangers and, more reservedly, the oilmen.[36] Benson, more significantly, suggested that many railroad men were attracted by federal regulation as a means of establishing stability within the industry. While all of these theories have varying degrees of merit, the only fruitful approach to the problem that has not yet been seriously explored is the role of the railroads. It is here that something new can be learned.

The precise authorship of the first significant federal railroad regulatory bill is not in doubt, but the motives behind it have been ignored too long. In early 1876, the independent oil producers of Pennsylvania convinced Representative James H. Hopkins of Pittsburgh to introduce a bill (H.R. 2725) in the House of Representatives forbidding rebates and rate discrimination, and to arrange a House investigation of the problem. The bill, which provided for enforcement by the courts rather than by a commission, was apparently written by the attorney for the Philadelphia and Reading Railroad, which was motivated by a dislike of certain of Standard's rate agreements with its competitors. The bill died in Committee and the investigation passed unnoticed for the most part. In November 1877, the Pennsylvania producers organized the Petroleum Producers' Union, and appointed E. G. Patterson to arrange for another bill to be presented to the House. George B. Hibbard, the Union's lawyer, drafted a bill similar in content and phraseology

[36] Benson, *Merchants, Farmers, and Railroads*, p. 212; Buck, *The Granger Movement*, chap. VI; Ida M. Tarbell, *The History of the Standard Oil Company* (New York, 1904), I, 167ff.

to the Hopkins Bill, and it was introduced in the House
in January 1878, by Lewis F. Watson of Pennsylvania.
The bill (H.R. 2546) was given to the Committee on
Commerce chaired by John H. Reagan of Texas, and
with the addition of an anti-pooling clause emerged as
the Reagan Bill (H.R. 3547).[37] Reagan regarded the
bill as essentially the earlier Hopkins Bill, however, and
freely acknowledged his debt to it.[38]

The motives of the Petroleum Producers' Union have
been ignored. The oil producers were not anti-railroad,
but anti-Standard Oil, and this explains why a railroad
attorney could have written the first basic draft of a
railroad bill for them. Quite the contrary, they were full
of sympathy for the railways. Save for the Erie, which
was pro-Standard, they claimed that Standard had vic-
timized the New York Central, the Pennsylvania, the
B. & O., and others—"They are its slaves without voice
or power in the oil trade, except as their master may
will."[39] Common sense indicated that rebates served only
the shipper. If the oil producers were correct, why should
railroads oppose their bill?

At the same time that they worked for the introduction
of a bill in Congress, the oil producers organized a massive petition and letter-writing campaign. Over 2,000
signatures of Pittsburgh businessmen and Pennsylvania

37 Gerald D. Nash, "Origins of the Interstate Commerce Act of
1887," *Pennsylvania History*, XXIV (July, 1957), 183-187; Tarbell,
History of Standard Oil, I, 167-171, 214-215.

38 See Reagan's statement in U.S. House of Representatives, Committee on Commerce, *Arguments and Statements*, House Misc. Doc.
No. 55, 47th Cong., 1st Sess., February 21-March 28, 1882 (Washington, 1882), p. 265. An interesting and largely correct contemporary account of the history of the law can be found in W. W.
Rice's speech in the House of Representatives on December 8, 1884,
reprinted as *Interstate Commerce* (Washington, 1885).

39 Petroleum Producers' Union, *A Brief History of the Standard
Oil Company* ([Penna.?] ca. 1880), p. 9. Also see Petroleum Producers' Union, *A History of the Organization, Purposes, and Transactions of the General Council of the Petroleum Producers' Unions
. . . From 1878 to 1880* (Titusville, Penna., 1880), p. 50.

oil producers flooded Congress in mid-1876 calling for "the passage of a Law to regulate Commerce, and prohibit unjust discriminations by Common Carriers."[40] In early 1878, over 14,500 signatures on petitions attacking rebates and rate discrimination arrived in the House alone from the citizens of Pennsylvania. The state legislatures of Pennsylvania, Nevada, and Indiana sent general resolutions to the House in 1879.[41] In early 1879, the National Grange began circulating a petition calling for "such laws as will alleviate the oppressions imposed upon us by the transportation monopolies. . . . The surplus of our farms is wrenched from us to enrich these giant monopolies." By early 1881, several thousands of these petitions had flooded the House, each signed by dozens of persons.[42] The farmers or oilmen were hardly indifferent. Indeed, these two groups overshadowed, by far, any other effort for federal railroad legislation via petitions.

Lee Benson's provocative study questions the significance of the Grangers and oilmen in the agitation for the Reagan Bill. He suggests that New York merchants were the most important single group working for the bill, but restricts his thesis by indicating "no implication is intended that they actually directed the final stages of the campaign, or that national railroad regulation was the product of their creation."[43] Despite the fact that they tried to influence the official position of the National Board of Trade from 1875 on, it is clear that until 1879 the Cheap Transportation and Anti-Monopoly interests in New York were primarily concerned with state rail-

[40] Petition in HR 44A-H 3.3, U.S. House of Representatives Records, National Archives, Record Group 233. Hereafter House Records in the National Archives are indicated as "HR," with the appropriate file number. Senate Records in the National Archives (Record Group 46), are indicated as "Sen," with the file numbers.
[41] Petitions in HR 45A-H 6.7.
[42] See HR 46A-H 6.6.
[43] Benson, *Merchants, Farmers, and Railroads*, p. 212.

road regulation. Although they continued to try to shape the National Board of Trade's railroad policy, and never succeeded in getting it to support the Reagan Bill, Benson points out that after 1882 the New York merchants ceased to be an important factor in the movement for railroad regulation.[44] But the movement for railroad regulation was to extend to 1887, and insofar as petitions to Congress are concerned, the Grange and oilmen were far more significant.[45] Benson indicates that, despite strenuous efforts, the New Yorkers could not swing the National Board of Trade behind the Reagan Bill.[46] In 1879 and 1880, the National Board of Trade explicitly refused to endorse the Reagan Bill, calling instead for federal regulation under a commission with powers to prevent "extortionate rates" but not to set others.[47] Hardly anyone in 1880 opposed such a plan, or something much stronger. The businessmen, clearly, were not terribly excited by railroad regulation during a period of continually declining rates. Reagan may have mentioned New York backing for his bill in 1878, but in 1882, when discussing the origin of support for his bill, Reagan gave no special emphasis to the New York merchants.[48] As we shall see, New York merchants later turned against

[44] *Ibid.*, pp. 230-231.

[45] Sen 47A-H 22, large and submitted by non-New Yorkers, is much smaller than the two massive petition campaigns organized by the Grange and oilmen. HR 47A-H 5.7, is still much smaller than the above-mentioned campaigns and almost entirely from small towns in the Midwest and West. Even granting a few New Yorkers engineered this campaign, the fact that the mass support for it came from the areas conventionally thought of as Granger only confirms the Buck thesis. Business groups outside New York began submitting a growing number of special petitions in 1880, but these were far outnumbered by rural petitions. See HR 46A-H 8.

[46] Benson, *Merchants, Farmers, and Railroads*, pp. 221, 225, 230-231.

[47] National Board of Trade, *Proceedings of the Eleventh Annual Meeting, Washington, December, 1880* (Boston, 1881), pp. 97-98.

[48] U.S. House, Committee on Commerce, House Misc. Doc. No. 55, 47:1, p. 263; Benson, *Merchants, Farmers, and Railroads*, pp. 214-217.

the Reagan Bill and took an increasingly conservative line.

The question remains: Was the basic aim of the New York merchants altruistically to "restore a more equal division of the profits of American enterprise and permit the continued functioning of the private enterprise system?"[49] The New York merchants, it must be concluded, were concerned for their own profits at the expense of the sorely pressed railroads and their fellow businessmen in other coastal cities, and the Eastern rate war of 1881 was in large part a result of their desire to attack other coastal shipping interests. Despite their rhetoric of Jeffersonian democracy, anti-monopoly, etc., many of the New York merchants were moved primarily by more mundane considerations. Francis B. Thurber, one of the militant leaders of the movement *and* a large wholesale grocer, advocated lower rates to New York City rather than to Boston and New England because of his city's greater volume. At the same time, he attacked lower freight rates granted to wholesalers in interior cities because they affected New York merchants negatively.[50]

The New York Board of Trade and Transportation, dominated by the advocates of regulation, clothed its actions in pious rhetoric which belied their real motives. The primary impetus behind the actions of the New York merchants was to maintain the preferential railroad rates that could guarantee their city's share of import and export shipping against the aggressively competitive railroads and merchants of Boston, Philadelphia, and Baltimore. Although they failed to maintain their share of the import and export trade in the face of rate wars, the New York merchants nevertheless frequently identified with the New York Central in their fundamental

[49] Benson, *Merchants, Farmers, and Railroads*, p. 242.
[50] F. B. Thurber, *The Relations of Railroads to the Public* (Washington, 1879?), pp. 2-3.

interests. They opportunistically followed any course designed to preserve their prerogatives or to expand them, and were unabashedly acquisitive in their ultimate ends. In June 1882, for example, the railroads leading into New York underwent a strike and refused to hire strike-breakers. The Board led the legal struggle for a writ of mandamus against the New York Central to compel it to carry freight. "For nearly ten years this Board has stood between the public and the corporations, defending the public rights . . . ," the New Yorkers boasted.[51]

The Railroads Consider Regulation

Railroad leaders, well before 1883, were fully aware that something more than cooperative goodwill would be required to bring order out of chaos in the American railroad system. Joseph Nimmo, Jr., head of the first government railroad statistics department, and later a leading champion of the railroads, told Fink in the late 1870's that pooling agreements would never work unless made legally enforceable.[52] By 1879 there was a general unanimity among pool executives, including Fink, that without governmental sanctions the railroads would never maintain or stabilize rates. In 1879, Nimmo could report, "At the present time railroad managers appear to be quite generally of the opinion that the only practicable remedy for the evils of unjust and improper discriminations, is to be found in a confederation of the railroads under governmental sanction and control, the principle of the apportionment of competitive traffic being recog-

51 New York Board of Trade and Transportation, *Report of the Special Committee on Railway Freight Grievances* (New York, 1883), p. 8 and *passim*. Also Benson, *Merchants, Farmers, and Railroads*, chap. II.

52 Joseph Nimmo, Jr., "Memorandum of April 15th, 1899: The Present Status of the Railroad Problem," typed carbon of a "confidential" memo in the Library of the Bureau of Railway Economics, Washington, D. C.

nized as a feature of such a confederation."[53] J. W. Midgley, chairman of the Southwestern pool, in 1879 decided ". . . I am strongly of the opinion that special authority is necessary to give permanence and assurance to apportionment schemes. Such result would be desirable not less to the public than to the railroads; and when, by proper representation, this is made manifest, there should be no difficulty in securing the necessary legislation."[54] Fink, while opposing the Reagan Bill in 1879, wanted the "*object* of the Reagan Bill . . . carried out." The means: legalized pooling and a permanent federal commission with powers to determine rates in the event of disputes among railroads, and to enforce their decisions in the courts.[55]

In early 1882, during House hearings on the Reagan Bill, Fink, while claiming he would prefer an investigatory committee of Congress first, made specific suggestions to the Committee on Commerce:

"The first step . . . should be to legalize the management of the railroad property under this [pool] plan and to abandon the antiquated notion that a government, or combination as it is called, of this kind is against public policy. It can be clearly shown that it is absolutely required for the public interest. The great defect in the present plan, and its great weakness, is that the co-operation of these railroad companies is entirely voluntary, and that they can withdraw from their agreements at pleasure. .

"I do not propose that the government shall compel the railroad companies to transact their business in the way I have described, but simply compel them, in case they voluntarily adopt that plan, to comply with the

[53] Treasury Department, *Report on the Internal Commerce of the U.S.*, 1879, p. 190.
[54] *Ibid.*, Appendix, p. 57.
[55] Gilchrist, *Business History Review*, xxxiv (1960), 40.

terms of their agreements. . . . This step alone I think would be sufficient to accomplish the purpose, because the self-interest of the railroads requires the adoption of this plan, and it is only the absence of authority to compel them to adhere to it that leads to disruption. . . .

"Another method that could be adopted by the government is to enforce the tariffs established by the railroads and approved of as reasonable and just by the government. . . . Some of the provisions of the 'Reagan bill,' with some modifications, could, if applied, aid the railroad companies in carrying out their plans, but they could not be effectively applied without the co-operation of the railroads. . . .

"I am free to say, however, that I have little faith that any law prohibiting the payment of rebates will be of much use. . . . Still a law of this kind could do no harm; it would aid me in performing the duties imposed upon me by the associated roads of the Joint Executive Committee."[56]

The major objection to the Reagan Bill among railroad men was its anti-pooling provision. It is quite evident that the idea of government rate fixing, the alleged bogey, was acceptable to many railroad men if accompanied by legalized pooling. And the idea of a railroad commission, although not included in the Reagan Bill, was attractive even to such railroad die-hards as Charles E. Perkins of the Chicago, Burlington & Quincy. When a similar proposal was made, Perkins in April 1878 wrote: "I don't see any danger in the Rice bill for Railroad Commissioners. There is no precedent for nearly every state has already provided for some kind of supervision of RRds. I think such men as Adams, Fink and Cooley who are named in the Bill as the first Board of Comrs. are just the *Kind* of men we want to study this

[56] U.S. House, Committee on Commerce, House Misc. Doc. No. 55, p. 189.

RR question instead of leaving it wholly to State politicians. . . . The public *will* regulate us to some extent—& we must make up our minds to it. . . . We can go to sleep and rest assured that their report will *not* be *communistic.* . . . We ought to try to pass the bill."[57] Deeply involved with the railroads, and author of the Rice Bill, Charles Francis Adams, Jr., by 1880 was proposing strongly that legalized pooling be made the keystone of all railroad legislation. In the same year, the *Railway World* suggested that enforceable pooling would solve the problem of rate discrimination.[58]

The House Committee on Commerce hearings of 1882 revealed disagreements among railroad men on particulars, but few indicated their opposition to legislation on any terms, and most had specific legislative alternatives to the Reagan Bill. Charles Francis Adams, Jr., presented the Committee with a bill, later called the Henderson Bill (H.R. 133), very much like his earlier Rice Bill of 1879 (H.R. 77). It proposed the President appoint three commissioners to investigate complaints concerning rates, services, etc., and "procure the data necessary to the gradual enactment of an intelligent system of national legislation regulating interstate railroad commerce."[59] Violation would be publicly reported, along with recommendations of legislation necessary to correct the abuse. The essentials of this proposal were endorsed by, among others, Wayne MacVeagh of the Pennsylvania, George R. Blanchard of the Erie, and Chauncey Depew.[60]

[57] Charles E. Perkins to John Murray Forbes, April 28, 1878, in Thomas C. Cochran, *Railroad Leaders, 1845-1890* (Cambridge, 1953), p. 431. Cochran's book is a goldmine for the period.

[58] Charles Francis Adams, Jr., *The Federation of the Railroad System* (Boston, 1880), pp. 10-11; *Railway World*, XXIV (January 10, 1880), 27-28.

[59] U.S. House, Committee on Commerce, House Misc. Doc. No. 55, 47:1, p. 159.

[60] *Ibid.*, pp. 16, 154, 210.

CHAPTER II

AGITATION FOR
A FEDERAL RAILROAD LAW
1884-1886

THE anarchy within the railroad industry deepened from
1884 through 1886. As the president of one line la-
mented, "It seemed to my mind as though something was
absolutely necessary to be done to save the railroads of
this country from utter ruin and destruction. . . ."[1] With
Vanderbilt, Gould, and the Pennsylvania battling each
other in the East, and "The Atchison . . . very bitter &
down on the Southern Pacific & will insist upon having
their fair proportion," freight rates for the nation declined by one-fifth between 1882 and 1886 and each
new mile of the 27,000 built during that period was
an additional provocation.[2] "The merchants are securing
the benefit of low rates, to which I suppose they do not
object," Henry Seligman wrote.[3] Fink's pool, despite its
usual efforts, could not control the crisis any better than
the earlier pools. "The great difficulty is not between the
roads which want to join," the president of the Michigan

[1] M. E. Ingalls of the Cincinnati, Indianapolis, St. Louis & Chicago
Railroad, quoted in Julius Grodinsky, *Jay Gould: His Business
Career, 1867-92* (Philadelphia, 1957), p. 505. Another factor increasing competition was the elimination of regional variations in
track gauges during the 1870's and 1880's, and the consequent
creation of alternative routes for shippers. See George R. Taylor
and Irene N. Neu, *The American Railroad Network, 1861-1890*
(Cambridge, 1956).

[2] Henry Seligman to Philip N. Lilienthal, February 24, 1886,
Henry Seligman Papers, Baker Library, Harvard Business School,
vol. 1; *Historical Statistics of the U.S.*, pp. 427-431.

[3] Henry Seligman to Philip N. Lilienthal, March 16, 1885, Henry
Seligman Papers, vol. 1.

Central wrote concerning the pools, "but in handling the roads which do not want to belong to any pool."[4] Even Morgan could not bring the combatants under control at this time.[5]

The Merchants and Legislation

Whether the passage of the Interstate Commerce Act was due to the demand of the public for equality of opportunity, as Walton Hamilton suggests, or "petty capitalist" pressures, as Lewis Corey claimed, it is clear that the merchants and manufacturers of the United States were not of one mind on the matter during 1884-1886, and New York had more than its share of divisions.

The first real sign of New York merchants' hesitation over the details of the Reagan Bill came in early 1884, when the New York militants at the National Board of Trade convention went through their futile annual effort to swing that body to a strong pro-legislation position. Simon Sterne, a veteran of the New York Board of Trade and Transportation, called for the passage of the Reagan Bill, but with a number of important amendments. A blanket refusal to allow pooling, Sterne thought, was probably an error. More important, a commission was needed to administer the law and was an "absolute prerequisite." Such a commission, chosen from railroad executives, would prevent the sort of laxity the courts had shown during the railroad strike of July 1883. Clearly, the New York merchants' strong anti-union sentiments were getting the upper hand. But the other delegates at the convention, reflecting on the cheapness of rates, refused to do more than endorse a proposal for a

[4] Henry B. Ledyard to J. W. Midgley, March 30, 1885, in Thomas C. Cochran, *Railroad Leaders, 1845-1890* (Cambridge, 1953), p. 391.

[5] Grodinsky, *Jay Gould*, pp. 504-512; Herbert L. Satterlee, *J. Pierpont Morgan: An Intimate Portrait* (New York, 1939), pp. 219ff.

national commission to study the railroad problem.[6] The railroad committee of the New York Chamber of Commerce, which included Thurber among its members, also came out in January 1884 for a Reagan Bill with a commission.[7]

The less subtle Iowa Legislature, the farmers and citizens of upper Wisconsin, and such merchant organizations as the Quincy and Pittsburgh Chambers of Commerce were the only groups unequivocally calling for *rate* regulation and the Reagan Bill. But, given the cheapness of rates in most places, in 1884 far more merchant groups wrote the Senate concerning a minor proposal on bills of lading, H.R. 7163, than for the Reagan Bill.[8]

In 1885, Thurber, representing the New York merchants, asked the National Board of Trade merely to endorse the principle of a railroad commission and regulation, and failed to signify explicitly the nature of these regulatory powers. With clear opposition among many merchants to the Reagan Bill, even Thurber's innocuous and conservative compromise was referred to a committee for emasculation.[9] By 1884 and 1885, the steam was out of the merchant agitation for federal regulation.

[6] National Board of Trade, *Proceedings of the Fourteenth Annual Meeting, Washington, January, 1884* (Boston, 1884), pp. 106-122, 125, 136.

[7] U.S. House of Representatives, Committee on Commerce, *Arguments and Statements*, 48th Cong., 1st Sess., January, 1884 (Washington, 1884), p. 131.

[8] See the petitions in HR 48A-H 6.8 and Sen 48A-H 23.

[9] National Board of Trade, *Proceedings of the Fifteenth Annual Meeting, Washington, January, 1885* (Boston, 1885), pp. 68-71. According to a member of his family, Simon Sterne "was frequently consulted in the preparation of the [Cullom] Interstate Commerce Act, and drafted some of its provisions." Simon Sterne, *Railways in the United States*, preface by "M. S. S." (New York, 1912), p. viii. Sterne had a more modest view of himself as "one who was consulted," and his official biographer suggests he thought fair rates—about which the Cullom Bill said little—was the key issue, and not pooling. John Foord, *The Life and Public Services of Simon Sterne* (London, 1903), pp 212-214.

Due to declining rates and their fear of labor troubles, the small group that remained interested had moved to an essentially conservative position.

In 1886, the year of decision, the pro-regulation merchants were in no mood to become radicals. It was obvious that legislation was imminent, since the Senate, long the obstacle to legislation, had voted for the initial Cullom Bill (S. 2112) in January 1885. A revised version (S. 1532) was favorably reported out of committee in February 1886 and passed in May. (The common impression that the Supreme Court's *Wabash Ry. v. Illinois* decision was responsible for action is largely incorrect, since that decision was handed down on October 25, 1886, and by that time both the Senate and House wanted legislation and were determined to have it. The only question was the form of the legislation.) The National Board of Trade endorsed the Cullom Bill in January but recommended the removal of the section calling for proportionately equal rates for short and long hauls. This contingency was the only aspect of the resolution objected to by Thurber, representing the New Yorkers.[10] The Board made it known that it did not want rate-making powers assigned to the commission which was to administer the act.

Merchants throughout the nation overwhelmingly supported the Cullom Bill as against the Reagan Bill, and left the farmers to take the radical position. The hearings of the Senate Committee on Interstate Commerce, held throughout the nation from May to No-

[10] National Board of Trade, *Proceedings of the Sixteenth Annual Meeting, Washington, January, 1886* (Boston, 1886), pp. 132-135, 142, 160.

The *Wabash v. Illinois* decision (118 U.S. 557) was inconsequential not merely because it was made well after all important parties decided to obtain federal regulation, but also because it outlawed a phenomenon—the regulation of rates by state commissions—that had no significant chance of becoming a widely accepted approach to regulation. By 1887, only eight states had assigned rate-making powers to their commissions.

vember 1885, clearly indicated that merchants wanted a commission to administer the bill, and a remarkably large number were willing to allow pooling or formally legalize it. Regional distinctions are not too important, although the New York Produce Exchange and the Mercantile Exchange tended to align themselves with the extreme conservatives by opposing any rate-making powers for the I.C.C.[11] The very minor merchant opposition to regulation in any form came from the giant shippers who benefited most from rebating and railroad chaos— Charles A. Pillsbury of Minneapolis, Gustavus F. Swift of Chicago, who strongly opposed pools and favored rebates, and Memphis merchants pleased with their excellent water competition with railroads.[12] Petitions and letters from merchant groups arriving in the House and Senate also overwhelmingly supported the Cullom Bill. In December 1886 and January 1887, however, when the compromise House and Senate bill was being formulated or considered, large numbers of Midwestern and Southern business organizations began calling for the elimination of the long-short haul and anti-pooling provisions—sections 4 and 5—or the defeat of the bill altogether in a few cases.[13]

The Railroads and Reform

By 1884 a large and important group of railroad men was ready and anxious to have federal railroad

[11] U.S. Senate, Select Committee on Interstate Commerce, *Testimony*, 49th Cong., 1st Sess., [May 20-November 18, 1885], (Washington, 1886), pp. 206, 214. For pro-Cullom Bill support, see *ibid.*, pp. 55, 72-73, 248-254, 646-722, 870-871, 880-900, 975ff., 1319ff., 1433. The actual *Report* of the Committee, a separate volume excluding testimony, contains a number of formal statements from merchants supporting the principles of the Cullom Bill. U.S. Senate, Select Committee on Interstate Commerce, Senate Report No. 46, 49:1, pp. 58-59, 71, 77, 94, 98, 100.

[12] U.S. Senate, Select Committee on Interstate Commerce, *Testimony*, 49:1, pp. 646ff., 1239ff., 1372ff.

[13] See Sen 49A-H 22 and HR 47A-H 7.10.

legislation—on their terms. Their motives varied. Some realized that voluntary efforts at pooling would never solve the problems of rate cutting, overexpanded facilities, and profitless rebates. Others, many of whom also shared this view, saw in addition that regulation was inevitable and that they had better define it to their own interest, or pass something to placate the public. The hearings held by the House Committee on Commerce in January 1884, clearly indicated that railroad men did not contest the principle of federal regulation, but only its form. John P. Green, vice-president of the Pennsylvania Railroad, frankly admitted "that a large majority of the railroads in the United States would be delighted if a railroad commission or any other power could make rates upon their traffic which would insure them six per cent dividends, and I have no doubt, with such a guarantee, they would be very glad to come under the direct supervision and operation of the National Government."[14] Although Green opposed legislation to prevent long-short haul discriminations, and the Reagan Bill specifically, he readily indicated his support for a commission and for the judicial review of rates.[15] Chauncey Depew also advocated a commission: "I think I can safely speak for the whole railroad interest of the United States that whatever may be the constitutional objections to the power of Congress, and they are certainly very great, and from the legal side I have grave doubts about it; however, from the practical business side, if there was a national board, with supervisory powers, fully authorized to investigate and report to Congress, I do not believe that there is a railroad, great or small, within the limits of this republic that would ever raise that constitutional question."[16]

[14] U.S. House, Committee on Commerce, *Hearings*, 48:1, January, 1884, pp. 1-2.
[15] *Ibid.*, p. 6.   [16] *Ibid.*, p. 39.

Albert Fink, of course, was more than anxious to get the House Committee to legalize pools and pooling contracts because they were "one of the best practical means by which the object of the Reagan bill can be attained."[17] Until such time as Congress was prepared to pass such legislation, Fink was ready to recommend the immediate passage of the Horr (H.R. 79) or Wilson (H.R. 2012) Bills, providing for a commission to collect data and recommend legislation.[18] Other railroad men appeared to oppose the Reagan Bill and favor a commission, although C. C. Dodge, a banker-director of the Atchison and Topeka, the Norfolk and Western, and other lines, indicated his support for the Reagan Bill *with* a commission. The radical critics of the Reagan Bill in Congress served to remind railroad leaders that a stern anti-railroad measure was a possible alternative to conservative reform.[19]

While public hearings were taking place, an illuminating correspondence was passing between Charles Francis Adams, Jr., then director, and soon to become president, of the Union Pacific, and John D. Long of Massachusetts, a newly elected member of the House Committee on Commerce. Reagan, Adams wrote to Long on January 3, 1884, was an opportunist and his bill might do "a great deal of ill." Adams opposed it. Only four years earlier, he told Long, he had tried to get Reagan to remove certain features of his bill and add a commission. "I assured him, and I was authorized to do so, that such a bill should encounter no opposition from the railroad companies in its passage." Adams had prepared a bill but Reagan rejected it.[20] Several days later Adams wrote Long again, this time with cynicism and a tone of bore-

[17] *Ibid.*, p. 66.   [18] *Ibid.*, pp. 40, 69.
[19] *Ibid.*, pp. 79, 131, 168ff.; *Congressional Record*, XVI, 48:2, pp. 40-47, 59ff., 861, 889.
[20] Charles Francis Adams, Jr., to John D. Long, January 3, 1884, John D. Long Papers, Massachusetts Historical Society.

dom. Long was interested in a substitute bill, and Adams, while too busy to write it, clearly knew what was needed. "What is desired, if I understand it . . . is something having a good sound, but quite harmless, which will impress the popular mind with the idea that a great deal is being done, when, in reality, very little is intended to be done." And, Adams concluded after a second thought, "As for the Reagan bill, I care very little now, whether it passes or not. For certain reasons, it seems to me best that it should pass. . . . I do not know that any great harm will result from letting him have it."[21] Still, Long was clearly thinking in terms of an opposition bill and Adams was ready to advise him on how best to go about writing one, ". . . taking the commissioner idea as the basis in an opposition bill,—and I regard it as containing all there is worthy of being in a bill,—that then it might be expedient to amplify it with provisions on other subjects, in order to render it popularly acceptable, and supply a demand for extreme legislation."[22] Long continued with his efforts to create a commission-centered bill, and soon had a draft for Adams. Adams, the founder of modern state commissions, cynic, and railroad president, with insight that could come only from experience, revealed to Long on March 1 why railroads were soon to bring all their weight behind the commission form of regulation. Indeed, he suggested the whole course of subsequent big business attitudes towards federal regulation: "If you only get an efficient Board of Commissioners, they could work out of it whatever was necessary. No matter what sort of bill you have, everything depends upon the men who, so to speak, are inside of it, and who are to make it work. In the hands of the right men, any bill would produce the desired results. . . ."[23]

[21] *Ibid.*, January 7, 1884.   [22] *Ibid.*, January 14, 1884.
[23] *Ibid.*, March 1, 1884. Adams' view was public knowledge. See *Congressional Record*, XVI, 48:2, p. 887.

The commission was to become the conscious avenue of salvation for pro-railroad legislators—their best defense against more radical demands. In addition it could serve the ends of the roads themselves. George R. Blanchard of the Erie, much less conservative than a few years earlier, was sufficiently chastened by rate wars, overexpansion, pool failures, and Grangers to swing into line. In an article in the *Chicago Railway Review* in 1884, he put forth his new views. The public—and the railroads—had a right to reasonable, non-discriminatory rates, without rebating. The Joint Executive Committee, he agreed, had been powerless to impose its views on the railroads. What was needed was "a national railway commission to co-operate with and not oppose this recognized committee. . . . The country therefore owes to railways conservative protection against radical assaults; and their co-operative traffic federations, which are intended, within just limits, to secure uniformity, stability and impartiality among railways, their patrons and the States, should be reinforced, ratified and legalized by an intelligent public conviction."[24]

Between May and November of 1885, when the Senate Committee on Interstate Commerce held hearings, dozens of key railroad men were called to testify or give statements to the Committee. With the exception of Charles E. Perkins of the C. B. and Q., whose record on regulation was hardly consistent, all were unanimous in advocating federal action of some type. Disagreements appeared on specific problems, but the principle of federal regulation was accepted as the only possible alternative to the chaos in the industry. As one railroad president bitterly declared: "The point reached since the beginning of 1884 in the prevailing contagion of depression and loss, from the effects of ruinous rates,

[24] G. R. Blanchard, *Traffic Unity, Popularly Called "Railway Pools"* (New York, 1884), pp. 30, 34. A reprint.

which were uncontrollable from a lack of adequate protection of railroad interests in the past, is not to be remedied by waiting upon 'the survival of the fittest.' This misapplied phrase of the scientist cannot furnish appropriate data in any recognition and adjustment of difficulties which may attend the commercial affairs of a people."[25] The large majority of the railroad executives—nearly all—favored a commission of some type. Many wished to have pools legalized, and quite a few called for anti-rebate laws. A number even called for various forms of rate regulation.[26] The Senate, which had blocked railroad legislation for nearly a decade, was ready to act. On January 18, 1886, nine months before *Wabash v. Illinois*, the Senate Committee on Interstate Commerce issued its report.

"The committee has found among the leading representatives of the railroad interests an increasing readiness to accept the aid of Congress in working out the solution of the railroad problem which has obstinately baffled all their efforts, and not a few of the ablest railroad men of the country seem disposed to look to the intervention of Congress as promising to afford the best means of ultimately securing a more equitable and satisfactory adjustment of the relations of the transportation interests to the community than they themselves have been able to bring about.

"The evidence upon this point is so conclusive that the committee has no hesitation in declaring that prompt action by Congress upon this important subject is almost unanimously demanded by public sentiment."[27]

A masterpiece of understatement!

[25] Senate Select Committee on Interstate Commerce, *Testimony*, 49:1, January 18, 1886, p. 819.
[26] *Ibid.*, pp. 108-109, 162-166, 333, 464-466, 599-601, 623-629, 819, 825, 835, 904-905, 1044-1047, 1204-1215, 1235, 1265.
[27] U.S. Senate, Select Committee on Interstate Commerce, Senate

There is ample evidence that the railroads' enthusiasm for regulation continued through 1886, especially as they witnessed another building boom of useless trackage. A director of the B. & O. announced in January that its president, Garrett, was ready for a federal commission to help solve inter-railway disputes.[28] The Pennsylvania Railroad, it is clear, swung completely behind the necessity of a law.[29] Some railroad men criticized the details of the Cullom and Reagan Bills, but not the principle. Add an amendment to forbid strikes, two presidents recommended.[30] Remove sections 4 and 5, suggested another.[31] William P. Shinn, a railroad expert who warmly endorsed the Cullom Bill, frankly analyzed the crucial value of legislation in the *Railway Review*:

"The rate wars which have of late years so devastated the finances of railroad companies, are all inaugurated and carried on upon inter-state traffic. They are detrimental alike to producer, transporter and consumer; they introduce elements of chance in transactions of business which should rest entirely upon supply and demand. . . .

Report No. 46, 49:1, p. 175. Also see Marshall M. Kirkman, *The Relation of the Railroads of the United States to the People and the Commercial and Financial Interests of the Country* (Chicago, 1885), pp. 30-43, for a railroad executive's opposition to the Reagan Bill and advocacy of a commission and federal regulation. Ida M. Tarbell, *The Nationalizing of Business, 1878-1898* (New York, 1936), p. 101, is an example of the conventional historical view that the railroads opposed any legislation. The railroad position on regulation, and its relationship to industry chaos and fear of radicalism, was analyzed before the House. See *Congressional Record*, XVII, 49:1, pp. 7290-7291.

[28] National Board of Trade, *Proceedings of the Sixteenth Annual Meeting*, p. 141.

[29] *Railway Review*, XXVII (March 12, 1887), 148.

[30] James C. Clarke, Illinois Central, to Shelby M. Cullom, April 28, 1886, in Cochran, *Railroad Leaders*, p. 301; letter of Frank Bond, Cincinnati, New Orleans, and Texas Pacific Railroad, June 18, 1886, in Sen 49A-H 22.

[31] Frederick J. Kimball, Norfolk and Western, to William Mahone, December 21, 1886, in Cochran, *Railroad Leaders*, p. 374.

"In the interests of producer, transporter and consumer, governmental regulation of inter-state traffic is necessary and desirable. . . .

"The leading railroad companies, which formerly (and as I then thought, unwisely) opposed such a commission, are now almost without an exception in its favor; not because, as has been charged, they expect to be able to control it, but because it places between the companies and the public a responsible organization to which both will acquiesce. . . . all experience goes to show that under the light of investigation nine-tenths of the complaints made, fail of substantiation, and thus grave causes of friction are removed.

"The good results of the railway commissions in the states of Massachusetts and New York are too well known to need more than a passing reference. . . ."[32]

On January 2, 1887, on the eve of the bill's passage, the *Chicago Inter-Ocean* correctly summarized the general railroad position: "Perhaps the strongest argument that can be presented in favor of the passage of this bill is found in the fact that many of the leading railway managers admit the justice of its terms and join in the demand for its passage. . . . The irregularities that have gradually crept into it [railroad system], got beyond their capacity to manage. . . . The effort to maintain rates was equally unsuccessful. Then came the last resort—the pool—but that, too, proved impotent. . . . And now, acknowledging the inefficiency of their own weak inventions . . . the managers are content to leave the settlement of the whole matter to the law-making power of the country. . . ."[33]

[32] William P. Shinn, "The Relations of Railways to the State," *Railway Review*, XXVI (March 13, 1886), 121-122.
[33] Reprinted in *Public Opinion*, II (January 8, 1887), 249.

The Nature of the Bills

Neither the Cullom Bill nor the Reagan Bill was intended to deal directly with the problem of rates, although Reagan was ambiguous about the matter. In January, 1885, he told the House, "this is not a bill to regulate freight rates, that it does not undertake to prescribe rates for the transportation of freight. I know the difficulties which would attend any measure attempting to prescribe rates of freight. . . . I simply propose to say they shall not discriminate in freight rates, but shall be just and equal in their charges to the public. . . ."[34] His bill, however, did not grant to any specific body the power or the criteria to determine precisely what was "just and equal." Cullom's Committee on Interstate Commerce concluded that "the principles upon which a schedule of charges should be arranged, either for a single railroad or for the entire system," were incapable of being determined.[35] (Years later Cullom claimed that he intended that the I.C.C., by implication, should have the power to decide a reasonable rate after a complaint and hearing.) Neither bill, it is clear, was designed to explicitly provide a standard for equitable rates and come to grips with the problem of effective regulation from the public's viewpoint. Yet is was precisely the problem of rates that was of central concern to Congressional spokesmen for Midwestern farmers and merchants, and although willing to support virtually any regulatory bill as a step in the right direction, these representatives condemned Reagan's Bill as a conservative sop to the railroads.[36]

[34] Speech of John H. Reagan, January 7, 1885, *Congressional Record*, XVI, 48:2, p. 533. Also see *ibid.*, XXXIX, 58:3, p. 2087.

[35] Senate Select Committee on Interstate Commerce, Senate Report No. 46, p. 182.

[36] Shelby M. Cullom, *Fifty Years of Public Service* (Chicago, 1911), p. 328; *Congressional Record*, XVI, 48:2, pp. 40-47, 59ff., 861.

The Reagan Bill explicitly forbade pooling; the Cullom Bill said nothing on the matter. Reagan, when in conference with the Senators to reconcile the two bills in December 1886, conceded on virtually every point of disagreement save pooling.[37] (As we shall see, because of the commission, Reagan actually got very little by these concessions. Section 4, providing for proportionately equal charges for short as for long hauls over the same line in the same direction, was left subject to special modifications by the commission.) Rebates were prohibited in both bills.[38]

Given the vagueness of the final act and the latitude of interpretation granted to the five-man commission, the struggle for the commission is of the greatest significance in the history of the first federal act. The commission determined who, in fact, attained their goals— the farmers and citizens, as is commonly thought, or the railroads, or the businessmen.

Reagan opposed a railroad commission both as a substitute for his bill and as a supplement to it. He felt that, as with the state railroad commissions, commission members and their appointments would be influenced by the railroads, and that the railroads would eventually dominate the commission. Reagan and his allies in the House wanted a specific bill that could be enforced directly by the courts without commission leniency. The fight for a commission in the House was led by John D. Long, who, taking his cue from Adams, was fully aware of its conservative potential. Opponents freely cited railroad support for a commission, and stated, in the words of Populist Senator Charles H. Van Wyck of Nebraska, that

[37] Cullom, *Fifty Years of Public Service*, p. 322. Also see U.S. Senate, Committee on Interstate Commerce, *Hearings . . . On S. 1534*, February-March, 1894, in Senate Doc. No. 39, 55th Cong., 2d Sess., April 15, 1897 (Washington, 1897), pp. 64-65.

[38] U.S. House, Committee on Commerce, House Misc. Doc. No. 55, p. 261; *Congressional Record*, XVII, 49:1, p. 7283.

"Annexing a commission with large salaries and little power is not what the people are demanding."[39] It was not until December 1886 that Reagan relented, thereby allowing a vague bill to be administered by a commission with ill-defined legislative, judicial, and executive powers.

If, in fact, the majority of the railroads had opposed the bill, as most historical accounts suggest, it is difficult to believe that the vote in favor of the final bill would have been as overwhelming as it was. The only alternative is the far-fetched assumption that these groups were politically powerless.[40] The compromise bill passed the Senate on January 14, 1887, by a vote of 36 to 12, and the House the following week by 219 to 41. For the moment, at least, everyone thought he was getting enough of the type of legislation he wanted to support the final bill. Senator Cullom was correct when he later said "the Act of 1887 was conservative legislation, but in Congress and among the people generally it was considered radical. . . ."[41] But in 1887 it was for the Interstate Commerce Commission to decide whether the Act would be conservative or radical.

[39] *Congressional Record*, XVII, 49:1, p. 3825. Also *ibid.*, XVI, 48:2, pp. 62, 167, 887. The debate, pro and con, is summarized in Robert E. Cushman, *The Independent Regulatory Commissions* (New York, 1941), pp. 45-54.

[40] Tarbell, *The History of the Standard Oil Company* (New York, 1904), II, 291, suggests that Standard opposed the bill; and E. G. Campbell, *The Reorganization of the American Railroad System, 1893-1900* (New York, 1938), p. 20, claims the railroads opposed the bill. Allan Nevins, *John D. Rockefeller: The Heroic Age of American Enterprise* (New York, 1940), II, 95-100, claims Standard took no position on the matter, and its Washington lobbyist, J. N. Camden, favored the Cullom Bill.

[41] Cullom, *Fifty Years of Public Service*, p. 327.

CHAPTER III

FORMATIVE YEARS OF THE
INTERSTATE COMMERCE COMMISSION
1887-1890

THE railroads, for the most part, welcomed the signing of the new railroad law on February 4, 1887. A few important railroad men, such as John Murray Forbes and William Bliss, regarded the Act with hostility.[1] But the dominant sentiment was expressed by the *Railroad Gazette* on February 18, when it admitted, "We do not ourselves apprehend any very destructive consequences, either industrial or political, from the present law."[2] According to the *Railway Review*, which summarized the matter, the new law was to be only the first step:

"The Pennsylvania Railroad officially states in the current annual report that it has 'favored the enactment of a proper law, which, while guarding the interests of the public, would afford to the railways the protection to which they are justly entitled in the conduct of their business.' This in reference to the passage of the interstate law.

"The leading and the progressive railways of the country have long entertained the same view of the matter as that expressed above. It is not the essential spirit of the new law that is now objected to, but the curious manifestations of that spirit in the obscure and contra-

[1] See John Murray Forbes to John M. Endicott, January 29, 1887, John Murray Forbes Papers, Massachusetts Historical Society; William Bliss to Chauncey Depew, January 20, 1887, in Thomas C. Cochran, *Railroad Leaders, 1845-1890* (Cambridge, 1953), p. 265.

[2] *Railroad Gazette*, XIX (February 18, 1887), 112.

dictory wording. . . . The probability is that important amendments will be required in order that the prime purpose of this legislation may be attained."[3]

In fact, the law *was* vague, and there was as yet no commission to clarify it. In February, a group of railroad executives met to discuss its meaning and ambiguities.[4] Two schools of thought emerged, one, led by Fink, advocating a free and broad interpretation of the new law, the other maintaining that it be treated literally. The *Railroad Gazette*, in siding with the literalists, felt that Congress should amend the law if it proved inadequate. "We think the law as it stands good enough to furnish a sound basis for something better. . . ."[5] One railroad president wrote, "We are all interested in the *bona fide* enforcement of the bill if it can be done, but none of us are willing to be sacrificed for the purpose of teaching the lesson of either its success or failure to the rest."[6]

But such apprehension was due to uncertainty as to whom President Cleveland might appoint to the new five-man commission. After all, Adams had predicted that "In the hands of the right men, any bill would produce the desired results . . . ," and even such die-hards as Charles E. Perkins had agreed that a commission was

[3] *Railway Review*, xxvii (March 12, 1887), 148. The conventional interpretation, of course, is that the railroads opposed the I.C.C. See, for example, I. L. Sharfman, *The Interstate Commerce Commission* (New York, 1931-1937), i, 39; Frank H. Dixon, *Railroads and Government: Their Relations in the United States, 1910-1921* (New York, 1922), p. 1; E. G. Campbell, *The Reorganization of the American Railroad System, 1893-1900* (New York, 1938), pp. 20-21; Chester McArthur Destler, "The Opposition of American Businessmen to Social Control During the 'Gilded Age,'" *Mississippi Valley Historical Review*, xxxix (March, 1953), 664. William Z. Ripley, *Railroads: Rates and Regulations* (New York, 1912), p. 456, takes the opposite view.

[4] *Railway Review*, xxvii (February 26, 1887), 118.

[5] *Railroad Gazette*, xix (April 1, 1887), 217.

[6] George Henry Watrous to "Mr. Henry," March 7, 1887, in Cochran, *Railroad Leaders*, p. 500.

the crux of the matter of regulation.[7] The railroads fully realized that the first commissioners would determine many of the crucial precedents that would shape the future of the law.[8] But Grover Cleveland was not the sort of figure to alarm railroad presidents overly much, for as a Buffalo lawyer he had worked for a number of railroads and was dubbed by his opponents as a "railway attorney." His interest in the problem of railroad regulation while President was minimal.[9]

As the law was being passed by the House and Senate, Senator Shelby M. Cullom, the author of the pro-railroad bill, wrote President Cleveland and suggested he appoint Thomas M. Cooley as chairman of the new Commission. On February 8, Cleveland offered Cooley the post.[10] The railroads themselves could not have chosen a more sympathetic regulator.

Cooley had made his reputation as a theorist of the constitutional limitations on governmental action; his position was best represented in the Supreme Court by Justice Stephen J. Field.[11] Charles E. Perkins stated in 1878 that Adams, Fink, and Cooley were the sort of men he would trust to regulate the railroads. And his confidence was well placed, for Cooley completely identified himself with the railroads' interests from at least 1882 on. When the Joint Executive Committee needed an arbi-

[7] Charles Francis Adams, Jr., to John D. Long, March 1, 1884, John D. Long Papers; Charles E. Perkins to John Murray Forbes, April 28, 1878, in Cochran, *Railroad Leaders*, p. 431.

[8] See William D. Bishop to George H. Watrous, February 20, 1887, in Cochran, *Railroad Leaders*, p. 262, for example.

[9] Lee Benson, *Merchants, Farmers, and Railroads: Railroad Regulation and New York Politics, 1850-1887* (Cambridge, 1955), pp. 181-182. See, for example, John H. Reagan to Grover Cleveland, July 7, 1888, Grover Cleveland Papers, Library of Congress, box 208.

[10] Shelby M. Cullom, *Fifty Years of Public Service* (Chicago, 1911), p. 229; Allan Nevins, ed., *Letters of Grover Cleveland, 1850-1908* (Boston, 1933), p. 131.

[11] Arnold M. Paul, *Conservative Crisis and the Rule of Law: Attitudes of Bar and Bench, 1887-1895* (Ithaca, N.Y., 1960), p. 12.

tration committee in January 1882 to decide on the fairness of rates to the major Eastern ports, Cooley was one of the three men chosen. As a result of his association with the railroads, Cooley was defeated for re-election to the Michigan Supreme Court.[12] In 1885 he was appointed receiver of the Wabash Railroad (a post he kept until he moved to the I.C.C.), and he continued as arbitrator for Fink's pool.[13] For several years he aligned himself with the most conservative railroad opponents of federal regulation, a position thoroughly consistent with his legal theory, opposing the desirability of new legislation and especially the granting of judicial powers to railroad commissions.[14] By 1887, however, Cooley was more the practical railroad administrator than the legal theorist, and was advocating the legalization of pooling with public sanction and control, in much the same terms as other pragmatic railroad men.[15]

Cleveland's other appointments were hardly designed to balance Cooley's strong pro-railroad predilections. William R. Morrison had been a Democratic member of the House for fourteen years, and after losing a Senate race was appointed to the Commission—a task for which he had no special competence. Morrison was chosen for purely political reasons and Cullom considered him to be

[12] *Report of Messrs. Thurman, Washburne & Cooley, Constituting an Advisory Commission on Differential Rates by Railroads* (New York, 1882), p. 3; Ernest C. Meyer, "Judge Cooley's Contributions to the Interstate Commerce Commission," *Detroit Law Review*, VII (March, 1937), 1. Pagination is from the reprint.

[13] See, for example, "Award of Arbitrator [Thomas M. Cooley] in Matter of Redivision of Chicago Eastbound Dead Freight and Live Stock Traffic," January 5, 1885, from Office of Chairman Albert Fink. A typed statement in the Interstate Commerce Commission Library, Washington, D. C.

[14] Thomas M. Cooley, "Railroad Commissions," *Railway Review*, XXIII (February 10, 1883), 71-72; U.S. Senate, Select Committee on Interstate Commerce, Senate Report No. 46, 49th Cong., 1st Sess., January 18, 1886 (Washington, 1886), pp. 9ff.

[15] Thomas M. Cooley, "Popular and Legal Views of Traffic Pooling," *Railway Review*, XXVII (January 8, 1887), 15-17.

nothing more than a "broken-down politician." Walter L. Bragg, another Democratic politician, had been on the Alabama Railroad Commission. Augustus Schoonmaker had been a political associate of Cleveland in New York, and later moved to greener pastures as a railroad attorney. But Aldace F. Walker was the only other appointee with any real knowledge of railroading—enough, in fact, to warrant his resigning in March 1889 to take over a railroad traffic association and eventually become chairman of the board of the Atchison, Topeka & Sante Fe. Save for the Western papers, which complained that there was no member of the Commission from their region, the press seemed favorable to the new appointees. And the railroads were hardly displeased. "Fortunately its present membership is not made up of the stuff that is liable to shrink from doing what it conceives to be its duty. . . ."[16]

The confidence of railroad men in Cooley was not misplaced. The law was, in many important particulars, quite vague. The new commission was given the opportunity to interpret its true meaning by over 1,000 complaints, grievances, and questions thrown at it within a few months, on a large variety of issues.[17] The first problem to which it addressed itself was section 4.

Section 4 provided that a railroad could not charge more for intermediate or short hauls over a longer route in the same direction than the price of shipping goods or transporting a person over the entire route. This part of the law was flexible enough—since it did not prevent, for example, a railroad charging much more for a small section of a long haul than for the remainder if the ag-

[16] *Railway Review*, XXVII (April 16, 1887), 220. Also see *Public Opinion*, II (April 2, 1887), 237-240; *Railway Review*, XXVII (April 2, 1887), 194.

[17] These complaints are in the Interstate Commerce Commission General Records, 1887-1900, General Services Administration Depot, Springfield, Virginia, filed in the first 1000 files. Hereafter referred to as "I.C.C. Records, Virginia."

gregate of the fractions was no larger than the charge for an unbroken long haul. The vested interests concerned with such inequities were many. Shippers in the West naturally tended to have the advantage over shippers in the East and Midwest, who had the larger volume and were charged proportionately more. In addition the Act of 1887 allowed the I.C.C. to "prescribe the extent to which . . . a common carrier may be relieved from the operation of this section of the act." Section 4 was theoretically capable of being applied whenever it aided a carrier, or being set aside if it damaged it.

The Interstate Commerce Commission was opened for business on April 5, 1887. The Southern railways were especially anxious to obtain relief from section 4, and it was temporarily granted in the "imperative" cases.[18] The Commission immediately embarked on an investigation of the matter, but until coming to a conclusion it unanimously decided to issue a temporary policy statement in a letter on May 18, from Cooley to J. A. Hanley, traffic manager of the Minnesota & Northwestern. The Hanley letter indicated that the Commission felt the Act was essentially flexible and that it was justified in taking a broad interpretation of it. "It must be assumed that Congress intended the general law, in its main features at least, to be a permanent law of the country," but temporary relief would be granted to applicants pending further investigation so "that harmful results from a sudden change in the law might thereby, to some extent, be averted."[19] Despite the growing clamor by shippers and farm towns to maintain section 4 where

[18] Interstate Commerce Commission, *First Annual Report, December 1, 1887* (Washington, 1887), p. 19.

[19] Thomas M. Cooley to J. A. Hanley, May 18, 1887, Interstate Commerce Commission Files, Interstate Commerce Commission Building, Washington, D. C., Letterbooks, vol. 2. Hereafter this source is indicated as ICC-2. The letter was also published in I.C.C., *First Annual Report*, pp. 122-125.

it benefited them, on June 15 the Commission handed down a magnificent triumph for the railroads in the Louisville & Nashville Railroad decision, written primarily by Cooley, which effectively guided I.C.C. policy for the next five years and allowed the railroads to suspend section 4 when it hurt them and maintain it when it was to their benefit.[20]

The carriers, the decision stated, could judge for themselves whether circumstances warranted suspending section 4, and they could alter their rates accordingly. If the Commission found the railroad misrepresented its justification, it could hold the railroad responsible later, but the consequences were left vague. Cases specially cited as warranting suspension of section 4 were railroads facing unregulated water competition—which immediately meant the South and coastal cities—railroads competing with foreign or intrastate lines, and "rare and peculiar cases." And, taking in the entire realm of regulation, anything the Act did not specify as unlawful was legal if it was so before the Act's passage. The Commission decided it could not and should not undertake the gigantic task of determining rates.[21] "It is now apparent that within certain limits the construction of the law is likely to be such as not to interfere for evil with existing trade relations," editorialized the *Railroad Gazette*. "The law as interpreted by the Commission and the courts must now provide the way to do what the roads were learning by costly experience to do for themselves. Perhaps it will, but if it does it will be one of the most successful pieces of legislation ever devised."[22]

The June 15 decision was broad and flexible, allow-

[20] Augustus Schoonmaker, "The Interstate Commerce Commission and Its Work," *Railroad Gazette*, XXIII (October 16, 1891), 725.

[21] E. B. Peirce, *Digest of Decisions of the Courts and Interstate Commerce Commission, 1887 to 1908* (Chicago, 1908), pp. 38, 272-274; I.C.C., *First Annual Report*, p. 66.

[22] *Railroad Gazette*, XIX (June 24, 1887), 422-423.

ing railroads to regulate themselves with I.C.C. sanction in the matter of discriminatory rates against locations. It "is capable of very general application . . . ," Aldace F. Walker wrote Joseph Nimmo, Jr., "and it is a fact that as a prevention of rate wars and destructive competition it is already recognized by intelligent railroad men as better than the pool."[23]

The railroads began exploiting their new liberty quite freely. New England, the South, and the transcontinental lines adjusted their rates accordingly.[24] When the first *Annual Report* of the Commission was issued in December 1887, the railroad journals took the occasion to heap praise on the I.C.C. and the honest men who ran it.[25] At the same time, using the new law as the authority, the railroads revamped their freight classifications, raised rates, eliminated passes and fare reductions, and revised their less-than-carload rates on all types of goods, including groceries. Led by the inimitable, militant Francis B. Thurber and the New York Board of Trade and Transportation, former merchant advocates of a federal railroad commission were reduced in 1888 to pleading for the principle of equal or near-equal rates for their less-than-carload shipments of pickles and cider. But the New Yorkers, their case argued by Simon Sterne, were left disappointed, for the I.C.C., in the Thurber case, held against them in early 1890. "Reasonable" differences in rates were allowed.[26]

[23] Aldace F. Walker to Joseph Nimmo, Jr., November 22, 1887, letter in the Interstate Commerce Commission Library, Washington, D. C. This letter is also an excellent, frank outline of the development of section 4.

[24] Edward Chase Kirkland, *Men, Cities, and Transportation: A Study in New England History, 1820-1900* (Cambridge, 1948), I, 519-522; I.C.C., *First Annual Report*, pp. 20-21.

[25] *Railroad Gazette*, XIX (December 9, 1887), 800; *Railway Review*, XXVII (December 17, 1887), 722.

[26] Peirce, *Digest of Decisions of the Courts and I.C.C.*, p. 445; Augustus Schoonmaker to William B. Allison, April 3, 1890, ICC-2, Letterbooks, vol. 6; Albert Fink, *Relative Cost of Carload and Less*

By 1890, the merchant organizations had had quite enough of the Commission's favoritism towards the railroads. The Detroit Board of Trade wrote the Senate in February that it wanted the Act repealed because it protected the railroads and their rates. Indianapolis agreed, and Boards of Trade and Chambers of Commerce throughout the Midwest and West sent in demands for the repeal of section 4. The Nebraska Farmers Alliance and the Producers Protective Association of Bradford, Pennsylvania, joined the chorus.[27] The National Board of Trade's annual convention in December 1890 suggested the law be revised to give the businessman means of breaking through administrative delays and the prejudices of section 4.[28] The Interstate Commerce Act was a bitter harvest for the farmers and merchants.

The Commission Defines the Law

The I.C.C.'s initial position on rates was as ambiguous as the section of the Act providing that rates be "reasonable and just." As early as May 16, 1887, Cooley wrote an inquirer that the Commission would not pass on the fairness of a rate, but in fact what he meant was that he would take no position on the matter with shippers but only with railroads.[29] Rates were only one example of an operational policy that was to guide the Commission under Cooley: informal opinions were to be given to railroads, but not to shippers. In a letter to A. B. Stickney, president of the Minnesota & Northwestern, on August 10, 1887, Cooley ventured an im-

---

Than Carload Shipments and Its Bearing Upon Freight Classification (Chicago, 1889); 3 *ICC Reports*, 473.

[27] Filed in Sen 51A-J 25 and HR 51A-H 6.11.

[28] National Board of Trade, *Proceedings of the Twenty-First Annual Meeting, New Orleans, December, 1890* (Boston, 1891), pp. 27, 53-64, 73.

[29] Thomas M. Cooley to J. S. Rawlings, May 16, 1887, I.C.C. Records, Virginia, file 602; also see files 1120 and 1133.

portant opinion on the means by which railroads might determine rates, without specifying, however, what they should precisely be. "It is greatly to be regretted, I think, that the roads could not come to a common understanding what rates they could afford to accept, + then fix such rates [and] abide by them."[30]

In the first *Annual Report* the Commission attacked rate wars at the same time as it paid homage to competition; it also implied it would oppose Congressional amendments to increase its rate-making powers. But section 1 of the Act gave someone, either the courts or the Commission, the power to judge whether rates were "unjust and unreasonable." So the Commission formulated criteria that removed the onus of responsibility for action from its shoulders. It suggested rates be "so apportioned as to encourage the largest practicable exchange of products between different sections of our country and with foreign countries. . . ."[31]

Such a definition could hardly pass muster, since it created more confusion than the Act. In 1890, the Commission formulated a more precise position, in large part based on its Thurber decision. "A reasonable rate is one that will make just and fair return to the carrier when it is charged to all who are to pay it without unjust discrimination against any. . . ."[32] The greatest good to the greatest number was the paramount consideration, although injury to some was unavoidable. Cost of service to the road was an important element, but so was the value of the product, and rates could be adjusted accordingly. And, most significant, cost of service to the road was more important than the profit of the shipper.[33]

[30] Thomas M. Cooley to A. B. Stickney, August 10, 1887, I.C.C. Records, Virginia, file 1119.

[31] I.C.C., *First Annual Report*, p. 36.

[32] Interstate Commerce Commission, *Fourth Annual Report, December 1, 1890* (Washington, 1890), p. 30.

[33] Peirce, *Digest of Decisions of the Courts and I.C.C.*, pp. 86, 352, 358.

Informal rulings to railroads and refusals to give informal opinions to shippers undoubtedly discouraged many shippers from embarking on uncharted and expensive battles with railroads. Cooley, on April 14, 1887, claimed that passing on informal or theoretical issues might prejudice the decision of a legal dispute in advance, and since most of the Commission's thousands of incoming letters during its first years consisted of undocumented complaints by shippers, its policy seemed reasonable.[34] The Commission soon decided it would "not express opinions on abstract questions, nor on questions presented by ex-parte statements of fact, nor on questions of the construction of the statute. . . ."[35] And although the Commission *often* told this to railroad men, it *always* told it to shippers, and not infrequently broke this rule, as it did many others, for the railroads.[36] As part of this friendly, informal *détente*, the Commission allowed the Western railroads to ignore an amendment to the Act in 1889 which required all rate increases to be filed with the Commission at least ten days before they went into effect. Instead, the railroads were told, rates could be sent along after going into effect.[37]

Until 1900 the average case before the Commission lasted not less than four years, and a refusal by the Commission to give a preliminary opinion to a shipper meant he had one of three alternatives. He could forget

[34] Thomas M. Cooley to T. H. Smith, April 14, 1887, I.C.C. Records, Virginia, file 183.

[35] William Morrison to William E. Royster, October 22, 1889, I.C.C. Records, Virginia, file 4598.

[36] See, for example, Edward A. Moseley to George J. Ermlich, December 17, 1889, file 4683; W. L. Bragg to M. N. Coe, February 10, 1890, file 4727; F. W. Clark to I.C.C., April 12, 1890, file 5264, all in I.C.C. Records, Virginia. In *Railroad Gazette*, XXI (August 30, 1889), 565, an anonymous railroad man complains of this practice.

[37] Charles S. Fee to Thomas Cooley, January 16, 1890; Edward A. Moseley to Charles S. Fee, February 28, 1890, in I.C.C. Records, Virginia, file 4866.

about it; or he could allow the Commission to mediate with the road in the hope that misunderstandings and errors could be worked out and the railroad would be charitable. "This method of disposing of complaints is believed by the Commission to be more useful than any other . . . ," the Commission wrote in 1887.[38] There is no record of shipper response or satisfaction with this method, and it essentially allowed the roads to judge themselves. The last alternative, of initiating a formal case against a road, was incredibly expensive and time consuming for the average shipper. For these reasons, and given the fact that the only shippers wealthy enough to undertake a case were usually in a position also to pass freight charges to their customers or bargain for rebates, formal cases were rare. During 1890 to 1900, only 180 cases were formally decided by the Commission —of the many thousands brought to its attention. In this context, railroad regulation essentially represented an internal class affair. The vast majority of farmers and the consumers were powerless and forgotten. It did not occur to the authors of the Cullom or Reagan Bills to create some formal mechanism for representing the "public interest" in railroad regulation, since it appeared almost axiomatic that shippers would eliminate any injustices through their appeals. Nor did it impress many politicians that the larger shippers and railroads might have more in common with one another than with an amorphous, unorganized mass of poorer farmers and workers; but for those few exceptions, who gradually found their spokesmen in Populism and the Democracy of William Jennings Bryan, government ownership of the railroads, and not regulation within private control, ultimately became the primary definition of "public interest."

[38] I.C.C., *First Annual Report*, p. 26; also U.S. Industrial Commission, *Final Report*, XIX, 420-422.

The Railroads and the New Law

Even Charles E. Perkins was ready to suggest a policy of "Let us ask the Commissioners to enforce the law when its violation by others hurts us."[39] And why not? The Commission was hardly hostile, and "there are many points in the Interstate Commerce law, which, if enforced, properly, would redound to the material interests of both the republic and railways," as one railroad man wrote.[40] Amendments should be added, most railroad men agreed, but in the meantime they wanted the Act to be applied. Railroad executives, indeed, were most anxious to see the law applied in cases where the Commission was unaware of violations, especially by their competitors, and they reported a number of them to Washington.[41] ". . . we would welcome the rigid and literal enforcement of every provision of the interstate commerce act," Charles Francis Adams, Jr., wrote in late 1888.[42]

For about six months after the formation of the Commission, railroad income grew because of the termination of many rebates, elimination of passes, and general conformity to the Act. Toward the end of the year, however, weaknesses began appearing as the aggressive few began granting rebates. The overexpansion of railroad mileage during 1886-1887 further undermined the railroad economy. Inevitably, attention was turned to the

[39] Quoted in Cochran, *Railroad Leaders*, p. 198.

[40] A. V. H. Carpenter to Edward A. Moseley, March 5, 1890, I.C.C. Records, Virginia, file 5236.

[41] See, for example, Charles Schiff to I.C.C., August 23, 1887, I.C.C. Records, Virginia, file 1273; A. G. Safford to George R. Blanchard, May 9, 1890, ICC-2, Letterbooks, vol. 6; Charles Francis Adams, Jr., to Thomas M. Cooley, January 31, 1889, Charles Francis Adams, Jr., Papers, Massachusetts Historical Society.

[42] Speech of Charles Francis Adams, Jr., December, 1888, in C. C. McCain, ed., *Compendium of Transportation Theories* (Washington, 1893), p. 183.

desirability of pools. The Commission, sympathetic to the railroads' plight, praised their voluntary associations and suggested that before a new law be passed railroads voluntarily respect their existing agreements and exploit the potentialities already in the law.[43] A few railroad leaders, such as Adams, agreed that the problem was the railroads' "want of good faith," and "The railroad system must heal itself; no act of Congress, or repeal of any act of Congress, will greatly help it."[44]

There was a middle way between growing anarchy and a bill making pools legally binding, and that was an organized effort to utilize the provisions of the Act to enforce a rate agreement. And although efforts to pass a pooling bill continued, the new compromise was tried as well. The organizational structure was the rate association, essentially the old pool continued without a division of freight and markets, but devoted solely to setting and maintaining rates—ostensibly still legal. When the I.C.C. was created, J. W. Midgley, representing the major Eastern and Midwestern pools, offered his association's services "to make the Act to Regulate Commerce practical and operative."[45] The Commission supported the efforts of the roads to work out a system of uniform classification of goods, and regarded the rate associations favorably.[46] The railroad associations desired something more concrete than sympathy, however, especially as rates began dropping and the restoration of

[43] I.C.C., *First Annual Report*, pp. 33-36; Thomas M. Cooley, *Address before the Boston Merchant's Association*, January 8, 1889 (n. p., 1889), *passim*. For the economic context, see Julius Grodinsky, *Transcontinental Railway Strategy, 1869-1893* (Philadelphia, 1962), chaps. XV-XVI.

[44] Adams, *Compendium of Transportation Theories*, pp. 178, 180.

[45] J. W. Midgley, "Growing Sentiment For a Properly Constituted Commission," [Circular Letter No. 39—'To Members'], April 28, 1905 (mimeo.), p. 9, in Sen 58A-J 36.

[46] I.C.C., *First Annual Report*, pp. 30-36; A. Schoonmaker to J. W. Midgley, June 27, 1890; W. Morrison to J. W. Midgley, July 3, 1890, in ICC-2, Letterbooks, vol. 7.

cutthroat competition appeared more and more likely.
"The strong lines, as a rule, so far as my observations of
the matter have gone," a railroad president calculated in
late 1888, "are anxious to make the Interstate Commerce
Act effectual, but the trouble is with the weaker lines.
. . . If a joint arrangement ordinarily known as a 'pool'
could be operative under the Inter-state Commerce Act,
I believe it would solve many of the difficulties. . . ."[47]

During the first days of 1889 the presidents of the
major Western roads, in the midst of a prolonged rate
war, were summoned to New York by J. P. Morgan and
several banking houses to devise ways of maintaining
rates and enforcing the Interstate Commerce Act. They
met with Cooley, Morrison, and Walker and, according
to Charles Francis Adams, Jr., the Commissioners
"desired greatly that some such organization should be
effected, with a view to co-operation with them . . . . they
would unite and act cordially with us in making it operative and effective. . . ."[48] The agreement that was reached
and signed by twenty-two roads was essentially designed to maintain rates, and although no formal shares
of freight were distributed, thereby keeping the contract
from appearing as if it were a complete pool, the executives were authorized to "take such steps as may be
proper, requisite and legal to secure to each Company its
due share of the competitive traffic."[49] Among the means
the association was to use to enforce the agreement was
notifying the I.C.C. of violations of law, a logical re-

[47] Henry B. Ledyard of the Michigan Central to James Clements,
November 21, 1888, in Cochran, *Railroad Leaders*, p. 404.

[48] [Interstate Commerce Law Association], *Proceedings of Conferences between Presidents of Railroad Lines West of Chicago and
St. Louis and Representatives of Banking Houses, January 8th and
10th, 1889* (New York, 1889), p. 17. For additional background,
see Grodinsky, *Transcontinental Railway Strategy*, chaps. XVII-
XVIII. The January meeting was the culmination of a series of
earlier conferences, as well as of a widespread debate among railroad
leaders.

[49] *Ibid.*, p. 14.

course, since the purpose of the group of railroads was "to exercise their power and influence in the maintenance of rates and the enforcement of all the provisions of the Inter-State Law."[50] The new organization of railroads, which appropriately dubbed itself "Inter-State Commerce Railway Association," was in fact nothing more than a massive railway effort to interpret and enforce, with Commission sanction, the Act of 1887. And to give itself the proper *imprimatur*, the new association induced Aldace Walker to resign from the I.C.C. and become its chairman.

"We feel satisfied that the law properly enforced will remove a great many of the difficulties that are now surrounding the management of railways," George B. Roberts, president of the Pennsylvania, told his fellow railroad presidents at the meeting.[51] "The Northwest Board for whom I speak," Marvin Hughitt of the Chicago and Northwestern declared, "favors as I said the Inter-State Commerce Law and wishes to see it enforced with all its provisions. . . ."[52] The arrangement was all assets, Chauncey Depew, now president of the New York Central, admitted. "While we avoid the pool so-called we do evidently under the sanction of the Inter-State Commerce Commission and without any amendment to the Inter-State Commerce law in general secure some machinery by which peace can be maintained."[53] Not all railroad men agreed. The Illinois Central stayed away from the meeting because it felt the rates the new association would set were legally unenforceable. It proved to be correct.[54]

Since the law was not being enforced at the present time, Adams wrote Cooley, "I feel, therefore, that the

[50] *Ibid.*, pp. 2, 10.   [51] *Ibid.*, pp. 22-23.
[52] *Ibid.*, p. 21.   [53] *Ibid.*, p. 28.
[54] See Stuyvesant Fish to Edward T. Jeffery, January 3, 1889, in Cochran, *Railroad Leaders*, p. 323.

enforcement of this act must soon become, if it is not now, a matter of mere self-preservation to the company I represent."[55] In February, ten of the major Eastern lines signed a similar compact, with Fink as its commissioner, designed "to aid in the enforcement of the provisions of the Interstate Commerce Law" and report all violations to the I.C.C.[56]

Morgan's efforts to impose stability and profit on the Western railroads were bound to failure even before the ink was dry on the new compact. The Far West had been the scene of excessive railroad expansion, especially in the Northwest, where the Northern Pacific and the Oregon and Transcontinental Railroads under Henry Villard were struggling with the Union Pacific in a battle of mileage.[57] By March 1889, barely enough time for the railroad presidents to get back from Morgan's, a rate war in the West sharply undermined the new organization's value, and by June the chaotic status quo was restored. And, ironically, Adams' Union Pacific was the center of the new rate war, as temptation overcame virtue. Efforts to reestablish the association in May 1890 failed, though in December 1890, Morgan reconstituted the organization with I.C.C. approval. At the same time, Gould, Huntington, and the Atchison, Topeka and Santa Fe interests also formed a rate organization in the Southwest. But both associations went through the traditional cycle of collapse and resurrection over the next several years.[58] In short, voluntary railroad agreements were no

[55] Charles Francis Adams, Jr., to Thomas M. Cooley, January 31, 1889, Charles Francis Adams, Jr., Papers.

[56] [Trunk Line Association], *Articles of Association of the Trunk Lines—Copy of Trunk Line Contract of February 20th, 1889* (Philadelphia, 1894), p. 7 and *passim.*

[57] The entire affair is discussed in James Blaine Hedges, *Henry Villard and the Railways of the Northwest* (New Haven, 1930); and for this period, Henry Villard Papers, Houghton Library, Harvard University, box 35.

[58] [Joint Rate Association], *Proceedings and Circulars of the Joint Rate Committee of the Trunk Line, Central Traffic and*

more successful with the new law and the intervention of Morgan than before.

The Southern Railway & Steamship Association revised its rules in 1887 to become a rate association, and substituted fines rather than boycotts against violators. The I.C.C. also worked with it to enforce its posted rates, but by 1893 the association had fallen apart, only to be patched together a few years later.[59] The Trunk Line Association, the Eastern equivalent of the Inter-State Commerce Railway Association, kept going for a number of years with only modest success, although Fink resigned less than one year after its formation.[60] Throughout the 1890's the railroads continued regional or highly specialized rate associations, many of which also tried to divide markets or assign quotas. Their efforts were merely formal and gratuitous.[61]

The effort to maintain rates by voluntary means proved no more successful after the Interstate Commerce Act than it had earlier, and the movement to legalize pools continued. Bills were presented to Congress, but despite substantial railroad support invariably failed. Aldace F. Walker, now playing his new role as spokesman for the responsible railroads, suggested that stable rates were all the shipper really needed, and, without

---

Western Freight Associations, 1889 and 1890 (Chicago, 1891), pp. 4, 8, 87, 91, 306; Julius Grodinsky, *Jay Gould: His Business Career* (Philadelphia, 1957), pp. 560-568, 583-584; Herbert L. Satterlee, *J. Pierpont Morgan: An Intimate Portrait* (New York, 1939), pp. 257-258; Grodinsky, *Transcontinental Railway Strategy*, chap. XIX.

[59] Hudson, *Quarterly Journal of Economics*, v (1890), 91; Charles S. Langstroth and Wilson Stilz, *Railway Co-operation* (Philadelphia, 1899), pp. 67-68; U.S. Industrial Commission, *Final Report*, House Doc. No. 380, 57th Cong., 2nd Sess. (Washington, 1902), XIX, 336-337.

[60] Joint Rate Association, *Proceedings . . . 1889*, pp. 126, 161.

[61] Industrial Commission, *Final Report*, XIX, 334-337; William Z. Ripley, *Railroads: Finance and Organization* (New York, 1915), pp. 588ff.; Langstroth and Stilz, *Railway Co-operation*, pp. 68ff.; I.C.C., *Fourth Annual Report*, pp. 22-25.

pools, rates would continue to fall.[62] Competition, the railroads claimed, was too dangerous. But even Cooley's public support of pooling could not change the unwillingness of Congress to make major amendments in the Act.[63]

[62] Aldace F. Walker, *Argument Before Senate Committee on Interstate Commerce, June 4, 1890* (Washington, 1890), pp. 3-5; also Aldace F. Walker, *Railway Associations* (Chicago, 1890).

[63] Thomas M. Cooley, speech of March 1891, in *Compendium of Transportation Theories*, pp. 248-249. For railroad support of pooling legalization, see Joseph Nimmo, Jr., *Pooling and Governmental Control of the Railroads* (Washington, 1888), pp. 3, 8; G. R. Blanchard, *Why Pooling Should be Legalized: A Letter to the Hon. Shelby M. Cullom, June 9, 1890* (n. p., 1890); *Joseph Nimmo, Jr., to Aldace Walker, May 26, 1890* (n. p., 1890), p. 6; W. L. Bragg to James A. Logan, April 18, 1890, I.C.C. Records, Virginia, file 5466; G. R. Blanchard, "Shall Railway Pooling Be Permitted," *Forum*, v (August, 1888), 652-665.

CHAPTER IV

COMPETITION AND CRISIS:
THE FAILURE OF REGULATION
1891-1897

IF railroads declined to cooperate voluntarily and Congress refused to legislate, some railroad leaders predicted in 1888, railroads would resort to outright mergers and consolidations in the hope of ending anarchy. ". . . unless railway managers can associate," Aldace Walker warned in 1890, "railway owners must combine."[1] In September 1891, reflecting on the lack of progress in attaining stability, Collis P. Huntington invited his fellow railroad men to embark on consolidations in order to end mutually destructive rate wars.[2]

The Depression of 1893 played havoc with the American railroad system, already weakened by rate wars and overextended mileage. In 1893, railroads with 27,000 miles of track were foreclosed, equivalent to over one-tenth of the total mileage, and during the next five years lines with a total of 41,000 miles were foreclosed.[3] Included were such major lines as the Baltimore & Ohio, Union Pacific, Northern Pacific, Atchison, Topeka & Santa Fe, and the Erie.

[1] Aldace Walker, *Railway Associations* (Chicago, 1890), p. 23; also Charles Francis Adams, Jr., "The Interstate Commerce Law," *Compendium of Transportation Theories* (Washington, 1893), p. 182.

[2] Collis P. Huntington, "A Plea for Railway Consolidation," in *Compendium of Transportation Theories*, p. 251. This article originally appeared in the *North American Review*, September, 1891. U.S. Industrial Commission, *Final Report*, House Doc. No. 380, 57th Cong., 2d Sess. (Washington, 1902), XIX, 345-348, ascribes much of the consolidation movement to the failure of pools.

[3] Stuart Daggett, *Railroad Reorganization* (Boston, 1908), p. v.

The consolidation movement that followed in the wake of numerous railroad reorganizations is too well known to require any detailed consideration here. By the end of the decade J. P. Morgan became the most important factor in the railroad sector of the economy, controlling the Erie, the Philadelphia & Reading, the Jersey Central, the Lehigh Valley, the Delaware & Hudson, the Northern Pacific, the Southern, the New Haven, and various other lines, not including important understandings or communities of interest with Vanderbilt, Hill, and the Pennsylvania. As E. G. Campbell, a careful student of Morgan's machinations, put it: "The extent of Morgan's influence among the railroads of the country at the end of the nineteenth century cannot be stated absolutely, but by virtue of voting trusts, interlocking directorates and communities of interest, it was immense."[4] It was immense, but was it large enough to control and stabilize the entire railroad system, and was Morgan's intervention designed to do so?

Morgan's reorganizations, like Edward H. Harriman's, were accompanied by large doses of overcapitalized stock, primarily common shares.[5] Indeed, a cumulative process of overcapitalization among the larger lines, and their inability to freely pass their growing fixed costs to the shippers in higher rates, meant that they were especially susceptible to bankruptcy and reorganization during depressions. Most of the smaller, minor roads, Campbell proved, fared a good deal better in the 1890's than the giant roads, and they were more

[4] E. G. Campbell, *The Reorganization of the American Railroad System, 1893-1900* (New York, 1938), p. 328 and *passim*. Campbell's study and Daggett's *Railroad Reorganization* are the two best studies of this phase of railroad history.

[5] Campbell, *Reorganization of the American Railroad System*, pp. 158-172, 321-323; Daggett, *Railroad Reorganization*, pp. 61-64. Francis Lynde Stetson, *Address Before the Economic Club of New York, June 5, 1907* (n. p., n. d.), pp. 5-6, defends the practice. Stetson was a key Morgan lawyer.

prosperous than in the 1880's.[6] Morgan weakened rather than strengthened many of his roads, such as the Erie, Southern, or the New Haven, and hardly prepared them for effective consolidation of the railroad system under unified, voluntary control. Service and safety often declined.[7] Many of Morgan's lines overexpanded into areas where competition was already too great. Stuart Daggett, summarizing the reorganization of eight major lines, four of which Morgan controlled, concluded: "If unrestricted capitalization has increased the load which the railroads have had to bear, unrestricted competition has impaired their ability to support any load at all. The forms which this competition has taken have been mainly two: first, the cutting of rates, either openly or by secret concessions; second, reckless extensions of line, generally followed by rate-cutting."[8]

Certainly it can be said that the basically competitive and semi-chaotic structure of the railroad industry was not significantly altered during the 1890's by the consolidation movement, rate associations, or the I.C.C. Rates continued to decline, and the Depression of 1893 increased the sharpness of rate wars for several years. Freight revenue per ton mile declined from .94 of a cent in 1890 to .73 of a cent in 1900.[9] Rebating continued, as railroads tried to encourage the growth and volume of their own major shippers or were forced by them to grant rebates for fear of losing their traffic. "We adjust the rates so as to enable him [the new manufacturer] to successfully operate. That is what is called promoting traf-

6 Campbell, *Reorganization of the American Railroad System*, p. 304. The Industrial Commission, in its *Final Report*, XIX, 412-415, reluctantly concluded that overcapitalization has no direct bearing on rates.

7 Campbell, *Reorganization of the American Railroad System*, pp. 334-341.

8 Daggett, *Railroad Reorganization*, p. 340.

9 *Historical Statistics of the U.S.*, pp. 428, 431; Industrial Commission, *Final Report*, XIX, 352.

fic, and is, of course, the only possible way in which a corporation like ours can succeed—by increasing its traffic."[10] And railroad mileage over the decade increased another one-quarter.

Even granting the enormous power of Morgan, his community of interests and alliances with other railroads were quite as important to him as his actual control, for Harriman, Gould, or the Pennsylvania were capable of doing enormous damage, and their relation to him was based on a good faith that was no more permanent than their interpretation of their own vital interests. As we shall see, such alliances were too shaky to avoid serious disagreements. It was always apparent to at least some railroad men that the concentration of control could not be extensive enough to eliminate competition. In 1887, there were 28 railroads with over 1000 miles of track, and, in 1900, there were 48 such systems with 60 per cent of the total U.S. mileage. Although many of these lines were controlled by similar interests, a sufficient number were autonomous to leave a significant group of independent and powerful railroads often capable of serious competition with one another. And despite mergers and bankruptcies, there were 1,224 operating railroads in 1900, a growth of over 200 since 1890.[11] While most of these were small lines, they increased the number of alternative routes between commercial centers.

The New I.C.C.

Cooley resigned from the Interstate Commerce Commission in September 1891, because of poor health, and

[10] Testimony of Milton H. Smith, president of the Louisville & Nashville, December 6, 1897, in U.S. Senate, *Railway Rates and Charges, Etc.*, Senate Doc. No. 259, 55th Cong., 2d Sess., May 6, 1898 (Washington, 1898), p. 10.

[11] U.S. Industrial Commission, *Report of the Industrial Commission on Transportation* (Washington, 1900), IV, 296-298; William Z. Ripley, *Railroads: Finance and Organization* (New York, 1915), p. 458; *Historical Statistics of the U.S.*, p. 429.

Morrison became the new chairman. Since Schoonmaker's term had expired in December 1890, and Bragg had died in August 1891, Morrison was the only member left from the original Commission. He continued as chairman until December 1897. The new Commissioners, while certainly not crusading, tended to give a more sympathetic ear to the shippers than had Cooley. Nevertheless, they continued many of their older, informal relations with railroads, some of which were clearly illegal. The Commission allowed railroad associations to file common rates for its members, and told inquiring roads that it would take no action if they did not have rates posted, as provided in the law, but merely available to interested parties.[12] These comparatively small items, however, were modest in their consequences in comparison with the Commission's custom of adjusting shippers' complaints informally. The railroad was under no legal obligation to respond to the Commission in such cases, and a goodly number apparently chose not to, thereby dragging out matters for the shipper and postponing their utilization of legally enforceable alternatives. The Commission admitted that these shippers had "been induced to delay action on their own part by reason of our having undertaken to bring about adjustment or better understanding of the facts by correspondence."[13] If the railroad was charitable the shipper was not greatly inconvenienced by this system.

In dealing with section 4, however, the informality of the Commission was more and more untenable. Not only did it inspire merchant groups to call for the elimination of section 4, or the abolition of the Commission alto-

[12] Interstate Commerce Commission, *Sixth Annual Report, December 1, 1892* (Washington, 1892), p. 39; Minneapolis & St. Louis RR Co. to Edward A. Moseley, January 15, 1897; J. D. Yoemans to Minneapolis & St. Louis RR Co., January 21, 1897, in I.C.C. Records, Virginia, file 36829.

[13] J. C. Clement to J. M. Culp, December 19, 1896, I.C.C. Records, Virginia, file 36795.

gether, but even caused the railroads to split over the issue. Roads with direct lines or short routes preferred section 4 and the possibility of interpreting it themselves; those with active terminal competition or circuitous routes found the arrangement disagreeable.[14] In light of these divisions and declining rates, the Commission in late November 1892, after five years, decided to require railroads to apply to the Commission if they wished to make exceptions to the long-short haul provision of the Act. The decision was appealed and went to the courts, where it was finally defeated in 1897.

In another instance the new Commission broke with its easy-going predecessors by asking Congress for an act to require a witness to testify or produce evidence in court cases growing out of Commission action, in return for immunity from prosecution in the matter on which he testified. The request was necessitated by the Supreme Court's *Counselman* decision of January 1892, which declared a witness did not have to testify if it might incriminate him, and also by a cavalier attitude towards Commission requests on the part of some railroads. In late 1891, for example, an agent of the I.C.C. asked the U.S. District Court in Omaha to subpoena Midgley and J. N. Faithorn of Aldace Walker's Western Traffic Association, the successor of the Interstate Commerce Railway Association. Walker wrote the Commission bitterly, "I have no hesitation in saying that the associations are the most potent instrumentality that exists in the direction of securing the maintenance of rates and putting an end to personal discriminations, rebates, manipulations and all manner of like devices. . . . All this machinery runs alongside the machinery established by the Interstate Commerce Act and is in aid of

[14] Aldace F. Walker, "The Amendment of the Interstate Commerce Law," *Independent*, XLV (June 1, 1893), 734. Also see Interstate Commerce Commission, *Eighth Annual Report, December 1, 1894* (Washington, 1894), p. 20.

its operation. I think it may fairly be said that this machinery of the associations practically represents nearly all that has been done until a comparatively recent date in the way of securing obedience to the requirements of the statute." For this reason the associations should enjoy immunity, and the Commission should deal with them directly rather than through the courts. "I had supposed that an understanding existed to the effect that the matter would be so treated."[15] Congress gave the I.C.C. its law in February 1893, and the Supreme Court upheld it three years later.[16]

Other steps to strengthen the Commission did not fare as well, however. A bill (S. 892) to give Commission findings legal force in court, which the Commission did not especially demand, met with strong railroad opposition and was defeated.[17] The Commission itself finally began cautiously requesting rate powers, and in so doing tacitly acknowledged that it did not have them at the time, long before the Supreme Court confirmed their judgment. Its 1893 *Annual Report* declared the Commission should "determine *what are just and reasonable rates for public carriage.* . . ."[18] But the Commission was essentially ambivalent, since it knew full well that rate wars made the problem of unjust rates largely academic. In its 1894 report the Commission concentrated on "The evils of unlimited power in the carriers to reduce rates . . . ," an objection with which few roads were likely to quarrel.[19] According to Martin A. Knapp, a forceful new

[15] Aldace F. Walker to I.C.C., November 28, 1891, in I.C.C. Records, Virginia, file 41959½.

[16] Interstate Commerce Commission, *Ninth Annual Report, December 1, 1895* (Washington, 1896), pp. 8-9.

[17] U.S. Senate, Committee on Interstate Commerce, *Hearings . . . Re S. 892,* 52d Cong., 1st Sess., February, 1892 (Washington, 1892), *passim.* Schoonmaker appeared representing the New York, Lake Erie & Western RR. *Ibid.,* pp. 70ff.

[18] Interstate Commerce Commission, *Seventh Annual Report, December 1, 1893* (Washington, 1893), p. 10. Italics in original.

[19] I.C.C., *Eighth Annual Report,* p. 24.

Commissioner, the shipper was often as able to exploit the railroad as be exploited himself. To produce a "stable equilibrium" between the two was the goal of regulation.[20] Legislation to end rebates and "authority to correct ascertained excesses in railroad charges," the Commission said in its 1895 *Annual Report*, would be desirable, along with court review.[21] Despite its sympathy for legalized pools under proper supervision, to be considered later, the I.C.C. was clearly beginning to break with the tradition of Cooley. And, for the first time, Commissioners were to begin disagreeing with one another and taking independent positions. But, as under Cooley, the Commission's primary definition of its function was essentially compatible with the interests of the railroads.

The Railroads, Self-Regulation, and the Commission

As the personnel of the Commission changed rapidly within a brief period, and a few of the Commissioners began showing signs of independence, apprehension arose among some railroad leaders. Cooley, George Blanchard reminisced, was a "practical" man in comparison with his successors.[22] The Act of 1887 did not appear to be having the desired results, the pools and rate associations had failed, competition was growing, and in addition to their persistent clamor for pooling legislation, the railroads also turned to their own resources. The consolidation movement, as I have already indicated, was one alternative. The pool was another, but it was a proven failure.

Sometime in 1892, Joseph Nimmo, Jr., began circulating a confidential memorandum on the need for

[20] Martin A. Knapp, *Speech Before the Railway Congress at Columbian Exposition, June 23, 1893* (Chicago, 1893), p. 13.

[21] I.C.C., *Ninth Annual Report*, p. 17.

[22] G. R. Blanchard, *Argument Before the Committee of the United States Senate on Interstate Commerce, March 2, 1894* (n.p., 1894), p. 24.

railroads to adopt a "policy of self-control." Nimmo was disturbed by what he saw as the new Commission's search for more power and independence. Morrison was "a narrow man, moved by prejudice, fond of power." If the railroads could agree on a plan of "self-imposed, legalized restraints," he would have it introduced in Congress and they might thereby "suppress ill-advised schemes."[23] The railroads were not, however, interested enough to cooperate with Nimmo's plan or the effort that year to revive a rate association east of the Mississippi, even though numerous, impotent associations existed in the West and in smaller areas throughout the nation.

In June 1895, the presidents of the major lines east of Chicago met to discuss the deteriorating rate situation, and for lack of an alternative, they decided to organize a "rate association." In November, after a number of preliminary meetings, thirty-one railroads signed an agreement, to become effective January 1, 1896, "To aid in fulfilling the purposes of the Interstate Commerce Act, to co-operate with each other and adjacent transportation associations, to establish and maintain reasonable and just rates, fares, rules and regulations. . . ."[24] The executives of the Joint Traffic Association were to seek to attain "legally" a proper share of the traffic for all participating roads. In August 1895, however, Senator William E. Chandler of New Hampshire began writing the I.C.C. about the proposed association, demanding its destruction. The Commission at first pleaded

23 Joseph Nimmo, Jr., "Confidential Memo," 1892. A three-page mimeographed letter. A copy may be found in the Library of the Bureau of Railway Economics, Washington, D.C.

24 [Joint Traffic Association], *Proceedings of the Board of Managers of the Joint Traffic Association, December 13, 1895, to June 30, 1896* (New York?, 1896?), pp. 25, 32-33, and *passim*.

it knew nothing about the matter; later it suggested the association did not appear to be illegal. Chandler was particularly irked by Knapp, whom he considered a defender of the railroads who ought to be fired. Such political pressure influenced the Commission, and in its 1895 *Annual Report*, dated December 1st, it elected to play safe by calling the new association illegal even before it received copies of the agreement and before the compact went into effect.[25]

The articles of the new association were no different, in principle, than those of the defunct Interstate Commerce Law Association, which the Commission had considered legal. Nevertheless, Morrison wrote Judson Harmon, the Attorney General, on December 26, 1895, declaring the Joint Traffic Association to be illegal. Harmon obtained an injunction against the association in January; the case was heard in court in April and dismissed in May 1896. The Supreme Court reversed the decision in October 1898.[26] Before the Supreme Court brought in its verdict, striking the most devastating blow to pools and rate associations ever delivered, the association failed in its aims on its own volition. Despite its exclusion of coal, coke, oil, iron ore, limestone, and all Southern traffic from the agreement, rates could still not be maintained, if only because a significant number of Eastern lines never bothered to join the association.[27] By mid-1897 George Blanchard, the association's commissioner, was again ready to try to attain a political solution to the railroads' problems. "Until a decision is

[25] All documents may be found in U.S. Senate, Senate Doc. No. 39, 54th Cong., 1st Sess., December 24, 1895 (Washington, 1895), *passim*; I.C.C., *Ninth Annual Report*, p. 98.

[26] U.S. Senate, Senate Doc. No. 287, 54th Cong., 1st Sess., May 25, 1896 (Washington, 1896), pp. 1-2. Industrial Commission, *Final Report*, XIX, 335, indicates the association was definitely a traffic pool.

[27] Joint Traffic Association, *Proceedings*, pp. 12-20, 27.

rendered I am letting things go in New York, and keep-ing my eye on Congress."[28]

Keeping one's eye on Congress became an ingrained habit among railroad men during the 1890's, even as they attempted to control the industry by voluntary means. The major objective of their legislative aspira-tions was the pool, with stringent rate-making powers, legally enforceable. Cooley had supported this senti-ment by making it clear that it was not railroad competition but the steadiness of rates that was desir-able.[29] Railroad men had had enough of competition, Aldace Walker admitted. "The phrase 'free competi-tion' sounds well as a universal regulator, but it regu-lates by the knife. Unless the weapon in turn itself is held in check it is too dangerous an agency to be en-dured."[30] But the railroads did not have to rely on ex-Interstate Commerce Commissioners such as Walker and Schoonmaker for their rationales, valuable though their seeming authority might be.[31] A. B. Stickney, presi-dent of the Minnesota & Northwestern, in 1891 began advocating handing the entire matter of rates and rail-road stability over to the Commission: "For a quarter

[28] J. T. Marchand to William B. Morrison, June 1, 1897, I.C.C. Records, Virginia, file 38645. Also see Interstate Commerce Com-mission, *Twelfth Annual Report, January 11, 1899* (Washington, 1899), p. 14; Industrial Commission, *Final Report*, XIX, 334-337, for the general rate associations situation.

[29] Thomas M. Cooley, *Speech Before the 3rd Annual Meeting of National Association of Railway Commissioners, 1891* (n.p., 1891?), pp. 14-19; Thomas M. Cooley, speech of March, 1891, in *Compen-dium of Transportation Theories*, pp. 7-19.

[30] Aldace F. Walker, *Speech Before the Sunset Club, Chicago, April 2, 1891* (Chicago, 1891), p. 6. Also see the agreement of another railroad executive, E. P. Ripley, in *ibid.*, p. 12.

[31] Aldace F. Walker, "Unregulated Competition Self-Destructive," *Forum*, XII (December, 1891), 505-518; Schoonmaker, *Railroad Gazette*, XXIII (1891), 725-726; Aldace F. Walker, *Speech Before the National Transportation Association, November, 1892* (Chicago, 1892); Augustus Schoonmaker, "Unity of Railways and Railway In-terests," *Compendium of Transportation Theories*, pp. 57-66.

of a century they [railroads] have been attempting, by agreements between themselves, to make and maintain uniform and stable rates. But as such contracts are not recognized as binding by the law, they have rested entirely on the good faith of each company, and to a great extent upon the capacity as well as good faith of each of the traffic officials and employees. In the past they have not been efficacious, and judging from experience and from our knowledge of the foibles of human nature, it is too much to hope for any sufficient protection to the rights of owners growing out of such agreements in the future. . . . Their alternative protection is the strong arm of the law. Let the law name the rates, and let the law maintain and protect their integrity."[32]

Pressure on Congress for action increased, and in late 1892 the I.C.C. polled railroads, shippers, politicians, etc., to find out how they regarded legalized pooling under Commission control. Fourteen out of fifteen railroads favored it, along with all the railroad associations, many shippers, and even John H. Reagan and Charles E. Perkins. The Commission then endorsed legalized pooling along with increased Commission power to enforce its orders and prevent abuse of the pooling privilege. A bill (S. 3577) embodying the essence of such a proposal was introduced in the Senate, and hearings in December 1892 found Walker, George B. Roberts of the Pennsylvania, Chauncey Depew, and M. E. Ingalls of the C. & O. arguing for it.[33]

The railroads' demand for legislation continued throughout 1893, and Walker publicly claimed the

[32] A. B. Stickney, *The Railway Problem* (St. Paul, 1891), pp. 222-223; also p. 162.
[33] I.C.C., *Sixth Annual Report*, pp. 47-55, 219-265; U.S. Senate, Committee on Interstate Commerce, *Hearings on S. 3577*, Senate Misc. Doc. No. 126, 53d Cong., 3d Sess., December 14, 1892 (Washington, 1893), *passim*.

Commission had given "tacit approval" to the pooling bill in the Senate.[34] Walker understated the case. The Commission's 1892 *Report* was explicit enough, and Wheelock G. Veazey, one of the new Commissioners, was making public declarations attacking the evils of low rates and proclaiming the need for pools.[35] The only time the Commission opposed a pooling bill, such as H.R. 4230, was when it was excluded from control over final rates.[36] But this contingency hardly put the Commission in opposition to the railroads, since most of them also wanted the power of the I.C.C. behind pooling agreements.

In 1894, the railroads were faced with three alternative pooling bills. One, introduced in the Senate by Orville Platt (S. 1039), merely legalized pools created by the roads themselves; since the enforceability of such voluntary agreements was debatable, the railroads opposed it. The Patterson and Storer bills in the House allowed pooling arrangements subject to Commission approval, but with no judicial review. The roads opposed this approach, and the Commission failed to approve it. The third alternative was embodied in S. 1534, introduced by Senator A. P. Gorman in January. This bill, which obtained the general support of the railroads, would have given the I.C.C. ten days to disapprove pool-

34 Walker, *Independent*, XLV (1893), 733. Also see G. R. Blanchard, *Reply to S. M. Cullom* [reprint of an article in *Railway Age and Northwestern Railroader*, April 14, 1893] (Chicago, 1893); James Peabody, "The Necessity of Railway Compacts Under Governmental Regulation," *Independent*, XLV (June 1, 1893), 737; Ossian D. Ashley, *Railroad Corporations and the People* (New York, 1893), pp. 24-25; Joseph Nimmo, Jr., *Form of Bill to Secure the Just and Orderly Conduct of the American Railroad System, July 17, 1893* (n. p., 1893).

35 W. G. Veazey, *Address Before the Railway Congress, Columbian Exposition, June 21, 1893* (Chicago, 1893), pp. 10-12.

36 See William Morrison to House Committee on Interstate and Foreign Commerce, November 1, 1893, in HR 53A-F 19.2. About a dozen different merchant organizations wrote the House Committee on Interstate and Foreign Commerce in 1893 supporting the demand of the railroads for legalized pooling. See HR 52A-H 9.1.

ing contracts submitted to it, although the Commission could order changes at any time, with the right of judicial review over their decisions. John K. Cowen, the attorney for the B. & O. who actually wrote the bill, told the Senators on behalf of the railroads that "we say unhesitatingly we are not afraid for one instant of the intervention of the Commission. We do not want an agreement to go into effect without their approval. . . ."[37] Knapp, representing the I.C.C., indicated the Commission wanted judicial review on the basis of evidence presented at Commission hearings, and complained that the Gorman Bill did not confer the explicit rate powers on the Commission that most railroad men wanted it to have. The Patterson Bill was preferable. In any event the Commission made it clear they were not opposed to what they considered to be the proper type of pool.[38]

The urgent need for a legislative solution to chaotic railroad rates never seemed greater than in 1894 and 1895. ". . . there is need of some system of governmental authority, not only to control the roads, but to protect them,—to protect them not so much against the public as against themselves and against each other," Aldace Walker wrote despairingly.[39] But despite the support of the Commission, the National Convention of Railroad Commissioners of the various states, and important merchant groups, action was not forthcoming.[40] Albert Fink, reflecting on the failure of voluntary cooperation, re-

[37] Senate Doc. No. 39, 55:1, pp. 57-58 and *passim*. Cowen's authorship is suggested in John K. Cowen to Senator M. C. Butler, March 14, 1894, in Sen 53A-F 15.

[38] Testimony of Knapp in Senate Doc. No. 39, 55:1, pp. 86-87; W. R. Morrison to M. C. Butler, January 7, 1894, in Sen 53A-F 15.

[39] Aldace F. Walker, "Has the Interstate Commerce Law Been Beneficial?" *Forum*, XVII (April, 1894), 215.

[40] I.C.C., *Ninth Annual Report*, pp. 100-101; National Convention of Railroad Commissioners, *Report of Committee on Pooling of Freight, etc., April 1894* (n. p., 1894); and petitions in HR 53A-H 14.7. Most merchant support came from the East, and most opposition from the Midwest and West.

peated his earlier conclusion that "If Congress would pass a law to this effect [legalizing pools], I would consider the whole railroad problem in this country settled, and upon truly American principles."[41] Ideological questions of laissez-faire and competition bothered almost no one.

Only the railroads were consistently interested in increasing federal regulation of the railroads throughout the 1890's. Neither merchants nor farmers offered significant opposition to their plans. Some merchants, especially in the East, actually aligned themselves with the railroads. It was clear to these merchants that rates were declining, and this alone took the impetus out of their earlier anti-railroad sentiment. But the proper regulation was never forthcoming, and in 1896 the Eastern roads tried to revive the pooling system, only to be defeated by their own weaknesses and, ultimately, the courts.

In 1897, the railroads were ready to embark on another unsuccessful campaign for federal regulation of pools. "It is not believed that intelligent railway managements object to proper regulation," Walker wrote at the beginning of the year. "On the contrary, there is a general and hearty desire apparent in all railway circles to secure in some way the extinction of illegitimate methods and the establishment of fair and reasonable rates which shall be honestly and honorably maintained." The "experiment of regulation by the general government through its control over interstate commerce has never been fairly tried," he added.[42]

Two pooling bills, one by Joseph B. Foraker and another by Cullom, were presented to the Senate. The

[41] Albert Fink, "The Legislative Regulation of Railroads," *Engineering Magazine*, IX (July, 1895), 629.
[42] Aldace F. Walker, "The Pooling of Railway Earnings," *Railway Magazine*, II (February, 1897), 122-123.

Foraker Bill (S. 1479) was essentially similar to the earlier Gorman Bill, but gave the I.C.C. twenty days to disapprove of a contract and power to change or modify rates with judicial review.[43] The Cullom Bill was based on section 6, which declared rebates illegal; it gave the Commission thirty days to condemn what were effective pooling agreements. The bills led to a dispute within the Commission, since much of the pressure for them was generated by a single Commissioner, Martin Knapp.

In April 1897, E. P. Wilson of the Cincinnati Freight Bureau received a letter from Knapp urging him to organize a conference of railroads, shippers, and the Commission to revise the Act of 1887, in light of the ban on rate associations handed down by the Supreme Court in the *Trans-Missouri* decision of March 1897. Word of the letter quickly spread, and on May 5 Morrison disassociated the rest of the Commission from it. Knapp wrote Cullom in early June and urged revision of section 5 forbidding pooling.[44] A group of freight bureaus met in Cincinnati to push for the passage of the Foraker Bill, but the Chicago Freight Bureau, the Chicago Board of Trade, and a few others decided they would support the Cullom Bill. Cullom, knowing full well Knapp was in favor of his bill, asked the Commission on June 11 to comment on a memorandum by George Blanchard claiming the Commission would support the Cullom Bill.[45] Morrison and Judson C. Clements responded to Cullom by indicating that they were personally opposed to his bill but that the Commission itself had no position. At the same time, they assured him that despite the recent Court decision against rate associations, they felt "com-

[43] Senate Doc. No. 39, 55:1, *passim*.
[44] W. R. Morrison to H. F. Dousman, May 5, 1897, I.C.C. Records, Virginia, file 38334; Martin A. Knapp to S. M. Cullom, June 1, 1897, in Sen 55A-J 29.
[45] J. Furley to I.C.C., June 7, 1897, file 38583; E. P. Wilson to William R. Morrison, June 5, 1897, file 38624; S. M. Cullom to I.C.C., June 11, 1897, file 38690, all in I.C.C. Records, Virginia.

mon carriers may now under section 6 of the act lawfully make and establish joint tariffs and all agreements incident and necessary to the establishment and maintenance of such joint tariffs over continuous lines operated by more than one common carrier. It thus appears that agreements among the carriers are lawful in matters where joint action is deemed essential."[46] Charles A. Prouty, a new Commissioner who had formerly been attorney for the Rutland Railroad, also came out later in the year against the existing bills because of their lack of sufficient Commission control, although he left the door open to better pooling legislation in the future. Knapp disagreed with his colleagues, however. He believed that the *Trans-Missouri* decision endangered every type of railroad cooperation, and although his bill was not perfect, Knapp again assured Cullom of his support.[47]

Courts and Chaos

According to conventional interpretations, the decisions of the Supreme Court on railroad regulation in the 1890's were almost consistently pro-railroad.[48] Although the confusion is in large part the result of a misunderstanding of what the railroads really thought their vital interests to be, the fact is that the Supreme Court was

[46] William R. Morrison and Judson C. Clements to S. M. Cullom, June 17, 1897, file 38690; also see J. C. Clements to J. Farley, July 13, 1897, file 38583, in I.C.C. Records, Virginia.

[47] Martin Knapp to S. M. Cullom, June 17, 1897, I.C.C. Records, Virginia, file 38690; Charles A. Prouty, "Railway Pooling—From the People's Point of View," *Forum*, XXIV (December, 1897), 454-460; Interstate Commerce Commission, *Eleventh Annual Report, December 6, 1897* (Washington, 1897), p. 49. See Charles Prouty, *Address Before the Nineteenth Annual Convention of the National Hay Association, Kansas City, Mo., July 16, 1912* (n. p., 1912), p. 11, for Prouty's early railroad connections.

[48] See, for example, Harold U. Faulkner, *The Decline of Laissez Faire, 1897-1917* (New York, 1951), pp. 188-190; Ida M. Tarbell, *The Nationalizing of Business, 1878-1898* (New York, 1936), p. 218; Charles A. and Mary R. Beard, *The Rise of American Civilization* (New York, 1934), II, 343.

functionally neither pro- or anti-railroad, nor pro- or anti-Commission on the issue of railroad regulation. It is widely assumed that the extension of capitalist power occurred through a process of judicial consolidation. This was not so, at least so far as the railroads were concerned, and, what is more important, the judicial revolution that did in fact occur proceeded on the basis of an economic theory that was fundamentally unrelated to economic reality. For the Supreme Court in the 1890's handed down decisions that hurt the railroads and important sectors of industry just as much as, if not more than, they did the Interstate Commerce Commission.

The Supreme Court was certainly conservative, and undoubtedly pro-business in the sense that it defined business welfare.[49] But the Court believed in laissez-faire and judicial supremacy, and took a *literalist* view of its application. The railroads and much of industry may have given lip service to laissez-faire, but really did not like the consequences of its workings, and operationally tried to work on anti-laissez-faire premises, with or without the aid of legislation. The Court was out of touch with the real needs of the railroads, and consequently did enormous damage to them.

Much of the later criticism of the Supreme Court's major decisions on railroads was based on the mistaken assumption that the Act of 1887 was actually effective. The long-short haul provision is the one possible exception, and here, in the *Alabama Midland Ry* decision of 1897, we find the Court imposing on the Commission a requirement that railroads did not first have to obtain permission to ignore section 4. This, in fact, had been the Commission's de facto policy from its formation until late 1892, and neither the I.C.C.'s policy nor the Court's

[49] This is as far as Arnold M. Paul, *Conservative Crisis and the Rule of Law: Attitudes of Bar and Bench, 1887-1895* (Ithaca, N.Y., 1960), goes in analyzing the Court in his otherwise detailed study.

decision prevented a shipper from resorting to the courts or the Commission. The Court's decision in this instance merely formalized the reality of section 4's death, since it was never applied until 1893, and only loosely thereafter, and was the only area in which the Court *may* be considered to have weakened the I.C.C.

So far as rate-making powers are concerned, the Court was correct in questioning during 1896, in the *Maximum Rate Case* (167 U.S. 479) and in the *Social Circle Case* (162 U.S. 184), whether the Commission ever had the ability to determine a rate in the first place. Reagan surely was extraordinarily vague about granting such rights, and denied that the Act ever granted rate-making powers. The I.C.C. itself, especially under Cooley, rarely demanded such powers. Its statements on rates varied from year to year; it was generally as concerned with rates that were too low as those that were too high.[50] The Commission's definition of a fair rate was never more specific or rigid than that of the Court. In its Thurber decision it talked vaguely of cost of service as being the minimum rate, just as the Supreme Court did in *Smyth v. Ames* in 1898. William Z. Ripley, indeed, suggests the Court saved rate regulation with this decision, although his judgment may be questioned.[51] The Commission's reaction to the *Maximum Rate* decision confirms my judgment that the Commission had a limited view of its rate-making powers. In the *Eleventh Annual Report* it reiterated that "The Commission has never claimed the right to prescribe the rate in the first instance."[52] At the same time, the Commission wished to be able to determine what was unreasonably high and

[50] See pages 53-54 and 69-70 *supra*.

[51] E. B. Peirce, *Digest of the Decisions of the Courts and Inter-state Commerce Commission, 1887 to 1908* (Chicago, 1908), pp. 352, 358, 371; Ripley, *Railroads: Finance and Organization*, pp. 318-319.

[52] I.C.C., *Eleventh Annual Report*, p. 15.

to fix a maximum rate. It is true that the Court caused havoc in the Commission, but it would be a mistake to think that the Court took powers from the Interstate Commerce Commission that the Commission claimed or ever really had. And it would be wrong to think that the Court attacked the I.C.C. because it wished to strengthen the railroads. Quite the contrary, it also imposed havoc on the railroads.

The *Trans-Missouri Freight Association* decision (166 U.S. 290) of March 1897 and the *Joint Traffic Association* decision (171 U.S. 505) of October 1898 meant the end of pools, rate associations, and voluntary efforts at self-regulation among railroads. All three were attacked as being restraints of trade under the Sherman Act. (The *Joint Traffic* decision was based on the Act of 1887 also.) The I.C.C. condemned these decisions just as it had the earlier ones applying to rates and section 4. "Certainly it ought not to be unlawful for carriers to confer and agree for the purpose of doing what the law enjoins."[53]

The Supreme Court left the railroad industry in a state of anarchy, without legal or voluntary relief. New legislation was the only means left open to the railroads.

[53] I.C.C., *Twelfth Annual Report*, p. 16. The *Addyston Pipe and Steel Co.* decision in 1899 applied the prohibition on price and market pools to industrial corporations as well.

CHAPTER V

THE MOVEMENT FOR REFORM
1898 THROUGH THE ELKINS ACT

THE standard version of the relationship of the Interstate Commerce Commission to the railroads throughout the 1890's assumes, in I. L. Sharfman's words, that "the entire period of almost two decades discloses a basic struggle for supremacy between the government and the railroads. . . ."[1] It is, however, a mistake to regard the Commission and the railroads as antithetical. After all, for years the Commission had tried to work with the railroads informally, and it extended sympathy to them when the Court left them helpless. The railroads, for their part, tried to enforce the law by voluntary measures, and advocated an extension of the Commission's power if it was accompanied by enforceable pooling legislation. Cooperation and sympathy rather than hostility and conflict are the dominant themes in the relationship between the Commission and the railroads.

The I.C.C. was ready to admit in 1897 that the Supreme Court had created a situation in which "The people should no longer look to this Commission for a protection which it is powerless to extend."[2] But it is at least debatable whether the Commission was prepared to extend protection to the public even with additional legislative powers. The Commissioners, by and large, had considerable confidence in most railroad leaders, and

[1] I. L. Sharfman, *The Interstate Commerce Commission* (New York, 1931-1937), I, 39.
[2] I.C.C., *Eleventh Annual Report, December 6, 1897* (Washington, 1897), p. 51.

clearly regarded them as responsible men. "I have found no instance in which the railroad companies were not apparently disposed to do what was right under all circumstances except in the matter of oil rates," Charles Prouty, one of the leading Commissioners, wrote to a complainant in early 1897.[3] Given such attitudes on the part of the Commissioners, it is not altogether surprising that the I.C.C. advocated legislative measures similar, if not identical, to those advanced by railroad men. The Commission was an outspoken advocate of legalized pooling, and condemned the Supreme Court's *Joint Traffic Association* decision quite as strongly as its *Alabama Midlands Ry.* decision. The present law was "wholly inadequate," the Commission declared in 1899, and legalized railroad rate agreements with Commission powers to fix maximum rates would be a desirable correction of the intolerable existing situation.[4] The concrete expression of this viewpoint was supported by the Commission in 1898 when Senator Shelby M. Cullom formulated it into a new bill (S. 3354).[5] Even Joseph Nimmo, Jr., who strenuously opposed granting any power over rates to the Commission, admitted by 1898 "That the Act to Regulate Commerce is a just and wise measure of legislation, dictated by true statesmanship, is strenuously maintained."[6]

The Commission could only give Congress advice, and it was generally ignored. It could, however, by its informal arrangements with railroads hope to shortcut

[3] Charles Prouty to J. F. Tucker, March 22, 1897, I.C.C. Records, Virginia, file 37523. One of the Commissioners during 1898-1899, William J. Calhoun, had been a lawyer for the Chicago & Eastern Illinois RR. *The In-Com-Co*, XII (September, 1929), 4.

[4] I.C.C., *Twelfth Annual Report, January 11, 1899* (Washington, 1899), pp. 16-20, 27.

[5] Testimony of Martin Knapp, U.S. Senate, Committee on Interstate Commerce, *Hearings . . . On Senate Bill No. 3354*, 55th Cong., 2d Sess., March, 1898 (Washington, 1898), pp. 3ff.

[6] Joseph Nimmo, Jr., *Criticism of the Eleventh Annual Report of the Interstate Commerce Commission* (n. p., 1898), p. 17.

the cumbersome legislative process and try to attain results by voluntary means. The final destruction of formal rate agreements during 1898 as a result of the Supreme Court decision left both the railroads and the Commission in a position of dependency on each other. Nimmo reported in early 1899 that: "The attitude of the commission in its last annual report seems to me to be somewhat in the nature of a bid for the cooperation of the railroads, in their attempt to secure from Congress autocratic power in the nature of the right to exercise administrative control of the railroads."[7] The railroads, under the leadership of John K. Cowen of the B. & O., were also trying to maintain rates by voluntary means, using the Commission as the instrument of control. "This plan of action of course falls far short of railroad self-government under legal agreements as to competitive rates," Nimmo commented, "but may be, and hopefully is, a step in that direction." Tacit rate and traffic agreements existed, Nimmo reported, and the Commission "seems to recognize the fact," but the arrangement was too unstable and called for more decisive action.[8]

The B. & O., in the hope of ending such instability, had the Commission call a meeting of railroad presidents in the early spring of 1899 in the hope of ending rebating and violations of rates. This arrangement restored some stability, and meetings between the Commission and railroad presidents continued at least until June 1899.[9] But new complaints of rebating began coming

---

[7] Nimmo, "Memorandum of April 15th, 1899: The Present Status of the Railroad Problem" (typed carbon in Bureau of Railway Economics Library), p. 9.

[8] *Ibid.*, pp. 9-10.

[9] U.S. Industrial Commission, *Report . . . of the Industrial Commission on Transportation* (Washington, 1900), IV, 6, 316; Joseph Nimmo, Jr., to Edward Moseley, May 4, 1899, file 45408; Paul Morton and George Harris to M. A. Knapp, June 7, 1899, file 45606; M. A. Knapp to Paul Morton, June 8, 1899, file 45606, all in I.C.C. Records, Virginia; Interstate Commerce Commission, *Thirteenth Annual Report, January 15, 1900* (Washington, 1900), pp. 8-11.

to the I.C.C. even as the railroad presidents were meeting, and in 1900 the seemingly inevitable rate cutting became more common and led to sharp rate wars in 1901.[10] The Commission, for the most part, placed its major emphasis on the need for legalized pooling, a position that not even the conservative U.S. Industrial Commission was willing to endorse.[11] Knapp, the successor of Morrison as chairman of the Commission, spoke publicly against railroad competition and for pooling with Commission control over rates: "The benefits supposed to result from railroad competition I believe to be greatly exaggerated. . . . I go to the extent of saying that we cannot have that free and fair competition in trade which is the condition of industrial freedom without methods and rates for public transportation which amounts to a monopoly."[12]

The intensive merger movement among railroads between July 1899 and November 1900, and the absorption of about one-tenth of the total mileage by other railroads, were the result of the failure of the pooling system as well as a by-product of the speculative mania sweeping the major stock exchanges in the wake of the restoration of prosperity in the economy. Pools had failed long before 1899, just as the merger movement

[10] Martin A. Knapp to M. H. Smith, April 29, 1899, file 45790; Stuart R. Knott to Martin A. Knapp, May 12, 1899, file 45790, I.C.C. Records, Virginia; U.S. Industrial Commission, *Final Report*, House Doc. No. 380, 57th Cong., 2d Sess. (Washington, 1902), XIX, 353.

[11] William Z. Ripley to Stephen B. Elkins, March 16, 1905, Stephen B. Elkins Papers, University of West Virginia Library, box 8, for the Industrial Commission's refusal to endorse pooling.

[12] Martin A. Knapp and Paul Morton, *Speeches Before the National Association of Merchants and Travelers, August 7, 1899* (n. p., 1899), pp. 7-8. Also see the report of the speeches in *Railway and Engineering Review*, XXXII (August 12, 1899), 448-452; Edward A. Moseley, *Speech Before the Pennsylvania Millers' State Association, September, 1900* (Washington, 1900). The latter favored the Cullom Bill.

in railroads had been unable to establish operational control over falling rates in most areas. Only two areas were an exception: in the Middle Atlantic region competition was virtually eliminated, and in the Southeast effective working alliances were created.[13] But the larger railroads and banking houses had for several years owned or controlled nearly two-thirds of the mileage, and it was certain of the large railroads who were most active in working for federal legislation. The problem was the aggressive small railroad, and frequently avaricious larger lines as well, and the consolidation movement never went far enough to eliminate these competitive troublemakers. Between 1900 and 1907, the peak year, the number of operating railroads increased from 1,224 to 1,564, although 847 totally independent lines existed in 1900 and only declined to 829 during the following decade.[14] When *all* lines are taken into account, it is the diffusion rather than concentration of the American railroad system that is of greatest significance to the political behavior of the major railroads.

The railroads did not neglect the legislative front as the merger movement within their ranks welded a number of lines together. They endorsed the pro-pooling position of the Commission, but let it and others take the initiative for the creation of a stronger Commission. Senator Cullom's revised bill (S. 1439), written primarily by Prouty and submitted to the Senate in December 1899, would have granted the Commission powers to determine minimum and maximum rates upon complaint, and to fix a uniform freight classification, but

[13] Interstate Commerce Commission, *Intercorporate Relationships of Railways in the United States as of June 30, 1906* (Washington, 1908), pp. 40, 474.
[14] *Historical Statistics of the U.S.*, p. 429; William Z. Ripley, *Railroads: Finance and Organization* (New York, 1915), p. 458. Also see the testimony of Thomas F. Woodlock, U.S. Industrial Commission, *Report of the Industrial Commission on Transportation* (Washington, 1901), IX, 462.

the Senate Committee on Interstate Commerce reported on it adversely and President McKinley had no interest in the railroad problem. And, as it stood, the railroads and Knapp opposed the Cullom Bill because it failed to include a pooling provision.[15] By 1900 the railroads were becoming increasingly concerned with rebates, a surreptitious form of rate cutting, and did not mind the prospect of Commission rate fixing if it were accompanied by judicial review and the right of pooling.[16] Commissioners Knapp and Prouty were the leading spokesmen for regulation, and railroad reaction to their proposals was perhaps best summarized by Paul Morton, vice-president of the Atchison, Topeka & Santa Fe, in commenting on a speech by Knapp in August 1899: "I am so much in sympathy with the changes in the Interstate Commerce Law, wished for by the distinguished commissioner who has just addressed you, that I can add very little to what he has said much on the subject. . . . I am very earnestly in favor of legalized pooling, and I do not object to the Interstate Commerce Commission having proper supervision over pool rates."[17] The significant contingency added by railroad men was the right of judicial review of Commission decisions.

There was another factor of growing consequence to railroad leaders, however. State regulation was beginning to grow more cumbersome, and was less controllable and more unpredictable than federal regulation. "I am

[15] Shelby M. Cullom, *Fifty Years of Public Service* (Chicago, 1911), pp. 328-330; U.S. Senate, Committee on Interstate Commerce, *Hearings on S. 1439*, 56th Cong., 1st Sess., January, 1900 (Washington, 1900), pp. 95, 114-116, and *passim*.

[16] See the testimony of railroad executives in Industrial Commission, *Report . . . on Transportation*, IV, 474, 565, 683-684; also *Aldace F. Walker to E. P. Bacon, April 23, 1900* (n.p., 1900), pp. 16-17. A number of railroad men wanted the government to control the building of new mileage as well. See Industrial Commission, *Report . . . on Transportation*, IV, 287, 492, 663.

[17] Knapp and Morton, *Speeches Before the National Association of Merchants and Travelers*, pp. 12, 14; *Railway and Engineering Review*, XXXII (1899), 451.

opposed to any construction of the old States Rights doctrine," Paul Morton stated in 1899. "For fear that this may grow, I would like to see all transportation . . . declared subject to federal supervision and amenable to the national commission."[18] In 1902, Samuel Rea, a vice-president of the Pennsylvania, sent Philander C. Knox, then Attorney General, an editorial from the *Wall Street Journal* for his consideration that reflected the mood of many railroad leaders: "The wiser heads in the railroad world see that there is a chance now, by conceding Government control over rates, to secure Government protection. . . . They see that sooner or later the public will demand rate control, and they see that if that demand be refused it will eventually be enforced without corresponding protection being given."[19] The railroads clearly were not politically naive.

The New Champion: Stephen B. Elkins

The year 1900 was especially propitious for the "wiser heads" among the railroad men, and the need for their leadership was never greater than at the opening of the century. Despite the re-emergence of a new generation of small merchants and businessmen actively interested, after a decade of relative apathy, in railroad legislation, the prospects of success for politically oriented railroad executives were never brighter. And by 1901 there was a new President who, unlike McKinley, was at least moderately interested in railroad legislation, and the channels of communication to him were open. In 1899, Shelby M. Cullom, certainly no foe of the railroads, had resigned as chairman of the Senate Committee on Interstate Commerce and was replaced by a far more active man, thereby ending the relative

18 *Ibid.*, p. 14.
19 *Wall Street Journal*, April 2, 1902, in Philander Knox Papers, Library of Congress, accession 9172, box 1.

lethargy in the legislative branch of government towards railroad legislation. His successor, Stephen B. Elkins of West Virginia, was to remain the chairman of the Committee for over a decade, and the most important single influence in Congress on matters pertaining to railroads during that time.[20]

Elkins was a classic example of a man who rose by exploiting political office for private gain. By 1875 he had climbed to the position of the largest landholder in New Mexico while serving as the U.S. District Attorney; and by a fortunate marriage to the daughter of Henry G. Davis, the coal, timber, and railroad magnate of West Virginia, he also became the largest mine owner in the Atlantic area. He and Davis controlled the West Virginia Central and Pittsburgh Railroad until 1902, when they sold it to the B. & O.[21] His remaining public manuscripts, as fragmented as they are, make it clear that Elkins was always an exceedingly blunt and direct politician who considered himself first and foremost a mine and railroad operator. "It would be very unfortunate for the owners of the West Virginia Central if the persons in charge of the larger systems upon which the West Virginia Central is now dependent to reach tide water should be unfriendly," Elkins was warned by E. D. Kenna of the Atchison, Topeka, & Santa Fe in 1899, while discussing the dangers of unwise legislation.[22] His peers knew Elkins could be talked to frankly. "Permit me to call your attention to the fact that West Vir-

[20] Cullom in later years claimed he resigned because of the pro-railroad orientation of his colleagues. But this bit of hindsight is largely incorrect, for he was a dedicated friend of the railroads in all but his final bill. See Cullom, *Fifty Years of Public Service*, p. 330.

[21] Gustavus Myers, *History of the Great American Fortunes* (New York, 1937?), chap. xxv; Oscar Doane Lambert, *Stephen Benton Elkins* (Pittsburgh, 1955), *passim*. Lambert's book is an official biography and uncritical.

[22] E. D. Kenna to Stephen B. Elkins, April 18, 1899, Elkins Papers, box 5.

ginia is a petroleum producer," H. H. Rogers of Standard Oil wrote him concerning a pending treaty, "and is likely to be benefitted by the treaty if it is favorably acted upon, for the reason that the French are very large consumers of petroleum."[23] In writing him about the Hanna Shipping Bill in 1899, John Cook also reminded Elkins, "Your large holding in the West Virginia coal fields, and in the railroad company moving the coal and coke to tidewater, necessarily gives you a large personal interest in this matter."[24]

The railroads had confidence in Elkins, and his involvement with them was continuous and detailed.[25] In response to his cooperation and dependency on them, the railroads returned favors. The C. & O., for example, in an election in 1900, offered to bring enough Republican miners into Morgantown to swing the election, and Elkins learned how to use the legislative skills of railroad attorneys.[26] During the impasse faced by the railroads at the end of the century as a result of the failure of their voluntary efforts and the Supreme Court's decisions, the rise of Elkins to the most crucial legislative position in the nation was indeed fortunate for the railroads.

The Emergence of a New Merchant Lobby

Ironically, it was also fortunate that at the very time the railroads needed legislation and Elkins assumed his key post the merchants and small shipping interests

[23] H. H. Rogers to Stephen B. Elkins, February 8, 1900, Elkins Papers, box 6.
[24] John Cook to Stephen B. Elkins, December 19, 1899, Elkins Papers, box 5.
[25] See, for example, E. R. Bacon to Stephen B. Elkins, June 9, 1897, box 5; President of the C. & O. Railroad to Elkins, June 7, 1900, box 8; Oscar C. Murray to Elkins, December 18, 1903, box 8, all in the Elkins Papers.
[26] J. W. Knapp to Stephen B. Elkins, April 21, 1900, Elkins Papers, box 7. Also see H. T. Newcomb to Stephen B. Elkins, September 26, 1906, Elkins Papers, box 8.

began adding to the clamor for railroad legislation. Although their motives and interests were different, these elements helped make legislators aware of the need for action, even though the action itself was directed and controlled by pro-railroad legislators. So long as the bill under consideration consisted of obviously pro-railroad pooling legislation the merchants and farmers regarded such measures indifferently, as they had the earlier Cullom pooling bill (S. 3354). Commercial groups and Granges alike were about evenly split on pooling legislation and largely apathetic, and no patterns of opposition or support by region or interests can be discerned.[27] But the creation of the League of National Associations in late 1899 led to the first significant small business activity for railroad legislation in nearly two decades.

The League was formed in late 1899 by an indefatigable Milwaukee grain merchant, Edward P. Bacon, who managed to arouse the interest of national commercial organizations in railroad legislation. At the request of the League, Charles Prouty of the I.C.C. revised the old Cullom Bill to exclude legalized pooling, and the League managed to get the Millers' National Association, the National Association of Manufacturers, the National Board of Trade, and about fifty national commercial groups to endorse it. With the millers serving as the prime mover and relying heavily on the Grange, Bacon was able to start a substantial petition campaign for the Cullom Bill (S. 1439) in late 1899 and 1900.[28]

[27] See the relatively small number of petitions in HR 55A-H 9.2 and HR 55A-H 9.11 sent to the House Committee on Interstate Commerce in 1898.

[28] U.S. Senate, *Hearings on S. 1439*, 56:1, pp. 6, 114-116, 303-341; U.S. House of Representatives, Committee on Interstate and Foreign Commerce, *Hearings*, House Doc. No. 422, 58th Cong., 3d Sess. [December, 1904-January, 1905] (Washington, 1905), pp. 6-8; petitions in HR 56A-H 10.1 and Sen 56A-J 21. The petition declared "said bill was framed by request of The Millers' National Association."

Bacon's organization was renamed the Interstate Commerce Law Convention and it continued as the major merchant spokesman for railroad regulation. But from 1900 to 1902 the work of the organization met with slight success; so long as only merchants supported a specific bill, it had little chance of passage.[29]

The Interstate Commerce Law Convention was basically the reaction of small shippers and merchants to the real and fancied rebating abuses of the railroads. Rebates were, in fact, extensive; but they went to the large shippers and manufacturers, few of whom identified or sympathized with Bacon's group.

An Anti-Rebating Law

Rebates could be initiated from several directions, and were hated by the railroads insofar as they were based on the power of large shippers to exploit the competitive railroad situation and threaten to take their goods elsewhere. Aggressive railroads, especially smaller lines, tended to use rebates to attract business or to stimulate the growth of key firms in their territory. Most railroads did not grant rebates on the basis of caprice or inherent maliciousness, as Ray Stannard Baker suggested, but because of unpleasant competitive pressures and the power of large shippers. Precise data on the extent of rebating is necessarily scanty, for, being illegal, combined rates, false classifications, underbilling

---

[29] Robert H. Wiebe, *Businessmen and Reform: A Study of the Progressive Movement* (Cambridge, 1962), *passim*, focuses on the fact of disunity among the merchant groups, attacking a somewhat simplified notion that business is always a unified, cohesive group on any specific issue. The point is well taken but obvious, and largely irrelevant to an understanding of the political process. It fails to evaluate or discuss who succeeded in politics, what the decisive big business or railroad groups wanted, and the social function of business in the political process and its relationship to the rest of society. Wiebe ignores the issue of who *really* has the power to direct the political process, and what is done with that power.

weights, and similar techniques concealed the practice; it was, however, certainly extensive and very costly to the railroads. I. L. Sharfman claims that rebates took about 10 per cent of the gross revenue of the railroads.[30]

The claimants to the authorship of the first major railroad measure since 1887—the Elkins Anti-Rebating Act of February 19, 1903—are numerous. But the real author was the Pennsylvania Railroad, and there is general agreement on this fact. Senator Joseph B. Foraker suggested in his autobiography that he was the major architect of the law; and Martin A. Knapp of the I.C.C. asserted that all its proposals were first advocated by his Commission—quite a different matter than actually writing the bill. However, all contemporary witnesses knew that most of the railroads were tired of rebating and that the Pennsylvania decided to resort to legislative means to end the costly institution.[31] But the details of the legislation deserve more consideration than they have received elsewhere, since they illus-

[30] Rebating is discussed in Industrial Commission, *Report . . . On Transportation*, IV, 52-54; William Z. Ripley, *Railroads: Rates and Regulation* (New York, 1912), p. 189; and Col. Augustus Pope to G. McPherson, February 17, 1908, on file in the Library of the Bureau of Railway Economics. Railroad opposition to the practice is discussed in Joseph Nimmo, Jr., *A Commercial and Political Danger* (Washington, 1902), p. 39; and alleged railroad support in Ray Stannard Baker, "Railroads and Popular Unrest," *Collier's*, XXXVII (June 9, 1906), 19-22. Sharfman, *Interstate Commerce Commission*, I, 35-36.

[31] Joseph Benson Foraker, *Notes of a Busy Life* (Cincinnati, 1917), II, 208; Martin A. Knapp to James R. Mann, March 29, 1906, James R. Mann Papers, Library of Congress. Also see Charles A. Prouty, *Address Before the Economics Club of Boston, March 9, 1905* (n. p., 1905), p. 6; Charles A. Prouty, "Competition and Railway Rates," *Illinois Manufacturers' Association Bulletin*, May, 1902, p. 8; Sharfman, *Interstate Commerce Commission*, I, 36; George E. Mowry, *The Era of Theodore Roosevelt, 1900-1912* (New York, 1958), pp. 123-124; Theodore Roosevelt to Henry Lee Higginson, August 15, 1907, in Elting E. Morison, ed., *The Letters of Theodore Roosevelt* (Cambridge, 1951-54), V, 751-752 (hereafter *Letters*). All of the above, save Foraker and Knapp, ascribe the authorship of the Elkins Act to the railroads in general or the Pennsylvania Railroad specifically.

trate the integral dependence of the railroads on political alternatives when voluntary means failed to attain rationalization, and suggest a continuation of the policy of trying to utilize the political process that began twenty-five years earlier, and which because of its usefulness persisted after 1903.

The ascent of Alexander J. Cassatt to the presidency of the Pennsylvania Railroad in 1899 was the single most important event in the movement to end rebating. Cassatt was an independently wealthy engineer dedicated to eliminating rebating and establishing stability in the railroad system. His commitment was a serious one, for he resigned from railroading from 1882 to 1899 because of the unwillingness of the Pennsylvania's directors to support his efforts to impose discipline over the Eastern railroads by a policy of consolidation and merger. In 1899, his program was twofold: to eliminate rebating to Pennsylvania customers and establish communities of interest between the major railroads in order to impose stability and control over the industry. Cassatt's effort to end rebating to Carnegie Steel led to the counter-threats of parallel Gould-Carnegie railroads and Pennsylvania entry into the steel industry, and finally resulted in the formation of the United States Steel Corporation as the solution to the threatened chaos of competition and expansion.[32] His community of interest policy concluded in an alliance with the Vanderbilt lines,

32 Details are found in James Creelman, "All Is Not Damned," *Pearson's Magazine*, XV (June, 1906), 543-554; Andrew Carnegie, "My Experience with Railway Rates and Rebates," *Century Magazine*, LXXV (March, 1908), 722-728; Burton J. Hendrick, *The Life of Andrew Carnegie* (Garden City, N.Y., 1932), II, 24-28, 128; George H. Burgess and Miles C. Kennedy, *Centennial History of the Pennsylvania Railroad Company*, *1846-1946* (Philadelphia, 1949), pp. 460, 513-515; Andrew Carnegie to Stephen B. Elkins, December 10, 1900, Elkins Papers, box 8; Andrew Carnegie to A. J. Cassatt, January 12, 1901; Andrew Carnegie to Charles Schwab, January 11, 1901, Andrew Carnegie Papers, Library of Congress, vol. 81.

as well as their joint purchase of 40 per cent of the
C. & O.'s stock. By the end of 1902, Cassatt had spent
$110 million buying into competitive Eastern railroads;
he spent another $45 million over the next four years.
During the same period, Vanderbilt's New York Central
also extended its control over other important regional
competitors.[33]

The official historians of the Pennsylvania Railroad,
commenting on Cassatt's policies, correctly suggest that
he "considered these expedients as but temporary, designed to save the situation only until stabilization could
be effected on a more permanent base. Certain it is that
he recognized the weakness of the Interstate Commerce
Act as one of the major evils to be overcome. He
therefore led the fight for the adoption by Congress of
the Elkins Amendment in 1903, and for other legislation
to increase the power of the Commission to enforce its
findings against rebaters and rate cutters."[34] The original
Elkins Bill (S. 3521) was written by James A. Logan,
general solicitor of the Pennsylvania, in 1901. The fact
that Logan wrote the bill was no secret at the time, and
he freely discussed the matter with the press: ". . . the
crudities of the law as existing have been discovered and
the necessity of a more direct means of enforcement of
the powers of the Government recognized. . . . For my
part, I have faith in the integrity of governmental
agencies; especially those of the dignity of the Interstate
Commerce Commission. I believe not only the shipper
but the carrier needs governmental help. . . . If this act
is passed, railroads can no longer be subject to the
dictation of the great shippers as to rates and facilities."[35]

[33] Burgess and Kennedy, *History of the Pennsylvania*, pp. 458-
460; Creelman, *Pearson's Magazine*, xv (1906), 550.
[34] Burgess and Kennedy, *History of the Pennsylvania*, p. 461.
[35] James A. Logan in *Railroad Gazette*, xxxiv (March 21, 1902),
208 (from an interview reported in the *Philadelphia Press*). Also

Although the Pennsylvania and other railroads wanted the abolition of rebating, and did not hesitate to tell President Theodore Roosevelt and Attorney General Philander Knox so, Bacon's Interstate Commerce Law Convention, and even Elkins at one point, were not quite so unanimous.[36] In January 1902, Elkins was toying with the idea of a comprehensive revision of railroad legislation along the lines of the Sawyer Bill (S. 3805) of 1893, a bill that had been written by Richard Olney while he was attorney for the Boston & Maine Railroad, and whose central innovation was a special railroad court.[37] But before committing himself to Olney's bill, Elkins decided upon Logan's bill, a less ambitious measure. "If this bill fails—and I am inclined to think it will,—then I am going to take up the judicial bill fashioned largely on the one you drew," Elkins reported to Olney.[38] But Logan's measure did not fail, and it was to be nearly eight years before Olney's bill was revived.

The first Elkins Bill (S. 3521) of early 1902 allowed the I.C.C. to set a new rate, upon complaint, for one year—subject to judicial review; established legalized pooling with Commission review of any pool actions violating law; made corporations as well as individuals

---

see U.S. House, House Doc. No. 422, 58:3, p. 4. John B. Thayer, a vice-president of the Pennsylvania, in *Speech Before the Buffalo Chamber of Commerce, April 18, 1907* (n. p., 1907), p. 20, denies the Act was written by the Pennsylvania, but only that "our company, with many others, aided with suggestions." It is true that the original bill was amended, but its basic aim was to eliminate rebating, and this section of the bill remained.

[36] See J. M. Dickenson to Philander Knox, March 17, 1902, and Charles M. Parker to Theodore Roosevelt, March 22, 1902, Philander Knox Papers, accession 9172, for examples of the desire of the railroads to end rebating.

[38] Stephen B. Elkins to Richard Olney, February 6, 1902, Richard Olney to Stephen B. Elkins, January 25, 1902, January 30, 1902, Richard Olney Papers, Library of Congress, vol. 93.

[38] Stephen B. Elkins to Richard Olney, February 6, 1902, Richard Olney Papers, vol. 93.

liable under the law; abolished imprisonment as a penalty; and, most important, permitted the Commission to petition a Circuit Court to investigate violations and enforce established rates.[39] But the Interstate Commerce Law Convention, with its 110 member organizations, was unwilling to support such a blatantly pro-railroad bill and swung its support to the Corliss-Nelson Bill (S. 3575), a measure with a strong anti-rebating provision but which also allowed the Commission to fix rates for two years upon complaint, after which time they could be reviewed by the courts. The major difference between the two bills was the legalization of pooling, since the first Elkins Bill accepted the principle of Commission rate fixing.[40] None other than Francis B. Thurber, who by this time fully supported the railroads' interests and called for legalized pooling, led the pro-railroad merchant opposition to the Nelson Bill. The Interstate Commerce Commissioners also opposed the Nelson Bill for a variety of different reasons, ranging from its failure to legalize pooling in Knapp's case to the fact that the Commission was not consulted first in Prouty's case.[41]

The differences between the Elkins and Nelson Bills were not insurmountable, at least not in Bacon's view, and "an understanding" was reached with Cassatt and Logan to modify the original Elkins Bill and for the merchants to remain neutral on the topic of pooling. Both the railroads and merchants supported the new Elkins Bill (S. 7038) and it quickly passed during

[39] U.S. Senate, Committee on Interstate Commerce, *Hearings, Railway Freight Rates and Pooling,* 57th Cong., 1st Sess. February-March, 1902 (Washington, 1902), pp. v-viii.

[40] *Ibid.,* pp. xv-xviii.

[41] U.S. House of Representatives, Committee on Interstate and Foreign Commerce, *Hearings on . . . H.R. 146, 273 . . . ,* 57th Cong., 1st Sess., April, 1902 (Washington, 1902), pp. 221, 273ff., 315-316, 340. Knapp was initially opposed to both bills. See U.S. Senate, *Hearings, Railway Freight Rates,* 57:1, p. 138.

February 1903, by a unanimous vote in the Senate and 250 to 6 in the House.[42]

The final Elkins Act was in reality much closer to the original railroad bill than the Nelson Bill, and not a genuine compromise. Corporations as well as individuals were made liable under the act, but imprisonment as a penalty was dropped from the law. Both the giver and receiver of rebates could be prosecuted, with fines up to $20,000 for an offense, and when the I.C.C. had "reasonable ground" to believe that rebates were being given a Circuit Court could be asked to try the case and enforce rates; the Attorney General could initiate proceedings as well. Although pooling was not recognized, joint rates were legal, and like all other rates, any joint rate filed with the Commission "shall be conclusively deemed to be the legal rate, and any departure from such rate, or any offer to depart therefrom shall be deemed to be an offense. . . ."[43] Such a provision for maintaining rates accomplished the same end as pools and rate associations; this had been the goal of the railroads for three decades.

The major railroads were delighted with the Elkins

[42] E. P. Bacon to William H. Graham, January 7, 1903, a form letter sent to members of Congress. Copy in HR 57A-H 11.1. Also see letter of E. P. Bacon to members of the Interstate Commerce Law Convention, December 19, 1904, in HR 58A-H 10.5. Support for the bill from merchant groups was extensive, although quite often the letters and petitions received in the House merely wanted stronger railroad legislation, and did not specify the Elkins Bill. See HR 57A-H 11.1 and Sen 57A-J 33. This vagueness on the part of merchants and farmers is reflected in U.S. Senate, *Hearings, Railway Freight Rates* . . . , 57:1, pp. 175-210 and *passim.* Allan Nevins, *John D. Rockefeller: The Heroic Age of American Enterprise* (New York, 1940), II, 516, claims Standard did not oppose the Elkins Bill, though there is nothing it could have done even if it had. But Theodore Roosevelt, who often tended to see opposition where there was none, was correct in stating that "No respectable railroad or respectable business can openly object to the rebate bill. . . ." Theodore Roosevelt to Lawrence F. Abbott, February 3, 1903, *Letters,* III, 417.

[43] E. B. Peirce, *Digest of Decisions of the Courts and Interstate Commerce Commission, 1887 to 1908* (Chicago, 1908), p. 1204.

Act, for the legal machinery of the government was now
to do what they had failed to accomplish themselves.
The law should have passed five years ago, the *Railroad
Gazette* declared: ". . . all that will be asked of the Commissioners by the public will be that they go ahead and
catch every law-breaking rate-cutter in the country."[44]

[44] *Railroad Gazette*, xxxv (February 20, 1903), 134. Knapp
endorsed the final Act. See Balthasar Henry Meyer, *Railway Legislation in the United States* (New York, 1903), pp. 323-326.

CHAPTER VI

PRESSURES FOR
RAILROAD LEGISLATION
1903-1905

THE merchants supporting the Interstate Commerce Law Convention were not particularly satisfied with the Elkins Act alone. In late 1903, they began agitating for the Quarles Bill (S. 2439), a revised version of the Nelson-Corliss Bill. The new measure, introduced in December 1903, gave the Commission power to suspend rates upon complaint, to fix definite rather than maximum rates without hearings, and to apportion joint rates—all subject to court review. The court, however, could suspend Commission rates. Failure to obey Commission rulings would subject violators to a $5,000 fine for every day of violation.[1] With Bacon's organization canvassing support for it, large numbers of individual and printed petitions began arriving in Congress throughout 1904 calling for Commission rate regulation in general and passage of the Quarles-Cooper Bill specifically.[2] Local Boards of Trade and Chambers of Commerce readily responded to Bacon's prodding, and even the National Association of Manufacturers in May 1904, strongly endorsed the principle of Commission rate regulation with judicial review. Save for the New York Board of Trade and Transportation, and a few

[1] U.S. Senate, Committee on Interstate Commerce, *Hearings, Regulation of Railway Rates*, Senate Doc. No. 243, 59th Cong., 1st Sess., [December 1904-May 1905] (Washington, 1906), I, 711-713, contains the text of the bill.

[2] In HR 58A-H 10.5, HR 58A-H 10.13, and Sen 58A-J 36. There are nearly 500 examples in this collection.

isolated local associations, merchant opposition to the Quarles Bill was concentrated in California.[3]

The Townsend Bill (H.R. 18588) was a much more serious proposition for both the merchants and railroads, and it actually passed the House in February 1905, with strong bipartisan support. It also allowed the Commission to fix definite rather than maximum rates and apportion joint rates, and maintained the same fine of $5,000 a day for ignoring Commission orders. Rates could be set only after hearings, however. It departed from the Quarles Bill by increasing the membership of the Commission to seven and appointing a "court of transportation" of five circuit court judges to serve as the only court of appeal for railroads or shippers short of the Supreme Court.[4] Merchant divisions on the new bill were even greater than over the Quarles Bill, though it followed much the same lines. Georgia peach growers, Cincinnati merchants, and Bacon's association, now claiming 512 member organizations, appeared before hearings on the various bills to advocate either the Quarles Bill, the Townsend Bill, or simply endorse the principle of Commission rate regulation. But the opposition did an excellent job of organizing in California, Wisconsin, Iowa, and Kentucky, as well as among railroad unions, and it was obvious that small business and merchants were quite divided.[5] It is also evident that much of the anti-legislation sentiment among merchants was controlled, since Louisville, Kentucky, alone accounted for nearly one-quarter of the large number of petitions

[3] National Association of Manufacturers, *Proceedings of the Ninth Annual Convention—1904, May 17-19, 1904, Pittsburg, Penna.* (New York, 1904), p. 236. U.S. Senate, *Regulation of Railway Rates*, Senate Doc. No. 243, 59:1, I, 165-169, for the New York Board of Trade and Transportation.

[4] Text of the bill in U.S. Senate, *Regulation of Railway Rates*, Senate Doc. No. 243, 59:1, I, 732-736.

[5] See *ibid.*, I, 126, 129, 266, 479-491; III, 1764-1765, 1840, 1926, 2005, 2112, 2364, 2503ff., 2684ff., 2743, 2756-2767; IV, 3811-3848, for serious merchant divisions.

arriving in Congress, and most of these apparently were produced on the same typewriter.[6]

Growing disagreements among merchants and small business organizations over the Esch-Townsend Bill illustrate the instability and fluidity of merchant interest in railroad legislation, and suggest that, in the last analysis, small businessmen were less important in the formation of federal regulation, despite their numbers, than the railroad men who knew precisely what they wanted. Merchant campaigns on the issue could be turned on and off by a variety of sources, and ultimately reflected the serious interest of only a small number of articulate, active individuals. During 1905, organized merchant groups managed to neutralize each other with their disagreements over the terms of regulation, and left the direction of affairs to the less ambivalent railroad leaders.

The major New York commercial organizations were opposed to either the Quarles or Townsend Bills, and the ability of an organization such as the New York State Chamber of Commerce to have its closely reasoned statements signed by such powerful figures as A. Barton Hepburn or Thomas P. Fowler made a good deal more difference than the obviously inspired petitions of small-town merchants.[7] In 1905, the National Association of Manufacturers was willing to endorse a stronger rebate law, but reversed its earlier position and explicitly rejected the principle of Commission rate-making powers with judicial review.[8] And it was organizations of the

---

[6] Petitions for 1905, both form and individual, are found in Sen 59A-J 58. These are mainly anti-legislation, though often opposed to rebates and discrimination as well.

[7] See Chamber of Commerce of State of New York, *On the Proposed Increase of Power to the Interstate Commerce Commission* (New York, 1905), p. 8 and *passim*.

[8] National Association of Manufacturers, *Proceedings of the Tenth Annual Convention, Atlanta, Ga., May 16-18, 1905* (New York, 1905), pp. 107-121, 214-215.

caliber of the N.A.M. that made the difference to politicians. When joined by smaller or less prestigious
groups, such as the Trans-Mississippi Commercial Congress, the merchant opponents of Commission rate making were quite as powerful as Bacon's Interstate Commerce Law Convention.[9]

Indeed, the N.A.M. was more powerful than Bacon's
largely paper organization, and was able to eliminate it
as a significant factor in shaping railroad legislation
by the end of 1905. Bacon called a meeting of the
association in October 1905, to endorse the principle of
Commission rate fixing. David M. Parry, president of
the N.A.M., arrived at the meeting with a large group
of supporters, and when Bacon refused to admit them
without their first endorsing his position, the N.A.M.
group immediately formed a rump convention with over
twice the number of delegates as remained with Bacon.[10]
The result was the collapse of the Interstate Commerce
Law Convention and the elimination of Bacon as a
serious factor in the regulation movement. So far as
the press was concerned, the October meeting of shippers
had rejected the idea of a law giving rate powers to the
Commission.[11]

The demise in 1905 of the shipper movement for
granting rate-making power to the I.C.C. illustrates
an important trend in the history of federal railroad
regulation. In the 1890's, the railroads alone advocated
legislation, and failed to get any. The Act of 1887,

[9] [Trans-Mississippi Commercial Congress], *16th Session of Trans-
Mississippi Commercial Congress, Proceedings, Portland, Ore.,
August 16-19, 1905*, p. 12. Copy in Sen 59A-J 60.

[10] *Railroad Gazette*, XXXIX (November 3, 1905), 137. A tran-
script of the meeting may be found, significantly enough, in Sen
59A-F 15. Robert H. Wiebe, "Business Disunity and the Progressive Movement, 1901-1914," *Mississippi Valley Historical Review*,
XLIV (March, 1958), 676, claims the delegations were evenly divided. But in either case the destruction of Bacon's association
was achieved.

[11] *New York Herald*, December 17, 1905.

however, was the result of years of both shipper and railroad support for the principle of the specific legislation, as was the Elkins Act of 1903 and successive legislation, including the Hepburn Act. What is important, in addition to the subsequent interpretation and implementation of the law by the Interstate Commerce Commission, is the detailed contents of any specific legislation which both shippers and railroads supported on the assumption that they were attaining at least some of their legislative goals.

Shipper sentiment for railroad legislation was often conservative in motive and variable in direction. The railroads were always able to find at least some shipper group willing to help serve as spokesmen for the railroad position, and the manipulation of the naturally divided shippers is a continuous feature of the history of agitation for national legislation. In the campaign for legislation in the 1880's, important shipping elements aligned themselves with the railroads behind the Cullom Bill rather than the Reagan Bill, and a shipper-railroad alliance in 1902 resulted in the passage of the Elkins Act and the achievement of the major legislative goal of the railroads. The inevitable diversity of interests among shippers, each with unique problems and products, always allowed the railroads to ally themselves with significant merchant and manufacturing groups, or to exploit the political sentiments created by others. Although Congress frequently acted out of solicitude for merchant and shipping interests—yet with ample concern for the economic health of the railroads as well— the ultimate beneficiaries were the railroads. In their diversity the shipping interests were crucial in the development of federal regulation of railroads from 1887 to 1916, but the basic catalyst in the regulation movement was the needs and position of the majority of the railroads, which the shippers supported by one means or another, consciously or unwittingly.

Roosevelt as Reformer

Historians have commonly assumed that Theodore Roosevelt's role in railroad regulation was a positive one based on a principled desire to make the industry responsive to public needs.[12] In reality, careful investigation shows that Roosevelt's commitment to railroad legislation and his concern for railroad reform have been sharply exaggerated. He gave no special thought to the problem until assuming the Presidency, and only then after a delay of several years. The role of Roosevelt in the movement for railroad reform deserves a major reconsideration.

It is not unfair to say that until 1904 Roosevelt had no serious interest in railroad legislation. His first message to Congress in December 1901 merely commented on the undesirability of rebates for shippers and railroads alike, and the need for legislation to correct it. The statement was brief, mild, and one of the less prominent aspects of the message.[13] The railroad section of his second message was even briefer, and consisted merely of a defense of Congress' power to legislate on interstate commerce, without proposing any specific legislation or action.[14] His third message to Congress in December 1903 ignored the topic of railroad regulation altogether, perhaps on the assumption that the passage of the Elkins Act, with which he had had but slight connection, solved the grievances of which he had earlier complained. Instead, Roosevelt commended Congress for

[12] John M. Blum, "Theodore Roosevelt and the Legislative Process: Tariff Revision and Railroad Regulation, 1904-1906," in *The Letters of Theodore Roosevelt*, IV, 1333-1342.

[13] [Theodore Roosevelt], *Messages and Papers of the Presidents, September 14, 1901, to March 4, 1909* (New York, n.d.), pp. 6654-6655.

[14] *Ibid.*, p. 6712.

enacting legislation during 1903 on "sane and conservative lines."[15]

It is clear that until 1903, at least on the topic of railroad legislation, Roosevelt was following his sincere lack of interest and not merely maneuvering for conservative support for the presidential nomination in 1904. It is evident that he allied himself with the conservatives of his party because he naturally found them most compatible. William Howard Taft, ironically, chided him about his reliance on the conservatives in early 1903, and Roosevelt, in a personal letter on March 19, insisted, "You are unjust to Senator Aldrich. My experience for the last year and a half . . . has made me feel respect and regard for Aldrich as one of that group of Senators, including Allison, Hanna, Spooner, Platt, of Connecticut, Lodge and one or two others, who, together with men like the next Speaker of the House, Joe Cannon, are the most powerful factors in Congress." Roosevelt admitted they were men he differed with at times, but also men of intelligence and integrity capable of being brought around to a reasonable position—leaders "not only essential to work with, but desirable to work with." Despite their commitments to special interests, "they are broad-minded and patriotic," and "it was far more satisfactory to work with them than to try to work with the radical 'reformers' like Littlefield."[16] Standpatters like Platt advised his Wall Street friends not to oppose Roosevelt, but to control him, since he was a safe conservative.[17]

Roosevelt, during 1904, had no definite commitment

[15] *Ibid.*, p. 6785.

[16] Theodore Roosevelt to William Howard Taft, March 19, 1903, *Letters*, III, 450.

[17] Although Platt was disturbed by Roosevelt's career after 1904, he favored Commission rate fixing with the right of judicial appeal before the rates went into effect. He died before the Hepburn Bill was passed. Louis A. Coolidge, *Orville H. Platt* (New York, 1910), pp. 515-519.

to any specific type of railroad regulation, and was not sure how much legislation he wanted. But he did believe in his conservative political friends, their integrity and reliability, and his ability to solve problems by gentlemen's agreements and understandings rather than by legislation. Their character was sufficient assurance of their good intentions when he did not agree with them, and their approach to problems was generally close to his own, if not identical.

Two incidents especially illustrate this weakness in Roosevelt in matters relating to railroad laws. In May 1904, the Interstate Commerce Commission decided that International Harvester was guilty of accepting rebates, a matter for which they should have been fined. Harvester officials went to William H. Moody, the Attorney General, and asked that the charges be dropped in return for their promise to end the practice. The arrangement was accepted by Moody and Roosevelt, and the incident marks the beginning of a long *détente* between Roosevelt and International Harvester that ignored the already existing laws.[18] The second incident, which was public, involved Paul Morton, Roosevelt's Secretary of the Navy and former vice-president of the Atchison, Topeka, & Santa Fe. The Santa Fe, the I.C.C. decided in February 1905, was guilty of granting rebates while Morton was an executive there. Morton, for his part, often represented the railroad cause while in the Cabinet, and was an important pipeline to Roosevelt. Among other things, he had managed to convince Roosevelt of the desirability of railroad pools.[19] When the affair broke in June, Morton naturally submitted his resignation to

[18] The early history of the *détente* is given in William C. Beer to Herbert Knox Smith, August 23, 1907, Bureau of Corporation Records, National Archives, Record Group 122, file 4902-1.

[19] E. H. Harriman to Theodore Roosevelt, December 2, 1904, *Letters*, v, 450; Theodore Roosevelt to Benjamin I. Wheeler, January 18, 1905, *Letters*, IV, 1105; Senate Doc. No. 180, 59th Cong., 1st Sess. (Washington, 1905), pp. 182-183.

Roosevelt. Although he accepted Morton's resignation, Roosevelt insisted on defending him; he asserted that Morton alone among the railroad leaders had selflessly fought for the abolition of the rebate system.[20] While Roosevelt realized he also had to order further investigations of the allegations against the Santa Fe—Moody recommended he do so—in ordering Moody to go ahead he stressed, without access to new facts, that Morton was innocent, that only the Santa Fe, and not its individual officers, be investigated.[21] Because of the case's importance, Moody assigned former Attorney General Harmon to investigate the matter, but he made no secret of the fact that he did not want to prosecute Morton's railroad. Harmon was contrary, however, and strongly advised prosecution of the Santa Fe on contempt charges. Moody, embarrassed, was forced to hand the matter over to the courts for a decision, but since his own attorneys were in charge of the prosecution, no judgment was brought against the Santa Fe.[22] Roosevelt's direction of the Morton affair indicated that personal loyalties, as well as his sense of public relations, were deep indeed.

Roosevelt's recommendation in his 1904 message to Congress was the result of an obvious need to meet the growing clamor of shippers for railroad legislation. Although it was quite general—a long paragraph stuck away in a not-too-prominent position—Roosevelt's proposal was more conservative than the fixed, rather than maximum, rate concept embodied in the Quarles or

[20] *Railway and Engineering Review*, XLV (June 24, 1905), 477; Theodore Roosevelt to Paul Morton, June 12, 1905, *Letters*, IV, 1213-1214; Theodore Roosevelt to William H. Moody, June 12, 1905, *Letters*, IV, 1210-1211; Theodore Roosevelt to Joseph B. Bishop, June 15, 1905, *Letters*, IV, 1105.
[21] Theodore Roosevelt to William H. Moody, June 17, 1905, *Letters*, IV, 1237-1238.
[22] *Railway World*, XLIX (December 29, 1905), 1029-1031.

Townsend Bills. "While I am of the opinion that at present it would be undesirable, if it were not impracticable, finally to clothe the Commission with general authority to fix railroad rates, I do believe that . . . the Commission should be vested with the power, where a given rate has been challenged and after full hearing found to be unreasonable, to decide, subject to judicial review, what shall be a reasonable rate to take its place. . . ."[23] Shortly thereafter, Roosevelt asked Senator Philander C. Knox, his former Attorney General and once a lawyer for Henry C. Frick, to prepare a bill embodying the ideas in his message to Congress. ". . . there is no other man in the Senate quite so well fitted to draft a bill and put it through."[24]

Roosevelt's 1904 recommendation was vague, and although he was not sure precisely what he wanted, it was clearly not the Quarles or Townsend Bills, and perceptive Congressmen immediately pointed to the conflict between the President's message and the Townsend Bill. Knox failed to produce a bill, so Roosevelt ordered Moody to write one in consultation with William P. Hepburn of the House. The actual drafting was done in the Attorney General's office, although Hepburn insisted on a special "Court of Commerce" and it was included in his first bill.[25] Since Roosevelt favored pools at this time, it is surprising that a section legalizing them was not included as well.[26] Had Roosevelt really

---

[23] Roosevelt, *Messages and Papers*, p. 6902.

[24] Theodore Roosevelt to Philander Knox, December 19, 1904, *Letters*, IV, 1073-1074. Roosevelt also consulted John W. Midgley, of pool fame, as well, reportedly, as Samuel Spencer and A. J. Cassatt, for their views; J. W. Midgley, "Growing Sentiment for a Properly Constituted Commission," April 25, 1905, in Sen 58A-J 36; *Congressional Record*, XXXIX, 58:3, p. 2025.

[25] William H. Moody to William P. Hepburn, February 18, 1905, *Letters*, IV, 1123n. Also see *Congressional Record*, XXXIX, 58:3, pp. 2010, 2064, 2098.

[26] Theodore Roosevelt to Benjamin I. Wheeler, January 18, 1905, *Letters*, IV, 1105.

been interested in having the Townsend Bill enacted—
and, despite confusion among House Republicans during the first months of 1905, he never was—he would
not have authorized the drafting of new legislation just
as the Townsend Bill was being passed in the House.

Roosevelt, with typical exaggeration, felt the railroads
were strongly opposed to his 1904 message, and he
enunciated a view, often repeated in other contexts, that
he was merely acting to save the railroads from themselves or from more radical legislation. ". . . such
increased supervision," he warned in his 1904 message,
"is the only alternative to an increase of the present evils
on the one hand or a still more radical policy on the
other."[27] The railroads, he wrote Lodge in May 1905,
"are very shortsighted not to understand that to beat it
[Hepburn Bill] means to increase the danger of the
movement for the Government ownership of railroads."[28]
The net effect of such thinking was to make Roosevelt
more defensive about his recommendations, and ultimately even more conservative. He deliberately tried to
reassure the railroads, in personal meetings and public
statements, that he could be trusted. In October 1905,
speaking at Raleigh, Roosevelt made it very clear that
"It must be understood, as a matter of course, that if this
power is granted it is to be exercised with wisdom and
caution and self-restraint. The Interstate Commerce
Commission or other government official who failed to
protect a railroad that was in the right against any clam-
or, no matter how violent, on the part of the public, would
be guilty of as gross a wrong as if he corruptly rendered
an improper service to the railroad at the expense of the
public. When I say a square deal, I mean a square deal—
exactly as much a square deal for the rich man as for the

[27] Roosevelt, *Messages and Papers*, p. 6902.
[28] Theodore Roosevelt to Henry Cabot Lodge, May 25, 1905,
Letters, IV, 1193.

poor man; but no more."[29] Roosevelt's equation of bribery with "clamor," whether justified or not, and his assumption that the railroads must be protected from the public if necessary, were the sort of professions that suggest a fundamentally conservative commitment on his part.

At the same time that Roosevelt was delivering speeches soothing to conservatives and dissociating himself from the Esch-Townsend Bill, James R. Garfield, the head of the Bureau of Corporations and a member of the "tennis cabinet," was holding meetings with Victor Morawetz, the Santa Fe's attorney, and Francis Lynde Stetson, Morgan's attorney. Roosevelt, in the meantime, continued indicating that he would not propose radical legislation to Congress—but that he would press for some legislation. In mid-November he wrote Ray Stannard Baker that, on the basis of the Attorney General's opinion, he regarded a definite rate law (the Quarles and Townsend Bills) as unconstitutional, and that only a maximum rate law would be legal. His open condemnation of the Townsend Bill, so carefully guided through the House as the Republican proposal, later exposed House Republicans to embarrassing Democratic jibes and forced them to retreat to the milder Hepburn Bill. Roosevelt also attacked the "swinish indifference" of state legislatures towards railroads, a group that condemned the railroads ten times for every one railroad offense to the people.[30] On November 27, 1905, a conference was held at the White House with Elihu Root, Taft, Garfield, Charles Bonaparte, Philander Knox, Knapp, and a group from the Commission. Root, Knox, Garfield, and Knapp, of course, were leading spokesmen for conservative action, and essentially sympathetic to

[29] *Railway and Engineering Review*, XLV (October 21, 1905), 750. Also see *Congressional Record*, XXXIX, 58:3, p. 2025.

[30] Theodore Roosevelt to Ray Stannard Baker, November 13, November 20, 1905, *Letters*, V, 76-77, 83. Also see *Congressional Record*, XL, 59:1, pp. 1981, 1998, 2247.

the railroads. According to Garfield, the result of the meeting was that "General principles agreed upon but it was distinctly understood that . . . [there] should [not] be an administration measure—that the Pres. is of course entirely free to favor any measure that he may deem wise. . . ."[31]

Roosevelt's message to Congress on December 5, 1905, was a cautious, carefully worded plea for railroad regulation that can leave no doubt as to his conservative motivation. While he indicated that "It is not my province to indicate the exact terms of the law which should be enacted," he suggested the general means in far greater detail than in any of his earlier statements. What was needed was Commission power to fix maximum rates if, upon complaint, the rates initiated by the railroads were found to be unjust. "This power to regulate rates, like all similar powers over the business world, should be exercised with moderation, caution, and self-restraint. . . ."[32] All Commission decisions would be subject to court review. Private-car lines should be brought under the act, and more stringent anti-rebating measures were required. Again and again Roosevelt reiterated that "The big railroad men and big shippers are simply Americans of the ordinary type who have developed to an extraordinary degree certain great business qualities. They are neither better nor worse than their fellow-citizens of smaller means. . . . It is in the interest of the best type of railroad man and the best type of shipper no less than of the public that there should be Governmental supervision and regulation of these great business operations. . . ."[33] Manhood and citizenship, Roosevelt indicated, were more important than uncontrolled profit-

[31] James R. Garfield Diary, November 27, 1905, vol. 23, James R. Garfield Papers, Library of Congress, box 106; also see the entries for October 12 and November 23, 1905, for conferences with Morawetz and Stetson.
[32] Roosevelt, *Messages and Papers*, pp. 6976-6977.
[33] *Ibid.*, p. 6980.

making, although "we have nothing but the kindliest feelings of admiration for the successful business man who behaves decently. . . ."[34] And at no point in his message did Roosevelt try to suggest that the purpose of his proposed legislation was to redress the existing distribution of wealth and power, to solve any basic defect in the existing social order. He was completely sincere when he declared:

"Let me most earnestly say that these recommendations are not made in any spirit of hostility to the railroads. On ethical grounds, on grounds of right, such hostility would be intolerable; and on grounds of mere National self-interest we must remember that such hostility would tell against the welfare not merely of some few rich men, but of a multitude of small investors, a multitude of railway employees, wage workers, and most severely against the interest of the public as a whole. I believe that on the whole our railroads have done well and not ill; but the railroad men who wish to do well should not be exposed to competition with those who have no such desire, and the only way to secure this end is to give to some Government tribunal the power to see that justice is done by the unwilling exactly as it is gladly done by the willing. Moreover, if some Government body is given increased power the effect will be to furnish authoritative answer on behalf of the railroad whenever irrational clamor against it is raised, or whenever charges made against it are disproved. I ask this legislation not only in the interest of the public but in the interest of the honest railroad man and honest shipper alike, for it is they who are chiefly jeopardized by the practices of their dishonest competitors. This legislation should be enacted in a spirit as remote as possible from hysteria and rancor."[35]

[34] *Ibid.*
[35] *Ibid.*, p. 6979.

Roosevelt had not only taken it upon himself to protect the railroads from each other, but to protect the railroads from a public capable of damaging them far more seriously than a traditionally sympathetic Commission could ever do.

At the same time that Roosevelt was trying to reassure the railroads of his conservative intentions, the Interstate Commerce Commissioners were making it known that they too opposed radical measures. The Commission refused to become involved in agitation for the Quarles or Townsend Bills, but instead enunciated general principles of legislation. Prouty suggested in early 1903 that while the Commission should have the right to consider rates, its decisions should be subject to the review of a special commerce court—an idea very similar to Elkins'.[36] The Commission's 1904 *Report* indicated that the Elkins Act left important loopholes for rebating, and that although the Commission could condemn a rate as unreasonable, it could not set a new one. To solve the problem, it asked for the power to set new rates after a complaint and hearings. Knapp, the chairman, moderated the Commission's request somewhat during 1905. New powers were desirable but secondary, he declared, and what was really needed were improved means of enforcing the law. Criminal penalties should be restored, and Commission orders related to enforcement should not be subject to court review.

By December 1905, both branches of Congress were in favor of strengthening the law; the question of how to do it remained.[37]

36 Charles A. Prouty, "National Regulation of Railways," *Publications of the American Economic Association* (Third Series), IV (February, 1903), 71-83. Elkins, in December, 1904, was again boosting Olney's commerce court bill. See Stephen B. Elkins to William H. Moody, December 12, 1904, William H. Moody Papers, Letterbooks, vol. 13.

37 Interstate Commerce Commission, *Eighteenth Annual Report, December 19, 1904* (Washington, 1904), pp. 6-8; Martin A. Knapp,

The Railroads and New Legislation

The new agitation for railroad legislation caught many railroad men off guard. Although the Elkins Act did not solve the rebating problem entirely, it had helped end what was equivalent to perhaps a 10 per cent drain on gross railroad revenues until 1903. From 1900 to 1905, railroad income rose for the first time in many years, both in freight revenue per ton mile and revenue per ton. Dividends nearly doubled.[38] The great incentive to railroad advocacy of federal legislation in earlier years had been declining rates and cutthroat competition. In a period of relative prosperity the railroads were less interested in legislation, even though Cassatt, James J. Hill, and others were said by some Congressmen to favor stronger legislation. The Elkins Act was probably all that many railroad men wanted for the time being. But despite this, it is clear that the principle of Commission rate setting with judicial review was not in and of itself alien to the railroads. They had been advocating it, in growing numbers, since John A. Wright's worried article in 1877 calling for federal protection of the railroads. In the 1890's, in conjunction with legalized pooling, it was accepted as desirable by many leading railroad executives. Indeed, the first Elkins Bill of 1902, written by a railroad lawyer, explicitly included a provision for Commission rate setting, subject to judicial review.

The more farsighted railroad leaders realized that the sentiment for regulation had to be channeled, and not a few, as we shall see, positively welcomed the opportunity for additional legislation. "The day has gone by when a

---

"National Regulation of Railroads," *Annals of the American Academy of Political and Social Science*, XXVI (November, 1905), 613-628; *Washington Star*, December 8, 1905.

[38] I. L. Sharfman, *The Interstate Commerce Commission* (New York, 1931-1937), I, 35-36; *Historical Statistics of the U.S.*, pp. 428, 431, 434.

corporation can be handled successfully in defiance of the public will, even though that will be unreasonable and wrong," Charles S. Mellen of the New Haven admitted in January 1904. "A public must be led, but not driven, and I prefer to go with it and shape or modify, in a measure, its opinion, rather than be swept from my bearings with loss to myself and the interests in my charge."[39] At the same time, not a few railroad spokesmen were becoming increasingly disturbed by the revival of state railroad regulation, and were attracted to federal regulation as a means of protection from the states.[40]

But railroad men did not favor either the Quarles or the Townsend Bills. Many of them appeared before the hearings of the Senate Committee on Interstate Commerce during December 1904 to May 1905, and nearly all opposed the specific legislation under consideration. A number of important facts stand out in the testimony of the railroad men. The first is their tone of moderation and avoidance of extreme positions.[41] More significant

[39] C. S. Mellen, speech to Hartford Board of Trade, January 21, 1904, carbon copy in Bureau of Corporations Records, file 541; James R. Garfield to C. C. Mellen, February 11, 1904, *ibid.*, compliments him on the speech.

[40] *Railway Age*, XXXVII (May 20, 1904), 960, for example.

[41] The common assumption that the railroad system as a whole underwrote a fantastic public relations program in 1905 attacking rate regulation as such is based on questionable grounds. The major evidence is the single page of conjecture and circumstantial material in *Collier's*, XXXIX (May 4, 1907), 13-15, and relied on by William Z. Ripley, *Railroads: Rates and Regulation* (New York, 1912), pp. 496-498. The problem with this article is that it gives only circumstantial evidence, no precise dates or durations, only one name (Samuel Spencer), and no proof of railroad support, general or specific. The major topic is a news bureau devoted mainly to fighting municipal ownership. Railroads undoubtedly fought the Quarles and Townsend Bills, but the real question is whether they fought rate regulation on any terms. The *Collier's* article throws very little light on this problem. Another contemporary article on the railroads and public relations is Ray Stannard Baker, "Railroads on Trial: How Railroads Make Public Opinion," *McClure's Magazine*, XXVI (March, 1906), 535-549. Baker gives no details of value, but contents himself with the assertion that the railroads controlled much newspaper sentiment and the Senate Committee on Interstate Commerce. Nothing is said concerning the railroads'

was the willingness of some to suggest different legislation—what they opposed was the specific measures of the Quarles and Townsend Bills, not the principle of federal regulation of railroads on their terms. Victor Morawetz of the Santa Fe praised the Commission and called for the vigorous enforcement of the Elkins Act, and court jurisdiction over fixing maximum rates. Others called for additional legislation on rebating. Only one railroad executive, A. B. Stickney, president of the Chicago, Great Western, strongly endorsed the principle of Commission rate regulation with court review.[42] The problem at hand was to defeat the Townsend Bill, and it is not surprising that many railroad men simply opposed rate regulation as such, with no further recommendations or contingencies.[43] Some of these adamant railroad executives, such as Walker Hines of the Louisville & Nashville and Samuel Spencer of the Southern, were more flexible when testifying on legislation to the House Committee on Interstate and Foreign Commerce. The railroads realized there was a necessity for regulation, Hines admitted, but they opposed the Quarles Bill. A. C. Bird of the Gould roads advocated "wholesome regulation" instead.[44]

Despite the poses and statements of railroad leaders before Congressional hearings, many of them inconsistent or designed to meet particular situations, the *Wall*

---

position on rate regulation or related issues. By implication only, it is hinted that they opposed it. Ironically, Baker's only specific evidence, *ibid.*, p. 548, indicates at least one railroad wanted stronger anti-rebating legislation. Also see footnote 6 of Chapter VII.

[42] For general pro-Commission, pro-legislation railroad views, see U.S. Senate, *Regulation of Railway Rates*, Senate Doc. No. 243, 59:1, II, 811-813, 829, 909-912, 1220-1221, 1299-1301; III, 2119 2133. Also see *Congressional Record*, XXXIX, 58:3, p. 2018.

[43] For this viewpoint, see *ibid.*, I, 234ff., 296; II, 1390ff., 1444ff.; III, 2250; IV, 2618ff.

[44] U.S. House, House Doc. No. 422, 58:3, pp. 179, 263; also see pp. 91-92. For straight railroad opposition see *ibid.*, pp. 216, 226ff.

Street Journal was probably correct when it editorialized in December 1904, that:

"Nothing is more noteworthy than the fact that President Roosevelt's recommendation in favor of government regulation of railroad rates and Commissioner Garfield's recommendation in favor of federal control of interstate companies have met with so much favor among managers of railroads and industrial companies. It is not meant by this that much opposition has not developed, for it has, but it might have been expected that the financial interests in control of the railroads and the industrial corporations would be unanimous in antagonism to these measures, which would, if carried into effect, deprive them of so much of their present power.

"The fact is that many of the railroad men and corporation managers are known to be in favor of these measures, and this is of vast significance. In the end it is probable that all of the corporations will find that a reasonable system of federal regulation is to their interest. It is not meant by this that the financial interests who are in favor of the administrative measures, approve of them exactly in the shape in which they have been presented by the President and Commissioner Garfield, but with the principle of the thing they are disposed to agree. It is known that some of the foremost railroad men of the country are at this time at work in harmony with the President for the enactment of a law providing for federal regulation of rates which shall be equitable both to the railroads and to the public."[45]

Railroad leaders and journals unequivocally attacked the Townsend Bill, but when it died in the Senate after passing in the House 326 to 17, they spoke more moderately than they had before Congressional hearings. B. D. Caldwell of the Delaware, Lackawanna, & Western in-

[45] *Wall Street Journal*, December 28, 1904.

dicated he might favor Commission rate making *if* the government were responsible for earnings.[46] The editorial response of the *Railway World* to the first Hepburn Bill, which included a commerce court, is significant: "This measure is an improvement over previous suggestions, and it may even be admitted that in some particulars the scheme of regulation which it outlines is preferable to that now in effect. The proposed reorganization of the Interstate Commerce Commission is especially to be commended."[47]

The journal asked only for the right of petition for injunctions to restrain any unconstitutional acts by the Commission—that is, the judicial review essentially granted by the bill.

Nor were railroad leaders unduly alarmed by Roosevelt's statements on regulation after the end of 1904. David Willcox of the Delaware & Hudson thought that rather than passing new laws those existing should be more vigorously enforced, but he was encouraged by Roosevelt's 1904 message opposing definite rate powers for the Commission.[48] Samuel Spencer, who took a much more conservative line when talking to Congressmen than to the members of the Traffic Club of Pittsburgh in April 1905, said: "At no time has the President's intention been to advocate Governmental regulation of railways which would inflict injury upon the investments in the properties. . . . He has never advocated, and he can be trusted never to advocate, the adoption of any regulation which does violence to the fundamental principles on which the Government is founded."[49]

[46] *Railway and Engineering Review*, XLV (January 14, 1905), 27.
[47] *Railway World*, XLIX (January 27, 1905), 75.
[48] David Willcox, "Proposed Interstate Commerce Legislation," *Railway World*, XLIX (February 3, 1905), 88; David Willcox, "Governmental Rate Making is Unnecessary and Would be Very Dangerous," *North American Review*, CLXXX (March, 1905), 410-429.
[49] Samuel Spencer, *Address Before the Traffic Club of Pittsburg*, April 7, 1905 (n. p., n. d.), p. 1.

Spencer admitted, "Under the provisions of the Act much good has been accomplished," and it was not regulation as such that was objected to, but direct control of rates and especially the Townsend Bill. Legislation to strengthen the Act in reference to rebates, to separate the Commission's investigatory from its prosecution functions, or to bring water carriers under the Act, was most desirable. So far as the provision for a commerce court was concerned, Spencer claimed "I speak with authority when I say that substantially every railway manager in the country will subscribe to that view, and aid in the accomplishment of the desired results."[50]

The railroad interests unreservedly opposed the Esch-Townsend Bill.[51] But numerous railroad men were sympathetic to so many of the specifics of the campaign for legislation that one must conclude, despite the commonly accepted version, that many essentially supported the movement for regulation in 1905 or were neutral toward it. Samuel Spencer, John W. Midgley, and other key railroad leaders were most anxious to have private-car lines placed under I.C.C. control, and refused to oppose any legislation per se. Midgley was pleased that "The most encouraging feature of the campaign for the suppression of private car abuses, unjust discrimination and other evils declared to be incident to transportation, is the insistence that if authority to set aside rates or classification held to be unreasonable is to be given, care should be taken that the body thus empowered be clearly competent—that is to say, should comprise some who have had actual experience in railroad affairs."[52] Midg-

[50] *Ibid.*, p. 1, and *passim*.

[51] For two examples, see *Railway World*, XLIX (May 19, 1905), 404-405; *Railway and Engineering Review*, XLV (May 20, 1905), 380.

[52] J. W. Midgley, "Growing Sentiment for a Properly Constituted Commission," April 28, 1905, p. 1, in Sen 58A-J 36. A brief version is found in *Railway World*, XLIX (May 5, 1905), 359-361. Also see Samuel Spencer, *An Address Delivered Before the Board of*

ley had confidence in Roosevelt's concern for "better" appointees. With court review of its decisions, Commission control over rates might not be so bad.

Henry Fink, a railroad executive and Albert's brother, probably made the longest defense of enlarging the Commission's power, on acceptable terms, by issuing a book on the topic. ". . . the Act to Regulate Commerce, not withstanding some imperfections, is a monument of legislative wisdom. . . . The amount of mischief that would have resulted from radical measures such as were, under pressure of popular prejudices, clamored for, it is impossible to conjecture."[53] Although not altogether consistent on every issue, and a strong opponent of the Townsend Bill, Fink made it clear that he was a friend of rate fixing and that Roosevelt was a safe, conservative President. However, the rate-fixing power should not be invested in the Commission, insisted Fink, but rather in legalized pools and traffic associations. Cooperation between these associations and the Commission, with greater Commission control over rebating, private-car lines, and water carriers, might create the basis for adequate control.[54]

After mid-1905, the railroads grew more apprehensive about the direction legislation might take, but their essentially positive attitude toward the idea of legislation as such could hardly have changed in so short a time after a commitment of decades.[55] The *Railroad Gazette*,

---

Trade of the City of Newark, October 11, 1905 (n. p., n. d.), pp. 5-6; J. W. Midgley, "Why Private Car Lines Were Overlooked in the Esch-Townsend Bill," *Railroad Gazette*, XXXVIII (April 14, 1905), 357-358.

[53] Henry Fink, *Regulation of Railway Rates on Interstate Freight Traffic* (New York, 1905), pp. 52-53.

[54] *Ibid.*, pp. 124, 224ff.

[55] According to Grenville H. Dodge on May 12, 1905, in a letter to William B. Allison, "The railroad people have almost all changed over from the view of accepting action by the commission on a reasonable rate to a determination to fight it. . . ." Quoted in Nathaniel W. Stephenson, *Nelson W. Aldrich: A Leader in Ameri-*

in October 1905, would have preferred a strict enforcement of existing laws before new legislation was enacted, though it admitted railroads needed protection from each other and from shippers, since rebating was still going on. Its editorial objections, it made clear, "should not be misunderstood to mean that government control of rates is not desirable. It is Government's right, and, when necessary, it is its duty."[56] It was very much encouraged by Roosevelt's Raleigh speech, his rejection of the Esch-Townsend Bill, and his advocacy of judicial review. His attack on the use of the Sherman Act to destroy rate associations was especially welcomed. "Surely here is a hopeful opportunity for agreement on a reasonable provision. . . . The country has been waiting for a powerful leader of public opinion to say this."[57] The *Railroad Gazette* made known the fact that "we are heartily in favor of legislation which will prevent rebates and discrimination," as well as further safety measures.[58]

The statements and speeches by Knapp and Roosevelt at the end of 1905, and the growing realization by the railroads that the Elkins Act had not gone far enough to solve the rebating problem, further consolidated railroad sentiment behind the regulation movement. The *Railway World* declared: "This article by Chairman Knapp will be read by railway men with lively satisfaction, and the *Railway World* regards it as containing a most comforting assurance against the evil consequences which are apprehended from the enactment into law of the President's program of rate regulation. We have con-

---

can Politics (New York, 1930), p. 275. As we shall see, this interpretation is of doubtful validity. The fact important bankers were for legislation in 1905 would have been sufficient to end much of the potential railroad opposition. Jacob H. Schiff is a case in point. See Cyrus Adler, *Jacob H. Schiff: His Life and Letters* (Garden City, N.Y., 1928), I, 43.

[56] *Railroad Gazette*, XXXIX (October 13, 1905), 333.
[57] *Ibid.*, October 27, 1905, p. 381.
[58] *Ibid.*, November 24, 1905, p. 477.

sistently opposed the proposition to increase the powers of the Interstate Commerce Commission, but on the other hand we have maintained that, providing speedy appeal could be made to the courts by railroads, little change would result from the operation of the Commission no matter how much its powers might be enlarged. . . . the interests of the railroads are safe in the hands of the courts. . . ."[59] The railroads fixed their attention on the role of the courts and judicial review in the rate-making process, a principle to which Roosevelt had already agreed. The *Railroad Gazette* liked those aspects of his message to Congress in December 1905 dealing with discrimination and private-car lines, and it was not frightened by his rate recommendations. ". . . we are inclined to prophesy," it remarked blandly, "that the portion of the President's address which deals with the strict matter of rate making . . . will produce results exceedingly small, while his frank efforts to promote corporate honesty and straight and open dealing will bear fruit out of all proportion to any railroad legislation this country has ever had."[60]

In mid-December 1905, perhaps in the hope of forestalling legislation, the leading officers of nearly all the roads west of Chicago met to discuss the increasingly widespread problem of rebating. It is more probable, however, that the railroads were genuinely disturbed by the growing practice of rebating. They decided to inform the Commission of all violations of the law, and they sent notice of their intention to the Commission.[61] The Commission was right, the *Railway World* declared, about the continuation of rebating, and the railroads found the practice most obnoxious. The journal welcomed

[59] *Railway World*, XLIX (December 1, 1905), 950.
[60] *Railroad Gazette*, XXXIX (December 8, 1905), 525. Also see the *New York Herald*, December 17, 1905, for the emphasis of the railroads on the desirable role of the courts.
[61] *Railway World*, L (January 12, 1906), 39.

Attorney General Moody's recent order to district attorneys to seek indictments against law-breakers.[62] At the very time that the passage of new legislation seemed imminent, the railroads realized a stronger law was especially timely. Moody's failure to prosecute the Santa Fe for a clear violation of the Elkins Act undoubtedly failed to give them any reassurance that the law as it stood would be adequately enforced. Congressmen debating the Hepburn Bill during the first months of 1906 were able frequently to cite examples of railroad leaders supporting the bill because of their antagonism toward private-car lines and rebating.[63] And that railroad men did not cite their voluntary agreement to enforce the law as a reason not to enact the Hepburn Act is indication that they were genuinely worried about the rebating problem. Contrary to the usual interpretation, by the end of 1905 the railroads were not hostile to railroad legislation that might be useful to them. They were not ready to break with a long tradition of reliance on political means to solve economic problems.

[62] *Railway World*, XLIX (December 22, 1905), 1022. Dolliver referred to this December meeting as proof of the need for further legislation. See his March 1, 1906 speech in *Congressional Record*, XL, 59:1, p. 3198.

[63] *Congressional Record*, XL, 59:1, pp. 1763ff., 1829, 1844, 1981, 2007.

CHAPTER VII

THE HEPBURN ACT

THE Hepburn Act has been generally regarded as a defeat for the railroads in particular and conservatism in general. "It was in 1906 that the railroads fought their fight to a finish against federal regulation," Frank H. Dixon wrote in 1922.[1] This impression was in part a by-product of the campaign of 1912, when Progressive Party publicists made the Hepburn Act one of the progressive monuments of Roosevelt's presidency—a victory allegedly snatched from the grips of conservative Senators and avaricious railroads.[2] Most historians have accepted this interpretation at its face value, and the standard treatment of the Hepburn Act has varied only in details and not in the basic analysis. John M. Blum, for example, has concluded that Roosevelt's claim to be a progressive in the generic sense is justified by his role in passing the Hepburn Act.

Although he admits the Hepburn Act was in many ways inadequate, Blum suggests the act "nevertheless earned for Roosevelt the opprobrious criticism of a large part of the business community and the tenacious opposition of a near majority of the United States Senate."[3] ". . . the Hepburn Act provided the precedent . . . by which federal regulatory agencies have promoted the na-

[1] Frank Haigh Dixon, *Railroads and Government, 1910-1921* (New York, 1922), p. 3.
[2] Judson C. Welliver, *Catching Up With Roosevelt* [reprint from *Munsey's Magazine*, March, 1912] (New York, 1912), p. 7, is one example of this.
[3] John M. Blum, "Theodore Roosevelt and the Hepburn Act: Toward an Orderly System of Control," in *The Letters of Theodore Roosevelt*, VI, 1561.

tional welfare."[4] By a politically astute policy of threatening tariff reform, Roosevelt was able to beat the conservatives in the Senate into line, and to force them to accept a new railroad law.[5]

The traditional interpretation of the Hepburn Act ignores too many crucial factors. The role of the railroads in the passage of the legislation and their reaction to what was going on have never been considered intensively or systematically. It is assumed that they opposed the Hepburn Bill because they were against the general extension of governmental control under any circumstances. Historians have concentrated on the debates in the Senate and Roosevelt's role rather than on the railroad journals or the statements of various railroad leaders. They have confused railroad opposition to the Townsend and Quarles Bills with opposition to the substantially different Hepburn Bill.[6] But even here, ignoring

[4] *Ibid.*, p. 1571.

[5] *Ibid.* Also see Blum, "Theodore Roosevelt and the Legislative Process: Tariff Revision and Railroad Regulation, 1904-1906," *Letters*, IV, 1333-1342; John Morton Blum, *The Republican Roosevelt* (Cambridge, 1954), pp. 82ff. Harold U. Faulkner, *The Quest for Social Justice, 1898-1914* (New York, 1931), p. 116, is an example of the standard historical interpretation of the problem.

[6] There were no hearings on the Hepburn Bill, but only on the Townsend and Quarles Bills. *Collier's*, XXXIX (May, 1907), 13-15, based wholly on thin circumstantial evidence, and whose reliability I have already criticized in footnote 41, Chapter VI, provides no data whatsoever to show the alleged railroad campaign extended beyond 1905. This item was used by William Z. Ripley, *Railroads: Rates and Regulation* (New York, 1912), pp. 496-498, as his major source of information for the contention that railroads as a whole fought rate regulation bitterly. Samuel Spencer was alleged to have been in charge of an anti-rate law campaign, and the railroads and the N.A.M. to have underwritten it. At its May 1904 convention, however, the N.A.M. passed a strong resolution for I.C.C. power to set rates, upon complaint, with judicial review. N.A.M., *Proceedings of the Ninth Annual Convention—1904 May 17-19, Pittsburgh, Penna.* (New York, 1904), p. 236. In May 1905, the N.A.M. was split, its Committee on Interstate Commerce calling for a renewal of its 1904 position, and the convention calling merely for a stronger rebate law if the existing one could not be more forcefully applied. N.A.M., *Proceedings of the Tenth Annual Convention, Atlanta, Ga., May 16-18, 1905* (New York, 1905), pp. 107-121, 214-215. Spencer, in April, 1905, as I have already indicated in Chapter VI, was publicly

the validity of this approach, historians have also over-dramatized and exaggerated the conflict in the Senate. Differences were not those of principle and basic political philosophies—between conservatives and progressives—but between detailed matters of emphasis. Nearly all Senators accepted the desirability of rate regulation and the principle of judicial review over Commission rate decisions. Whether that review was to be broad or narrow does not, it seems to me, warrant the assumption that the conflict between Roosevelt and certain Senators was over substantive matters, or that they disagreed fundamentally on the desirability of rate regulation.

On December 19, 1905, after a conference at the White House that included Elihu Root, Moody, and S. H. Cowan, a representative of livestock interests, Senator Jonathan P. Dolliver introduced S. 2261 in the Senate as the Administration's proposed railroad legislation, announcing "It is not drawn in a spirit of hostility to the railroad system of the country. . . ."[7] The actual draft was written by the Commission along the lines of the earlier Hepburn Bill, but the provision for a commerce court was removed. A number of other measures on railroad rate fixing were introduced in the Senate at about the same time as the new Hepburn Bill. Joseph B. Foraker of Ohio, whose sympathy for railroads and business has never been questioned, presented a rate bill which allowed all rate complaints to go directly to the courts. Foraker insisted that he was a friend of railroad regulation, but he must be regarded as a literal-minded

---

praising Roosevelt and endorsing the principle of new legislation to strengthen the law, although not in the direction of the Esch-Townsend Bill. Samuel Spencer, *Address Before the Traffic Club of Pittsburg, April 7, 1905* (n. p., n. d.). Henry F. Pringle, *Theodore Roosevelt* (New York, 1956), p. 294, appreciates the fact that Roosevelt did not endorse the Esch-Townsend Bill.

[7] *Washington Post*, December 20, 1905. The original bill is in U.S. Senate, Senate Doc. No. 292, 59th Cong., 1st Sess., March 28, 1906 (Washington, 1906).

maverick. His proposal never obtained any support, and the railroads either ignored it or considered it to be a cumbersome, unworkable scheme that might seriously undo many of the positive aspects of the Commission in hearing complaints.[8] Elkins, too, proposed a bill that established a court of commerce, allowed the Commission ninety days to review a rate before it went into effect, forbade pooling but allowed agreements between carriers subject to Commission approval, forbade railroads to mine or sell coal and iron ore, and left the general control of rates in the hands of the Commission. The bill was vague and not too explicit, and some of Elkins' friends regarded it as Roosevelt's work. While this appears most unlikely, and it is probable Elkins was in fact motivated by a desire to prevent the Commission from having extensive rate-making powers; his bill received no significant support and Elkins was eventually to swing behind the Hepburn Bill.[9] The Elkins Bill was too vague, the *Railway World* commented, and it "does not commend itself as a desirable substitute for other bills now before Congress."[10]

Henry Cabot Lodge differed with Roosevelt over the Hepburn Bill on details rather than on principles.[11] Boies Penrose, one of the more conservative members of the Senate, was lined up behind the Hepburn Bill by pressure from A. J. Cassatt, president of the Pennsylvania Railroad.[12] Philander Knox, now a member of the Sen-

[8] Everett Walters, *Joseph Benson Foraker: An Uncompromising Republican* (Columbus, 1948), pp. 215ff.; Joseph Benson Foraker, *Notes of a Busy Life* (Cincinnati, 1907), II, 209-211; *Railroad Gazette*, XXXIX (December 1, 1905), 502-503.

[9] Oscar Doane Lambert, *Stephen Benton Elkins* (Pittsburgh, 1955), pp. 271-276; Stephen B. Elkins to Nelson Aldrich, October 11, 1905, Nelson Aldrich Papers, Library of Congress, box 29, suggests the purpose of the bill was to modify the law in a "safe" way, according to Elkins' interpretation of safety.

[10] *Railway World*, L (January 26, 1906), 91.

[11] John A. Garraty, *Henry Cabot Lodge* (New York, 1953), p. 227, suggests this, and the facts, as we shall see, bear him out.

[12] Lambert, *Elkins*, p. 269.

ate, had favored Commission rate regulation with judicial review since at least 1903, and he was to ally himself with Lodge, Aldrich, and Elkins in the Senate.[13] That they all agreed with the basic purpose of the Hepburn Bill—to end rebating and fix criticized rates—cannot be doubted.

Unlike earlier contests over railroad legislation, shippers and the general public were strangely apathetic during the debate over the Hepburn Bill. The demise of the Interstate Commerce Law Convention meant that the petitions and resolutions that had deluged earlier Congresses as a result of organized campaigns were largely absent. Nor did the railroads, despite the common impression that they militantly campaigned against the Hepburn Bill, fill the Senate with anti-regulation petitions and letters.[14] When the Hepburn Bill was submitted to the House, the *Railway and Engineering Review* admitted "the Hepburn Bill is in many respects very much better than some of the other propositions that have been advanced," but it wanted minimum as well as maximum rates fixed by the Commission. ". . . the fixing by Congress, through the medium of a commission, the limits above and below which the railroads may not go will be a long step toward effecting a needed readjustment in the railroad charges of the United States."[15]

[13] Speech of Philander Knox, in *New York Herald*, December 3, 1903.

[14] See Sen 59A-K 19, which has well under 100 petitions and letters on the topic, mainly from shippers and Granges; and Sen 59A-J 52, which has a long petition from shippers for the Grosscup Plan for special courts of transportation to pass on rates immediately. Sen 59A-J 58, which covers this session of Congress, has a very large number of petitions from shippers against the Quarles and Townsend Bills only. Also see U.S. Senate, *Rate Legislation*, Senate Doc. No. 249, 59th Cong., 1st Sess., March 5, 1906 (Washington, 1906), a 42-page collection of telegrams, submitted by Elkins, from shippers in Iowa, Minnesota, South Dakota, and Wisconsin. Obviously part of an organized campaign, these telegrams are either in opposition to the Hepburn, Townsend, and Quarles Bills, or, in many instances, simply *for* judicial review.

[15] *Railway and Engineering Review*, XLVI (January 27, 1906),

Although it is the struggle for the passage of the bill in the Senate that is of major interest, the debate over the House version of the Hepburn Bill (H.R. 12987), which was approved by a vote of 346 to 7 in early February 1906, reveals much of contemporary Congressional attitudes toward railroad regulation, their motives and confusions. Without doubt, the majority of the House members were primarily concerned with the interests of the "shippers" and the "people." Yet they also made it amply plain they did not want to damage legitimate railroad interests. (They were frequently reminded that the railroads also favored an end to private-car and rebating practices.) If they waxed hot over the dangers of the "trusts" and "monopolies," terms they usually applied inconsistently and inappropriately, many also expressed a belief in the need for reform to head off socialism, and not a few recognized that the railroads also wanted freedom from the bargaining power of the giant shippers. The dominant concern among House members, in the last analysis, was less with the function of the Hepburn Bill, a problem few had clear thoughts on, than with the Constitutional and legal issues it allegedly raised.[16]

When the Hepburn Bill arrived in the Senate after passing the House, it granted the right of review to the courts and in effect allowed them to decide how broad judicial review of Commission decisions might be. In January 1906, Roosevelt was resisting steps to add more radical amendments for fear the bill might get

---

61. Samuel Spencer of the Southern, in "Railway Rates and Industrial Progress," *Century Magazine*, LXXI (January, 1906), 380-387, probably written before Roosevelt's 1905 message and certainly before the revised Hepburn Bill was submitted, directed a strong line of attack on the Esch-Townsend Bill, but admitted the Commission had the right to review the administrative decisions of railroad executives.

16 *Congressional Record*, XL, 59:1, pp. 1763ff., 1770, 1829, 1831-1832, 1844, 1847, 1904, 1981, 1996, 2002, 2007, 2104.

bogged down altogether.[17] Although there was substantial debate in the Senate on whether granting rate-making functions to a Commission was in fact granting legislative functions to an administrative body, too many Senators agreed on the desirability of delivering rate powers to the Commission to worry about Constitutional niceties. The major issue was the role of judicial review, and since Roosevelt as well as everyone else agreed it was necessary in one form or another, there can be little doubt that the theoretical distinctions that developed in the course of a more or less regular four-month consideration of the bill have been subsequently exaggerated by historians.

The review issue centered about two problems. The first was what was to be done with new evidence submitted to the court of review that had not been previously submitted to the Commission by a railroad. The so-called radicals wished to have the evidence given to the Commission first, so that it could report on it and, if necessary, adjust its case accordingly. The advocates of broad judicial review thought this would tend to result in a denial of due process of law. The second and more important topic of controversy was to what extent the courts should be allowed to issue injunctions setting aside Commission orders. Some said no prohibitions or injunctions should be imposed, others wanted explicit limitations on the courts; a compromise position called for delays on injunctions until hearings could be held.[18]

Railroad men worried about these legal questions far less than the eloquent and circumlocutious lawyers in the Senate. They wanted judicial review, of course, but the fine distinctions did not seem to bother them, and a

[17] Theodore Roosevelt to Chester I. Long, January 31, 1906, *Letters*, v, 142-143.

[18] Robert E. Cushman, *The Independent Regulatory Commissions* (New York, 1941), pp. 74-76, has the clearest legal summary of the complicated debates.

few, such as Cassatt, sided with the advocates of narrow court review.[19] Prouty assured them in February that he, for one, thought it would be foolish for the Commission to fix rates that would not return a fair profit, and that under the Hepburn Act "The railways will make their rates in exactly the same manner that they have. . . ."[20] A. B. Stickney, president of the Chicago, Great Western, was now far less an exception than he had appeared a year earlier when the railroad executives testified against the Townsend and Quarles Bills. ". . . under present conditions, without effective support from the law, railroads are powerless to prevent rebates and kindred devices . . . ," he told the Chicago Real Estate Board. "The country is indebted to Theodore Roosevelt for his courageous course in regard to legislative control of rates."[21] Traditionally a supporter of federal regulation and close to the Pennsylvania Railroad, the *Railway World* was pleased by the House version of the Hepburn Bill and concluded: "This Hepburn measure appears at present to be far milder than has been anticipated, but its true effect cannot be disclosed until interpreted by the courts. If the amendments which are apparently to be insisted upon by the Senate . . . are adopted we can see nothing in the measure threatening the interests of the railroads."[22] The Hepburn Bill, the *Railway and Engineering Review* commented in decidedly moderate terms, would be the basis of discussion and compromise in the Senate.[23] Even the outright opponents of Commission rate making, surprisingly few in number at this point, were re-

[19] Theodore Roosevelt to Alexander J. Cassatt, February 22, 1906, *Letters*, v, 162. Also see John G. Johnson to W. H. Moody, February 19, 1906, Philander C. Knox Papers, ac. 9172, box 1, in which an attorney of the Pennsylvania Railroad indicates they support the Hepburn Bill.

[20] Charles A. Prouty, "The President and the Railroads," *Century Magazine*, LXXI (February, 1906), 652.

[21] *Railroad Gazette*, XL (February 2, 1906), 120.

[22] *Railway World*, L (February 9, 1906), 123.

[23] *Railway and Engineering Review*, XLVI (February 10, 1906), 96.

strained in their terms.[24] Passage of the Hepburn Bill did not threaten the end of their world.

Indeed, much of the drama and excitement attributed to the debate over the bill in the Senate, which has been interpreted to mean that the bill was somehow radical or sharply opposed, has been exaggerated. "The newspapers have been making a mare's nest out of rate legislation in the Senate," an anonymous Republican Senator complained in mid-February, "when, as a matter of fact, it has been obvious to me for a month that there would be no difficulty whatever in getting a bill perfected by the Committee on Interstate Commerce which will receive nearly every vote in the Senate, and that without anything like a long debate."[25] Although perhaps too optimistic on a few points, the Senator was correct on the essentials. Indeed, some advocates of the Hepburn Bill in the Senate were disturbed by the political liabilities attached to the large conservative support for the bill. Dolliver's major speech in the Senate for his bill was decidedly a conservative one. Allison, Spooner, Dolliver, Nelson, and Long were not precisely radicals, and the word quickly got around that the House members from Pennsylvania and New England who voted for the Hepburn Bill were not unmindful of pro-regulation pressures being exerted by the Pennsylvania Railroad and the New Haven.[26]

Until the very last week of February, Roosevelt frustrated the less conservative Senators by clearly allying himself with his old friend Lodge and his associates. On February 12, addressing the Senate, Lodge came out unequivocally for rate control with judicial review, and the *New York Sun* reported that the radicals felt betrayed by Roosevelt's implicit support of the Lodge speech, although they might have predicted his course somewhat

[24] See, for example, Edgar J. Rich, *Address Before the Massachusetts Board of Trade, February 7, 1906* (Boston, 1906).

[25] *New York Post*, February 10, 1906.

[26] *Ibid.*; speech of Dolliver in *Congressional Record*, XL, 59:1, pp. 3192-3204.

earlier.[27] Over the next few days it was reported almost simultaneously that Roosevelt was very much inclined to appoint several railroad men to the Commission if the Hepburn Bill passed, that he would accept any amendments to the bill acceptable to Philander Knox, in whom he always had great confidence, and that he was moving toward a more narrow definition of judicial review.[28] It is not unlikely that all of these reports had at least a substantial measure of truth in them. On February 19, Roosevelt wrote Cannon about sharpening up the bill to assure the conservatives that it clearly provided for judicial review.[29] On the same day he saw Knox about Knox' proposed amendment on judicial review, a measure designed to please the Senate Committee on Interstate Commerce; and Charles S. Mellen of the New Haven, identified by the press as an early supporter of the bill, also saw the President about restricting the access of small lines to terminals through the bill.[30]

Knox, perhaps with some prodding from Moody, decided instead to submit his own complete rate bill to the Senate with a broad measure of judicial review. This move, which came on February 22, apparently caught everyone by surprise, and allowed Aldrich, who represented Eastern manufacturing rather than railroads, to get the Hepburn Bill out of Committee unamended. It was now on the floor, subject to additional amendments, because of strong Democratic support. Having temporarily fallen out with the conservatives, nearly all of whom favored some form of rate legislation, Roosevelt was forced to rely on the Democrats and, in particular, on "Pitchfork" Ben Tillman of South Carolina, whose

27 *New York Sun*, February 14, 1906; *New York Tribune*, February 13, 1906.
28 *Chicago Chronicle*, February 14, 1906; *New York Times*, February 19, 1906; *New York Tribune*, February 19, 1906.
29 Theodore Roosevelt to Joseph G. Cannon, February 19, 1906, *Letters*, V, 157-158.
30 *New York Herald*, February 20, 1906.

colorful expressions and quasi-Populist tendencies Roosevelt had freely criticized for years.[31]

Despite his distaste for Tillman, with whom he had refused to talk for four years, March 1906 was presumably Roosevelt's radical month for railroad legislation. But his reliance on the Democrats was actually something of a feint, politically designed to push Lodge, Elkins, Aldrich, and their group somewhat closer to his own compromise notions on judicial review. It is certain that Roosevelt resisted the efforts of advocates of narrow judicial review, such as Spooner, to limit the number of stays the courts could put on Commission orders. He was more interested in getting the House bill passed as it stood.[32] He did comparatively little to improve his relations with Tillman, and was pointedly telling the press that Congress was full of "ignorant men" after the Tillman-Gillespie resolution calling for an Interstate Commerce Commission investigation of coal and oil trusts was passed. Indeed, Roosevelt and Tillman were exchanging strong words during the second week of March, and it was Lodge who came to Roosevelt's defense.[33]

Roosevelt's half-hearted posture was met in kind by only a few railroad spokesmen during March. Stickney, of course, continued his agitation for Commission rate regulation. The *Railway World*, reflecting the views of the Pennsylvania more than any other line, suggested that: "If the proposed rate law should prove to be an effectual remedy it ought not to work a hardship to the carriers because . . . there is no outcry that rates are excessive. The proposed law is based on claims of dis-

[31] *Washington Post*, February 23, 1906; *St. Louis Republic*, February 23, 1906; Nathaniel W. Stephenson, *Nelson W. Aldrich: A Leader in American Politics* (New York, 1930), pp. 293-295.

[32] Theodore Roosevelt to Edward P. Bacon, March 9, 1906, *Letters*, v, 173-174.

[33] *Washington Post*, March 13, 1906; *Congressional Record*, xxxx, 59:1, 1906, pp. 3668ff.

crimination and if discrimination is actually removed so that all shippers, big and little, are on an equal basis the railroads should not be the sufferers."[34] The main object of the legislation, to destroy rebating and stabilize rates, was not lost to such railroad groups in the course of the legal debate over court review. Even the *Railroad Gazette*, which decided in early March that the Hepburn Bill was unworkable and unconstitutional as it stood, concluded that there was little to fear if it passed.[35] At the end of the month Charles S. Mellen of the New Haven, an old supporter of the bill, came out against it, although he hedged his opposition by declaring that any law to end discriminations was welcomed—with proper safeguards. At about the same time, Andrew Carnegie decided to endorse the Hepburn Bill.[36]

Amid this maneuvering by Roosevelt and the railroads, a few disturbing signs emerged showing they really had a great deal in common. For better or worse, at least some contemporaries regarded the Hepburn Bill as being in large measure a railroad inspired bill. On March 14, Senator Rayner of Maryland told the Senate that the suspending clause of the Hepburn Bill had been "suggested" by the railroads themselves, and upon cross examination offered Foraker the name of the railroad lawyer concerned for his private information.[37] Whether true or not, a number of individuals and papers believed it at the time. The *New York Press*, on March 16, de-

[34] *Railway World*, L (March 9, 1906), 211. Also see A. B. Stickney, "Legislative Regulation of Railroad Rates," *Political Science Quarterly*, XXI (March, 1906), 28-37.

[35] *Railroad Gazette*, XL (March 9, 1906), 217-218.

[36] *Ibid.*, March 30, 1906, p. 322; Theodore Roosevelt to Andrew Carnegie, March 28, 1906, *Letters*, V, 201. Ferdinand H. Graser, "Purpose and Work of the Interstate Commission," *Railway World*, L (May 11, 1906), 389-391, is another example of a railroad viewpoint fundamentally in support of the Hepburn Bill.

[37] Speech of Senator Rayner, March 14, 1906, *Congressional Record*, XL, 59:1, p. 3779. An additional discussion of railroads and regulation is found in *ibid.*, p. 3728.

cided Rayner was too modest—the railroads had written
the entire bill, and "This explains why the railroad lob-
bies did not raise a note of public or private protest
against the Hepburn bill in the House."[38] If the facts
were not documented, at least the logic of the criticism
seemed relevant. Foraker certainly accepted Rayner's
allegation, for several weeks later he was identifying
Mellen and Cassatt as supporters of the Hepburn Bill.[39]
After all, the railroads did not sit idly by without reason.

During April, Roosevelt moved to come to some final
arrangement on the Hepburn Bill. Having established
relations with those who advocated broad judicial review
as well as those favoring narrow review, he was in a
position to work with both sides. In April, as Blum right-
ly maintains, Roosevelt showed his masterful abilities as
political tactician—he played the role sufficiently well to
gain support for his position from all sides. On March
31, Moody, Prouty, Dolliver, Allison, Cullom, Clapp,
and Long met at the White House and agreed to a simple review by the circuit courts to determine whether a
contested order was beyond the Commission's rights.
This, in effect, was the House interpretation and meant
broad judicial review over the Commission's decisions.
It also meant new Republican backing, and Elkins announced his support for the bill "with great pleasure,"
though Tillman indicated he would oppose the Long
amendment to the bill embodying the new compromise.[40]
But Knox, Foraker, and Aldrich were not yet ready to
go along, although Elkins was now ready to treat the
bill as his own, and conferences between Elkins and
Roosevelt over the next two months indicate the President
relied on Elkins heavily from this point on. Yet Elkins'
position was not a conversion as a result of the March 31

[38] *New York Press*, March 16, 1906.
[39] *Congressional Record*, XL, 59:1, April 5, 1906, p. 4779.
[40] *Brooklyn Eagle*, April 2, 1906; *New York Press*, April 1, 1906;
New York Herald, April 1, 1906; *New York Times*, April 2, 1906.

White House meeting, for on March 29 he told the Senate: "I favor the bill. I will vote for it, and have always intended to do so, but prefer to amend it and make it a better bill."[41] "We have already taken occasion . . . to ask whether the Hepburn bill need be feared," the *Railroad Gazette* said, commenting on the new turn of affairs. "We may add our full belief that it need not be."[42]

To circumvent the new breach in his informal *détente* with Tillman, and to gain Democratic support, Roosevelt called in Overman of North Carolina, Daniel of Virginia, and other key Democrats.[43] But it should not be thought that in switching from one faction to another Roosevelt was allying himself with any comprehensive view of the economy or American society, whether conservative or progressive. He was, in essence, merely gathering support from all sides. Nor should it be thought that the disagreements between the Tillmans and Aldriches were as sharp as has been commonly portrayed. It is true, as the *New York Herald* declared, that Tillman "has not liked the spectacle of Messrs. Cassatt and Mellen and other prominent railroad men paying frequent visits to the White House." But Aldrich made it clear "I expect to see the pending bill so amended that both the Senator from South Carolina and myself will vote for it."[44] "So far as I know," Aldrich announced on the Senate floor, "there is no Senator sitting upon this side who does not sympathize fully with the Senator from Texas [Bailey] and the President of the United States in a desire to secure effective and proper legislation with reference to the regulation of railroad rates."[45] Rumors

41 *Congressional Record*, XL, 59:1, p. 4436. See also *ibid.*, p. 4832; Lambert, *Elkins*, pp. 278-279; *The Letters of Theodore Roosevelt*, VI, 1598-1599.

42 *Railroad Gazette*, XL (April 6, 1906), 347.

43 *Brooklyn Eagle*, April 5, 1906; *New York Press*, April 6, 1906; *Washington Post*, April 6, 1906.

44 *New York Herald*, April 7, 1906.

45 *Congressional Record*, XL, 59:1, April 5, 1906, p. 4778.

were rife, perhaps deliberately so: Roosevelt was allegedly supporting Senator Bailey's nonsuspension amendment for narrow court review at the same time that he
was definitely supporting Senator Long's broad review
amendment, or supposedly a broad review amendment
of Knox's.[46] The basic realities within the Senate at the
beginning of April should not be obscured by such
juggling and maneuvering. The *New York Tribune* correctly analyzed the situation on April 8:

"Congress has become almost unanimous for the great
principle he [Roosevelt] advocates, and federal control
of the rates charged by common carriers is now assured.
Despite exaggerated reports regarding differences between the President and the Senate, they are a unit in
their view of the important principle involved. . . .

"The fact that Congress is unequivocally committed
to the principle advocated by the President seems likely
to be lost sight of in the turmoil attending the adjustment of minor details of the legislation. Despite the war
and rumors of war between the President and the leaders
of the Senate, the fact remains that both Houses of Congress, by almost unanimous vote, will respond to the
chief recommendation of the President. . . .

"The tendency to magnify all differences between the
President and Congress, and the vast importance of the
entire subject, have led to such exaggerated accounts of
their present divergent views as largely to becloud the
facts and mislead the ordinary observer as to the actual
situation."

Even the railroads were content, the *Tribune* concluded.
The only question in the entire debate was when a contested rate would go into effect as a result of judicial
review. The possibility of not passing any rate bill
whatsoever was never considered.

[46] *New York Herald*, April 8, April 10, 1906, contains all of these
rumors.

The so-called radicals in the Senate—Tillman, La Follette, and Bailey—made their last stand in April for the Bailey amendment to prevent the suspension of Commission rate orders by the courts. Roosevelt played all sides against each other during this controversy. He opposed the Bailey amendment because he unjustifiably believed that the conservatives would support it and have the entire bill declared unconstitutional.[47] At the same time, Roosevelt resisted new measures proposed by Knox for fear of losing support for the Hepburn Bill. And he moved to work with the Senate Democrats more closely than he had for a month.[48] By the end of April it was clear the Senatorial conservatives would have their way. Prouty, Knapp, and the I.C.C. came out for judicial review in a general manner that strengthened the hand of the conservatives.[49] The conservatives were winning by sheer attrition, and interest in the bill lagged sharply by late April. La Follette, seeing the way the tide was running, called for the passage of the Bailey amendment and then lashed out against the entire Hepburn Bill as a half-way measure. He demanded that Congress introduce a scientific rate-making standard based on railroad valuation.[50] But the Senate radicals had very little strength at this point, and on April 30 the Senate voted to close debate on the topic. The *Railroad Gazette* editorialized: "There are two strong economic reasons why Congress should pass what is commonly known as a rate bill this session. The first of these is that the small

[47] Theodore Roosevelt to Knute Nelson, April 11, 1906, *Letters*, v, 209.

[48] Theodore Roosevelt to Philander C. Knox, April 22, 1906, *Letters*, v, 215; Theodore Roosevelt to William B. Allison, April 12, 1906, *Letters*, v, 210.

[49] *Washington Post*, April 20, 1906; also printed in U.S. Senate, Senate Doc. No. 394, 59th Cong., 1st Sess., April 21, 1906 (Washington, 1906).

[50] *Washington Star*, April 19, 1906; *New York Herald*, April 24, 1906.

shipper under the present system suffers a grievous wrong in the delay of the law and the cost of litigation. . . . The other reason is the existence at the present time of a strong public feeling against corporations in general and the railroads in particular. . . . As we have pointed out in these columns, this feeling cannot be disposed of by a policy of doing nothing. If a bill is not passed it seems sure that a national party will grow up, having as its principal platform a basis of hostility to railroads and to corporate interests which will do far more harm than any legislation now contemplated."[51] Although the journal had specific criticisms of minor aspects of the Hepburn Bill, and thought its criteria for a just rate too vague, it felt the bill met the evil of extortionate rates "in a simple and effective manner."[52]

With over fifty amendments to the Hepburn Bill in the Senate, and debate closed, Nelson Aldrich entered the picture and solved all differences among the Republicans. The "Allison" amendment was introduced in the Senate on May 3, and superseded the Long and all earlier compromises on the nature of judicial review. As Blum has suggested, the new amendment was merely the House version of judicial review, and allowed the court to determine the scope of its own power of review over a particular case.[53] Although all factions, save La Follette, supported it, the Allison amendment represents a clear victory for Nelson Aldrich and the Senators he represented. Allison was sick in bed when "his" amendment was presented to the Senate, and several days earlier Aldrich passed copies of it out to newspapermen with the injunction that they refer to it as Allison's measure.[54] Second thoughts and recriminations were not

[51] *Railroad Gazette*, XL (April 27, 1906), 418.

[52] *Ibid.*, p. 419.

[53] Blum, "Theodore Roosevelt and the Hepburn Act," *Letters*, VI, 1569-1570.

[54] *Washington Post*, May 5, 1906; also see *New York Tribune*,

far behind the compromise, however. Senator Bailey, on May 11, attacked Roosevelt for capitulating to the conservatives, and the next day Tillman accused the President of betraying an understanding they had reached, via Moody, to support narrow review. Roosevelt issued his first defense, significantly, through Lodge, and a few days later denied all.[55] One can hardly attribute Tillman's attack to a disillusioned naïveté. Everyone knew Roosevelt had been playing both sides of the street since the beginning of the year.

Despite growing attacks from Knox and Foraker as well as Bailey, the Hepburn Bill was passed by a Senate vote of 71 to 3 on May 18. A last minute change, removing "in its judgment" from the section on judicial review, undoubtedly picked up a few radical votes, although La Follette continued to oppose the bill.[56] Foraker was the sole Republican to vote against the measure; Aldrich was out of town at the time, although this cannot be interpreted as opposition, since the following week he and Crane visited the White House for the first time since February.[57] Elkins took the bill to the conference with the House, and it was essentially the Senate version that was signed into law on June 29.

The New Act and the Railroads

The new act was basically a refinement of the Elkins Act, and certainly not a radical departure from it. The law was extended to cover express and sleeping-car companies, pipe lines, and private-car lines. Section 1 made it illegal for a railroad company to transport goods, save

---

May 4, 1906; *New York Press*, May 6, 1906; Stephenson, *Aldrich*, pp. 310-312.

[55] *Brooklyn Eagle*, May 12, 1906; *Washington Star*, May 13, 1906; *New York Tribune*, May 15, 1906. Also see Theodore Roosevelt to Henry Cabot Lodge, May 19, 1906, *Letters*, v, 273-275.

[56] *Washington Post*, May 19, 1906.

[57] *New York Press*, May 24, 1906.

timber and its products, in which it had direct or indirect interest—the "commodity clause" aimed at the anthracite railroads. Sections 4 and 5, concerning long-short haul discriminations and pooling, were not altered in any way. Section 6 was changed to require 30 instead of 10 days notice to the Commission and the public in the event of a rate change, slightly altered the terms forbidding rebates, and provided for a fine for rebating three times the sum or value of the rebate received. Section 10 restored a maximum imprisonment of two years as a possible penalty for violating the law, and section 11 enlarged the membership of the Commission from five to seven. Section 15 dealt with rates, and was potentially the most important. Upon complaint of a shipper or railroad, the Commission could "determine and prescribe what will be the just and reasonable rate or rates, charge or charges, to be thereafter observed in such case as the maximum to be charged; and what regulation or practice in respect to such transportation is just, fair, and reasonable." All orders were to take effect in not less than 30 days, and were to last a maximum of two years, unless "suspended or set aside by a court of competent jurisdiction." The total absence of any criteria for rates or court action meant the act was subject to the broadest possible interpretation. It is for this reason that La Follette was to remark that section 20, imposing a standard bookkeeping system on the railroads, was the most useful part of the entire act. The Commission could not intervene against a rate until a shipper was ready to take the time and money to initiate a complaint, and the law did not even attempt to deal directly with the major source of shipper grievances, the long-short haul discriminations.

The railroads, during the final weeks of discussion of the bill, indicated growing support where before there had been none, and enthusiasm where support had existed before. In at least one instance, railroad backing for the bill that had been of prime importance was revealed now that the political liabilities of a public railroad endorsement of the bill could not ruin the chances for its passage. Even the *Railway and Engineering Review*, which had been the most reluctant of the major railroad journals to support legislation, asserted the law was inevitable and began calling for specific additions, such as granting to the Commission the power to classify freight, or for changes, such as removing pipe lines from coverage under the law. The *Railway World*, as usual, regarded the Hepburn Bill casually and favorably. On the shippers' side, the National Association of Manufacturers' convention in May endorsed Roosevelt's railroad policy, returning, in effect, to the old position of Bacon's Interstate Commerce Law Convention.[58]

In June, even before the final vote was taken, the public was officially informed of what had often been rumored: A. J. Cassatt had long favored federal rate regulation, and was an ardent proponent of the Hepburn Bill. In an authorized article in *Pearson's Magazine*, Cassatt was portrayed in heroic tones and his role in the passage of the Elkins Act was spelled out in considerable detail. So far as the Hepburn Bill was concerned, Cassatt was unequivocal, thereby indicating his position on legislation at the conferences with Roosevelt during the first half of 1906, conferences about which Tillman had so complained. In Cassatt's words:

"I have for several years believed that the national Government, through the Interstate Commerce Commission, ought to be in a position to fix railroad rates whenever the rates established by the railroads themselves

[58] *Railway World*, L (June 8, 1906), 474; National Association of Manufacturers, *Proceedings of the Eleventh Annual Convention, New York, May 14-16, 1906* (New York, 1906), pp. 116-118.

are found, after complaint and hearing, to be unreasonable; provided, of course, that there shall be the right of appeal to the courts.

"Let the Government regulate us. For my part and for my associates in the Pennsylvania Railroad Company, I am generally heartily in accord with the position taken by President Roosevelt, and we have been all along; I told the President himself when he made his first recommendation on this subject to Congress, more than four years ago, that I believed him to be in the right."[59]

For years the Pennsylvania had tried to eliminate rebating and instability in the railroad system. As their official historians put it, "The object having been thus obtained by legislation, the Pennsylvania, in 1906, sold all of its stock in the Chesapeake and Ohio and a majority of its holdings of Baltimore and Ohio and Norfolk and Western. . . ."[60] The Pennsylvania's 1906 *Report* frankly admitted that "through the passage of recent amendments to the Interstate Commerce Law and the enforcement of its provisions the maintenance of tariff rates had been practically secured, it was deemed advisable to sell a portion of the securities heretofore acquired."[61] The Pennsylvania's reliance on political means to solve its economic problems had been justified.

It is confusing, in light of the obvious fact that the large majority of the railroads supported the passage of the Hepburn Act, or were neutral toward it, to find nearly all recent American historians firmly convinced that the railroads wholeheartedly opposed the bill. Prouty went to some pains to assure railroad men that the new law would

[59] Quoted in James Creelman, "All is not Damned," *Pearson's Magazine*, XV (June, 1906), 551-552.

[60] George H. Burgess and Miles C. Kennedy, *Centennial History of the Pennsylvania Railroad Company, 1846-1946* (Philadelphia, 1949), p. 462.

[61] Quoted in *ibid.*

not be implemented rashly.[62] George W. Perkins, whose firm had an investment of some consequence in the matter, wrote his superior, J. P. Morgan, that the new railroad bill "is going to work out for the ultimate and great good of the railroads. There is no question but that rebating has been dealt a death blow."[63] The conventional interpretation of the Hepburn Act ignores the fact that for thirty years the American railroads, through voluntary and political means, had tried their utmost to devise means to *maintain* rates. In 1906, they finally attained their goal and also retained their power to take the initiative in determining rates. But even overlooking the role of the railroads in earlier legislative movements, the conventional version suffers from a logical inconsistency. The votes for the Hepburn Bill in both the House and Senate were nearly unanimous. Unless one maintains that the railroads were totally powerless politically, which was hardly the case, the votes for the Hepburn Bill can only be understood as an indication that enough important railroads essentially backed the measure, or were neutral toward it, to make such an overwhelming vote possible.

The immediate response of the railway journals in the months following the passage of the act certainly indicated a favorable attitude. The *Railway and Engineering Review*, once slow to commend the bill, praised the commodity clause and found nothing to object to in its rate provisions. The law's precise meaning was uncertain, and litigation would follow, but the journal hoped legislation to allow pooling would be tacked on the Act.[64] "The enforcement of the new rate law will,

[62] Charles A. Prouty, "The Rate Bill: What It Is and What It Will Do," *American Monthly Review of Reviews*, XXXIV (July, 1906), 70.

[63] George Perkins to J. P. Morgan, June 25, 1906, George W. Perkins Papers, Columbia University Library, box 16.

[64] *Railway and Engineering Review*, XLVI (July 14, 1906), 535-536.

I believe, be of the greatest benefit to all the railroads and the other common carriers," G. J. Grammar of the New York Central declared in July. He predicted that the elimination of free passes and services under the act would soon lead to shipper demands for its repeal.[65] The *Railroad Gazette* read the act carefully and decided it had criticisms of the commodity clause, insurance provisions, and aspects of through-rate fixing, but it praised the rebate, anti-pass, and statistical sections:

". . . on the whole there does not seem to be serious ground for belief that its operation will be harmful if it is administered with intelligence and if it is construed by the courts in accordance with the general understanding as to the intentions of Congress. . . .

"When carefully analyzed, it will be found that the new law makes surprisingly few fundamental changes in the act of 1887, as supplemented by the Elkins act, and that, in the main, it is confined to legislation intended to facilitate the carrying out of the intention of Congress in framing the original act. It lays down no new rule for determining the legality of a rate, and any rate that was lawful under the old law is now a lawful rate under the new law."[66]

Railroad executives, in any event, took steps to implement the law and after conferences and evaluation made the changes required in their operations.[67] The New York Central ended free storage facilities for New York flour merchants, the Chicago and Eastern Illinois Railroad began charging shippers for switching, and free loading privileges and car service in Philadelphia came to an end. (The American Shippers' Association protested the new filing rules under the law.) The *Rail-*

---

[65] *Railway World*, L (July 27, 1906), 620. A. B. Stickney, *ibid.*, urged firm enforcement of the new law.
[66] *Railroad Gazette*, XLI (August 3, 1906), 91.
[67] *Railway World*, L (August 24, 1906), 707-708.

way World summarized the feeling in late August, happily concluding that "notwithstanding the fears of many that railroads would be hurt by the operation of the law, no complaint has been heard from railroad men against its general provisions. On the contrary, the complaints are coming from the shippers, who were supposed to be the chief beneficiaries of the law."[68] The *Railway and Engineering Review* by September was most enthusiastic about the new law. Extending the notice of rate changes to 30 days kept the exporters from playing the railroads against each other by threatening use of alternative ports. And, so far as the commodity law was concerned, "The underlying principle of the law which prevents railroads from entering into competition with their customers is sound and will be perpetuated, with the result that the 'Industrial Roads' will go out of business. They ought never to have been allowed to begin it."[69]

The Commission, in the opinion of the *Railroad Gazette*, had begun its work under the new law in a moderate and tolerant manner: "The American railroad problem, as we see it, calls for the exercise of a considerable amount of Federal police power to prevent unjust and extortionate practices roughly grouped under the names rebate and discrimination. The new Interstate Commerce Law provides this police power, but along with it there are introduced serious elements of inflexibility and complexity not less than that which existed heretofore. . . . It seems clear that we need the police power without the paternalism, and if our railroads can be kept out of national politics long enough for the Hepburn experiment to clarify the situation, it seems probable that we shall get it."[70]

[68] *Ibid.*, August 29, 1906, p. 729.

[69] *Railway and Engineering Review*, XLVI (September 15, 1906), 714.

[70] *Railroad Gazette*, XLI (September 28, 1906), 253. Also see *ibid.*, October 5, 1906, pp. 278-279, for praise of the Commission.

The same theme of giving the new law a chance to operate before undertaking additional legislation was echoed by E. H. Harriman, who indicated he recommended such an approach as one who had favored the enactment of the Hepburn Act.[71] Virtually all railroad men or journals that expressed their views on the topic were optimistic that the new law would result primarily in good for the railroads, and the complaints of the shippers must have buttressed their belief. The *Railroad Gazette*, in mid-October, probably summarized the dominant view when it concluded, "On the whole we think the outlook for the future is bright, and we hope that the Commission and carriers combined will be able to put a stop to the abuses which have been largely responsible for [state] anti-railroad legislation and anti-railroad sentiment. . . ."[72] Virtually no one in railroad circles questioned the assumption that railroads and the Commission could cooperate on terms favorable to the railroads. Precedent was, after all, on the side of the railroads.

The Weaknesses of the Hepburn Act

The Hepburn Act of 1906 gave the Commission authority to determine a rate, upon a complaint and hearing, that was "just, fair, and reasonable" without giving the slightest criterion of what those terms precisely meant. Since the law included nothing on uniform classification it was impossible to prevent different railroad systems in the three major classification regions from charging substantially different rates for identical services. Many of the railroads wished to have this inconsistency ended, since it was a source of rebating, and a

[71] E. H. Harriman, speech in Kansas City, Mo., November 20, 1906, in *ibid.*, November 23, 1906, p. 140.
[72] *Ibid.*, October 12, 1906, p. 304.

number of conservative Senators, including Aldrich, Elkins, Crane, and Foraker, wanted a standard for rates
included in the bill. In effect, they desired an even stronger bill in reference to rates.[73] In addition, by not creating
Commission control over long-short haul discriminations,
the 1906 Act failed to attack the major source of shipper
grievances. Cost as a criterion of rates was too difficult
a standard, given the thousands of rates and the many
variables to calculate. La Follette's criteria for rates determined by a valuation of railroad property and a fair
rate of return was possibly relevant to over-all rates, but
it was too difficult to apply to specific rate controversies.
In practice, the Commission referred to other rates under
similar conditions to decide what to do about a complaint,
and used a cost-of-service and value-of-product standard
where it was also known or applicable.[74] There were
no means, under the 1906 Act, of rationally implementing the rate provision, and there were too many variables, involving tens of thousands of rates established by
over one thousand railroads, to hope to devise a practical
formula to overcome this paradox. More important, the
initiation of rate complaints was still left to the shippers
and other railroads, and, despite La Follette's urgings in
1906, Congress did not create any formal means to allow the Commission to initiate rate complaints on behalf
of the non-shipping "public" that ultimately paid all
the bills. Such a mechanism was ignored not because of
its probable impracticality, but because the world of the
I.C.C. was limited to shippers and railroads. "We don't
see anybody but the railroads and the shippers," Prouty

[73] U.S. Senate, *Railroad Rate Legislation: Views of the Minority*,
Senate Report 1242, Part 2, 59th Cong., 1st Sess., June 28, 1906
(Washington, 1906), p. 5.
[74] For a discussion of this problem, see M. B. Hammond, *Railway
Rate Theories of the Interstate Commerce Commission* (Cambridge,
1911), pp. 185-192; I. L. Sharfman, *The Interstate Commerce Commission* (New York, 1931-1937), III-B, 8-11.

once declared. "We don't see any other lawyers but railroad and shipping lawyers."[75]

The administrative structure of the Commission was improved by the 1906 law, and it has often been cited that the number of formal complaints disposed of by the Commission during the two and one-half years after the passage of the Hepburn Act was about one-quarter greater than the amount processed during the previous eighteen years. About 9,000 complaints arrived at the Commission during its first eighteen years, but due to the administrative policies initiated by Cooley, without authorization in law, all but 878 were disposed of informally. A mere change of administrative procedure would have meant a radical increase in formal complaints long before 1906, and would not have required new legislation.[76]

These weaknesses and strengths in the law were certainly known to contemporaries, for the railroads and Senatorial conservatives would have chosen to fight the bill on a more fundamental issue than judicial review had they opposed it en toto. Lincoln Steffens complained that Roosevelt allowed Cassatt to amend the bill, and that the President ultimately took his stand with Aldrich.[77] La Follette fought bitterly to have the law altered, and although we may question the efficacy of his proposal of using physical valuation of the railroads as the basis of rates, his insights into Roosevelt's approach to the legislation deserve careful attention. Roosevelt, concluded La Follette, "acted upon the maxim that half a loaf is better than no bread." To La Follette, "A halfway measure never fairly tests the principle and may utterly discredit it. It is certain to weaken, disappoint,

[75] Quoted in Marver H. Bernstein, *Regulating Business by Independent Commission* (Princeton, 1955), p. 158.

[76] Ripley, *Railroads: Rates and Regulation*, pp. 522-523; Sharfman, *Interstate Commerce Commission*, I, 41.

[77] Lincoln Steffens, *Autobiography* (New York, 1931), pp. 514-516.

and dissipate public interest."[78] Roosevelt could have obtained much more than the weak Hepburn Act, La Follette wrote. But holding himself up as an apostle of moderation, Roosevelt criticized standpatters and directed "an equally drastic attack upon those who were seeking to reform abuses. These were indiscriminately classed as demagogues and dangerous persons. In this way he sought to win approval, both from the radicals and the conservatives. This cannonading, first in one direction and then in another, filled the air with noise and smoke, which confused and obscured the line of action, but when the battle cloud drifted by and quiet was restored, it was always a matter of surprise that so little had really been accomplished."[79]

[78] Robert M. La Follette, *La Follette's Autobiography* (Madison, Wis., 1913), p. 388.
[79] *Ibid.*, p. 479.

CHAPTER VIII

THEODORE ROOSEVELT
AND REGULATION, 1906-1908

ROOSEVELT managed to attain a major railroad bill for his kudos, and the remaining two years of his presidency clearly illustrate his genuine and consistent desire to avoid damaging the interests of American railroads. His conflict with Harriman, which plays a major role in political histories of the period, had very little to do with the other railroads, and Roosevelt reiterated this again and again. "The aim of the National Government is quite as much to favor and protect honest corporations, honest business men of wealth, as to bring to justice those individuals and corporations representing dishonest methods."[1] From the passage of the Hepburn Act to the end of his presidency, Roosevelt moved to extend federal support to the railroads. He was considered by many railroad men as their best friend. His sixth message to Congress in December 1906 included a passing reference to a maximum hour law as being desirable for railroad workers and everyone else, but the request was couched in sufficiently vague terms to avoid exciting any specific interests. In his seventh message to Congress, Roosevelt requested action on a law to control overcapitalization, but he made it clear that he would not deprive railroads of investment funds and that all unjust efforts to reduce rates would be strongly resisted by the federal government. The following month, January 1908, Roosevelt

---

[1] See Roosevelt's seventh annual message in [Roosevelt], *Messages and Papers of the Presidents, September 14, 1901, to March 4, 1909* (New York, n. d.), p. 7076.

called on Congress to permit traffic and rate associations to control the rates and regulations of interstate lines, subject to Commission supervision.[2]

Nothing came of these public requests, and Roosevelt made no serious attempt to implement any of them. His major railroad activity took place away from the public view, and on an informal basis. If the President did not have legislative power, at least he had administrative machinery at his command that could have as strong an influence on the railroads as any written laws. The result was a series of informal, administrative decisions, at least some of them violations of the law, that were to gain for Roosevelt the support and confidence of many of the major American railroad interests.

Roosevelt's private solicitude for the railroads was shown by a number of incidents, perhaps the most important of which was the New Haven Railroad case. Under the presidency of Charles S. Mellen, though actually controlled by J. P. Morgan, the New Haven embarked on a program of attempting to consolidate the entire New England railroad system under its auspices.[3] To achieve its goal it watered its own stock to obtain capital for mergers, advanced large sums of money to important politicians, as well as to the Republican National Committee, and gradually developed a reputation for dishonesty which was scathingly denounced and extensively documented at the time by Louis Brandeis.[4] In March 1907, however, the New Haven was ready to acquire

2 *Ibid.*, pp. 7035, 7079-7080, 7130-7131.

3 That Mellen was Morgan's tool is brought out in *Official Stenographer's Report of the Testimony of Charles S. Mellen and Edward D. Robbins Before the Hon. Charles A. Prouty at Boston, Mass., May 2, 1913* (Boston, 1913), p. 26 and *passim.*

4 See Interstate Commerce Commission, *New York, New Haven & Hartford Railroad Co., Evidence . . . Relative to . . . Financial Transactions. . . .* [also printed as Senate Doc. No. 543, 63:2] (Washington, 1914), I, 907, 922-923; II, 2098ff., for the complete record. Louis Brandeis' discussion of the entire matter is in *Other People's Money—And How the Bankers Use It*, 2nd edn. (New York, 1932), chaps. IX, X.

the most important link in its plan, the Boston & Maine Railroad, and bought a substantial quantity of B. & M. shares from the New York Central. But a merger of this magnitude could hardly be effected without the approval of the federal government, since an anti-trust suit could be unleashed against the New Haven as easily as it had been against the Northern Securities Company. On March 11, 1907, J. P. Morgan called Roosevelt and asked for an appointment for himself and a number of railroad men.

The ostensible and public reason for the visit was the deteriorating railroad situation. Roosevelt was publicly attacking Harriman as a malefactor of wealth—because of a dispute over political donations, however—and rumor had it that the Interstate Commerce Commission was therefore contemplating a general attack on railroads. The rumor, of course, was without foundation, for even Garfield, certainly no foe of the railroads, was complaining about the same time that so far as the I.C.C. was concerned, "I think them as a body timid."[5] Rumor also had it that Roosevelt was instigating state attacks on the railroads, which, as we shall see, hardly any serious observer could believe. More important, the decline in stock prices at that time caught many railroads and interests short. Morgan and his group were going to the White House, it was reported, to find out what the federal government intended doing.[6]

Roosevelt received the overture from Morgan and railroad men with mixed feelings. He wanted them to announce their willingness to cooperate with the new law—Roosevelt insisted on seeing opposition where there generally was none—and finally concluded "They

[5] James R. Garfield Diary, January 25, 1907, vol. 25, Garfield Papers, box 107.

[6] *Commercial and Financial Chronicle*, LXXXIV (March 16, 1907), 592, summarizes these rumors and follows this version.

are now showing wisdom" on this count.[7] Morgan and four railroad executives, including Mellen, saw Roosevelt on March 12, "as to what steps might be taken to allay the public anxiety as to the relations between the railroads and government."[8] At least one contemporary press account suggests that they discussed the relation of the Sherman Act to the railroads.[9] A number of years later Mellen admitted that more tangible matters were considered, namely the proposed merger between the New Haven and the Boston & Maine that Morgan was now in a position to effect. Roosevelt, at the meeting itself, admitted he was not a lawyer and could not assure Mellen of the legality of the merger, but as Mellen reported it, "the reasons I gave him why it seemed to me desirable to buy the Boston & Maine shares, he said, appealed to him, and if there were no legal questions involved, and if he were in my place, he would be disposed to do what he plainly saw I was disposed to do—that is, acquire the shares."[10] Roosevelt sent Mellen to Commissioner Lane, and Mellen then returned to see Roosevelt, who repeated his earlier position that immunity would be granted the New Haven unless there was something illegal about the merger. By June 1907, the New Haven had gained full control of the Boston & Maine.[11]

Mellen had warned Roosevelt that either the New Haven had to acquire the Boston & Maine or that Harriman, the Canadian Pacific, or the Grand Trunk Railroads might. This threat was all that was necessary to

[7] Theodore Roosevelt to John A. Sleicher, March 12, 1907, *Letters*, V, 617-618.

[8] Morgan in the *Washington Star*, March 12, 1907.

[9] *Commercial and Financial Chronicle*, LXXXIV (1907), 592.

[10] I.C.C., *New Haven . . . Financial Transactions . . .* , I, 765-766.

[11] *Ibid.*, I, 766; *U.S. v. The New York, New Haven & Hartford RR Co., Original Petition [July, 1914] in the District Court of the United States, Southern District of New York* (Washington, 1914), pp. 47-49.

play on Roosevelt's hatred of Harriman, now at fever pitch because of Harriman's public revelation that Roosevelt had helped the Republicans obtain large donations from him during the 1904 campaign.[12] Mellen felt justified in writing to H. M. Whitney in May that "The Washington situation I have, I think, completely cared for. One never knows for a certainty regarding matters there, but the ground has been carefully plowed and every chance for trouble considered and I think successfully eliminated."[13] Roosevelt, perhaps to protect himself, consulted government attorneys concerning his actions and the legality of the New Haven's moves, and they confirmed his decision.[14]

The New Haven affair was one in which Roosevelt showed his personal weaknesses for his friends to the extent of ignoring the factual and well-documented attacks of Brandeis and his associates. Loyalty to friends and family, whose character and motives he never questioned, was typical of Roosevelt throughout his career. Indeed, it would almost seem as if Roosevelt had an essentially personalist approach to politics, ignoring ideology and interest in behalf of reducing issues to one of personal morality and "character." The only limitation on this interpretation is that Roosevelt acted consistently in behalf of a position which was conservative in effect if not in rhetoric. And the consequences of his actions were therefore no different from those of less well-mannered or blunter politicians, such as Foraker and Aldrich.

The New Haven affair was intimately tied to the interests of Roosevelt's friends and family. Morgan's allies in the grand merger venture were Lee, Higginson and Co., and Kidder, Peabody and Co. During August 1907, and the rising financial crisis, Lodge wrote Roosevelt that

[12] George Kennan, *E. H. Harriman* (Boston, 1922), ii, 192-208.
[13] I.C.C., *New Haven . . . Financial Transactions . . .*, i, 766-767.
[14] Theodore Roosevelt to Charles J. Bonaparte, June 20, 1907, *Letters*, v, 693.

his assignment of two federal agents to investigate the New Haven—both of whom advised against prosecution —as well as some of his recent speeches, were only disturbing the troubled financial waters. Roosevelt regretted the investigation, absolution or not, and assured Lodge there would be no suits. So far as his speeches were concerned, "I have also stated that we are acting in the defense of property."[15]

In October 1907, Mellen wrote Roosevelt and arranged for a meeting of himself, the President, and Herbert Knox Smith of the Bureau of Corporations. Mellen wanted the President's approval to sell the New Haven's steamship interests to Charles W. Morse, giving him a monopoly in the region. Roosevelt strongly opposed the step and, in Mellen's words, told him, "if you do not sell your lines to Mr. Morse I will promise you, so far as I am concerned, that you shall have no trouble while the law remains as it is; you shall experience no trouble from me in your ownership of what you now have."[16] Herbert Knox Smith, Prouty, and Knapp participated in the conference, and when a misunderstanding with Roosevelt developed, several weeks later, about the nature of the agreement, Smith was able to confirm Mellen's version.[17]

The continued attacks of Brandeis, and the facts revealed by a Massachusetts state investigation of the road, made it apparent that the New Haven was relying on dubious financing in its extension of control over the region's railroads. Roosevelt, who condemned excessive overcapitalization, was disturbed by the road's spiralling capitalization, which more than quadrupled over the decade from 1903 on. In January 1908, he wrote his

[15] Theodore Roosevelt to Henry Cabot Lodge, August 14, 1907, *Letters*, v, 750.
[16] I.C.C., *New Haven . . . Financial Transactions . . .* , I, 875.
[17] *Ibid.*, pp. 875-878.

former brother-in-law, George Cabot Lee, Jr., a partner in Lee, Higginson, that he was considering prosecuting the New Haven, "where I went, if anything, beyond the verge of propriety in condoning offenses."[18] Even the House of Morgan was fully aware of the New Haven's internal chaos, and while it issued defenses and public denials of mismanagement, it also moved to protect itself. "Mr. Mellen is getting the New Haven road into considerable of a muddle by his financial methods, and this I think, is becoming more or less the general opinion," George W. Perkins wrote Morgan in May 1908. "We have been quietly selling our New Haven debentures, as opportunity permitted."[19] On May 22, 1908, Roosevelt filed suit against the New Haven under the Sherman Act. But the President was not enthusiastic about his action, and he immediately vacillated. Lodge wrote him that Brandeis, the key enemy of the New Haven, was really the tool of Harriman and Kuhn, Loeb. Roosevelt responded to Lodge with more sophistication than he had to Mellen, but he was unwilling to damage the interests of Morgan, with whom he had already established several firm *détentes* concerning the promised good behavior of International Harvester and United States Steel.[20] Roosevelt failed to prosecute the New Haven case, and Taft dropped it altogether. It was not until Woodrow Wilson's administration, and the financial collapse of the New Haven, that the federal government again intervened in its affairs.

Roosevelt moved in several other areas to improve his

[18] Theodore Roosevelt to George Cabot Lee, Jr., January 13, 1908, *Letters*, VI, 907. *Interstate Commerce Commission Reports*, XXXI, July 11, 1914 (Washington, 1914), pp. 33ff., gives data on capitalization and where it went. The records of the Massachusetts trial are in the Boston & Maine RR Records, Baker Library, Harvard Business School, boxes 2-4.

[19] George W. Perkins to J. P. Morgan, May 15, 1908, George W. Perkins Papers, box 19.

[20] Theodore Roosevelt to Henry Cabot Lodge, May 28, 1908, *Letters*, VI, 1040.

position with the railroads, and especially to maintain friendly relations with the Morgan interests. Traffic agreements, clearly a violation of the law, were being quietly re-established by various railroads. Roosevelt was aware of the fact, and his response is interesting, for it was in reality an application of the "rule of reason" to violations of the law. In May 1907, he suggested a policy to Attorney General Charles J. Bonaparte that certainly guided his actions in the New Haven case and undoubtedly kept him from investigating other breaches of the law: "There are so many injurious violations of the law requiring the entire time and force of the Department of Justice that it is not deemed advisable to abandon such cases in order to devote the time of courts and officers to associations which, altho perhaps technically violations of law, are not in fact unreasonable or injurious."[21] In light of the fact that the Department of Justice filed only five cases in 1905 under the Sherman Act, fourteen in 1906, eleven in 1907, and eight in 1908, and could hardly have been considered overworked (Harding filed twenty-six in 1921 alone, and on a smaller budget), we must regard the President's action as a tacit acceptance of "reasonable" violations of law.

In the same year, the Interstate Commerce Commission began giving its famous "conference rulings" on allegedly obscure or ambiguous aspects of the new law, for which it had no statutory authorization, notifying shippers but primarily railroads whether certain general actions for which there were no precedents in earlier rulings would be deemed legal by the Commission. By early 1911, the Commission issued over 300 such rulings. This policy was an enormous boon to the railroads, and filled businessmen in other industries with admira-

[21] Theodore Roosevelt to Charles J. Bonaparte, May 26, 1907, *Letters*, v, 674.

tion for the legal security and certainty given the rail-roads—and was to be continuously referred to in the agitation for a national Trade Commission.[22] That such rulings often effectively deprived shippers of their recourse to legal action was quite another matter.

Roosevelt's major aid to a specific railroad interest, however, was his circumvention and effective destruction of the commodity clause of section 1 of the Hepburn Act forbidding railroads to transport goods in which they had a direct or indirect interest. With the exception of the anthracite carriers of eastern Pennsylvania, the great majority of railroad interests favored the clause. Elkins, who sold his railroad interests in 1902 and viewed the problem as a coal producer, had a similar clause in his substitute for the Hepburn Bill, which did not have such a provision until Tillman and Elkins put it in and had it included in the final compromise bill. The House of Morgan, the largest single interest in anthracite rail-roads in 1907, regarded the clause with considerable hostility. Technically, they had until May 1, 1908, to dispose of their properties.

Most major railroads owning coal companies did so indirectly or via stock, and they resorted to considerable manipulation of legal control in order to avoid their sale under the commodity clause. A number of companies fully expected the clause to be declared unconstitutional, and took no steps to dispose of their holdings. In January 1908, the Department of Justice decided it would not enforce the law against the anthracite railroads—accounting for over 90 per cent of the output of the industry—if they promised to obey a future Supreme Court decision on the matter. Theoretically the law should have been applied until suspended by a court, and

[22] Interstate Commerce Commission, *Twenty-First Annual Report, December 27, 1907* (Washington, 1907), pp. 5-6; I.C.C., *Conference Rulings of the Commission, April 1, 1911* (Washington, 1911).

there should not have been any question about railroad conformity to a final court ruling. The arrangement was illegal, but it certainly pleased the Morgan interests.[23] Roosevelt, so far as these interests were concerned, talked softly and left his big stick at home. He never tried to enforce the commodity clause during his presidency, though in May 1909 the Supreme Court validated it, excluding, however, indirect control of coal companies via stock companies. The result was a spate of new stock companies in anthracite, and the commodity clause was effectively circumvented in this period.[24]

The Railroads Face the States

The railroads realized long before 1900 that the federal regulation of railroads offered them protection, actual or potential, from harassment by the states. To undermine the new Interstate Commerce Act, the *Railway Review* suggested in 1887, would only lead to "more and worse 'granger' legislation."[25] Despite modest success in controlling some state legislatures, railroads found local governments were more responsive to the people and more likely to be radical. "Oh Lord pity us in Neb and preserve us from the results of a populist legislature and State government," one harried railroad man wrote the I.C.C. in 1897.[26] Paul Morton of the Santa Fe was disturbed in 1899 by the tendency of states such as Iowa and Texas to set rates that discriminated against out-of-state merchants and manufacturers: "I am opposed to any construction of the old

[23] See George W. Perkins to J. P. Morgan, April 21, 1908, George W. Perkins Papers, box 19, for example.

[24] Eliot Jones, *The Anthracite Coal Combination in the United States* (Cambridge, 1914), pp. 73ff., 187-203, is the best treatment of the problem.

[25] *Railway Review*, XXVII (June 4, 1887), 328.

[26] J. R. Buchanan to James D. Youmans, February 27, 1897, I.C.C. Records, Virginia, file 37153.

States Rights doctrine that is intended to obstruct inter-state commerce or curtail its freedom. . . . We do not want a system of domesticated protection adopted by any of our States, calculated to destroy commerce between States. . . . For fear that this may grow, I would like to see all transportation, that which passes between two points in the same State, as well as interstate traffic, declared subject to federal supervision and amenable to the national commission."[27] After 1900, the problem of state regulation became substantially more burdensome to the railroads. State taxes on railroads increased from $35 million in 1893 to $74 million in 1907, and to $134 million in 1915. The average state taxes per mile of railroad, a better criterion, increased 71 per cent from 1900 to 1910.[28]

Federal Commissioners, traditionally, had been sympathetic to the railroads. Even Prouty, whose reputation was that of a militant, was by 1906 an advocate of legalized railroad pools.[29] In the period immediately following the passage of the Hepburn Act, however, state regulation became especially cumbersome, and most of the major litigation seeking to define the legitimate boundary between state and federal regulation dates from this period. The *Minnesota Rate Case*, decided by the Supreme Court in 1913, was initiated when the Minnesota Railroad Commission manipulated the heretofore identical rates from Duluth, Minnesota, and Superior, Wisconsin, adjacent cities, so that the cost of shipments between Duluth and points within Minnesota was lower. In the *Shreveport Case* the argument centered

[27] Martin A. Knapp and Paul Morton, *Speeches Before the National Association of Merchants and Travelers, August 7, 1899* (n. p., 1899), p. 14.

[28] Thor Hultgren, *American Transportation in Prosperity and Depression* (New York, 1948), p. 299; Bureau of Railway Economics, *The Conflict Between Federal and State Regulation of the Railroads* (Washington, 1911), Bulletin No. 15, p. 13.

[29] *Railway World*, L (November 30, 1906), 1019.

on the ability of the Texas Railroad Commission to fix intrastate rates well below the competitive interstate standards. In 1902-1907, twenty-two maximum fare laws and nine maximum rate laws were passed by the states.[30] In a few states, railroad regulation became a leading, if not the most important, issue in politics, Alabama being the most notable.[31] The railroads had two defenses against the states: the courts, which consistently defended the supremacy of the federal regulatory power over the states, but took over six years to complete their work; and the Interstate Commerce Commission and federal government—on the scene, rapid, and essentially cooperative.

Paul Morton wrote Roosevelt at the beginning of 1907 about the threat of state railroad legislation. Roosevelt's answer to the problem was simple, and acceptable to the railroads: "I quite agree with you that there is a danger in ill-directed agitation, and especially in agitation in the states; but the only way to meet it is by . . . conferring upon the national Government full power to act."[32] The railroads, Roosevelt often insisted, were being saved by the federal government from dangerous attacks. Roosevelt, however, was quite wrong in suggesting that they failed to appreciate the value of federal regulation.[33] On March 12, 1907, B. F. Yoakum, chairman of the board of the Rock Island, visited Roosevelt at the White House on the same day that Morgan and his delegation saw the President. (The

[30] William Z. Ripley, *Railroads: Rates and Regulation* (New York, 1912), p. 630.

[31] James F. Doster, "The Conflict Over Railroad Regulation in Alabama," *Business History Review*, XXVIII (December, 1954), 329-342, gives the case history.

[32] Theodore Roosevelt to Paul Morton, January 24, 1907, *Letters*, v, 563.

[33] Theodore Roosevelt to Henry Lee Higginson, February 11, 1907, March 28, 1907, *Letters*, v, 584, 633-634; Theodore Roosevelt to Charles Evans Hughes, October 20, 1908, *Letters*, vi, 1302, reiterates this theme.

press claimed that Morgan also talked to Roosevelt about state railroad laws, but he probably spent much more time on the New Haven.)[34] Yoakum was concerned solely about the state attacks on railroads, and upon leaving the White House declared the "railroad men are willing that the supervision of the railroads be centralized in the national government." This "would restore confidence and give the people to understand that the railroads wish to observe the laws, and it would stop the hostile legislation in various states."[35] At about the same time, editorials in such major journals as *Harper's Weekly* and the *Outlook* sympathized with the plight of the railroads in the hands of the states.[36] An I.C.C. ruling against the Minnesota Railroad Commission in the Duluth case made it appear as if only the national government could be trusted.

As state action became sharper, railroad opinion favorable to the I.C.C. increased in tempo. "I would not if I could materially change the laws thus far enacted by Congress," William C. Brown of the New York Central told the Buffalo Chamber of Commerce in April 1907.[37] Robert Mather, vice-president of the Rock Island, confessed to the National Civic Federation in October 1907 that he had once opposed rate regulation before the Senate Committee on Interstate Commerce, which had recommended legislation. "I come here to-day to admit that the action taken in pursuance of that recommendation was wise, and to advocate an enlargement of the rate-making power of the Federal commission." The reason: since 1906 the states have been setting rates and im-

[34] *Commercial and Financial Chronicle*, LXXXIV (1907), 592.

[35] *Washington Star*, March 12, 1907, in *Letters*, V, 617-618n.

[36] "The Railroads and the States," *Harper's Weekly*, LI (August 24, 1907), 1224-1225; *Outlook*, LXXXV (March 23, 1907), 627-629; J. D. Evan, "Federal vs. State Regulations," *Van Norden Magazine*, II (August, 1907), 53-56.

[37] William C. Brown, *Address Before the Buffalo Chamber of Commerce, April 18, 1907* (n. p., 1907), p. 17.

posing regulations "in a degree unparalleled in any previous period."[38] ". . . the operations of our railroads should be regulated properly by wholesome and fair laws; and quite as necessary that they should not be regulated improperly," James J. Hill concluded in the mildest verdict of all.[39]

Roosevelt, until the end of his presidency, championed the supremacy of federal over state regulation, and gave special emphasis to the topic in his last message to Congress, in December 1908. In a facile but not-too-consistent analysis, the President equated the doctrine of states' rights with opposition to federal regulation, and suggested the advocacy of state regulation was usually reactionary in motive.[40] And, when it was not reactionary, it was naïve. Only the federal government could provide unified, effective control. By 1908, there were very few railroad leaders ready to disagree with the President. Indeed, by the end of Roosevelt's presidency, the I.C.C. had broken into a routinized pattern of adjudicating the problems of the railroad industry without concern for the larger interest of a public not immediately involved in the day-to-day issues preoccupying the railroads, Commission, and wealthier shippers. To borrow the apt description of the life-cycle of all regulatory commissions made by Marver H. Bernstein, the Commission had fallen into its period of "maturity": "Its functions are less those of a policeman and more like that of a man-

[38] National Civic Federation, *Proceedings of the National Conference on Trusts and Combinations, Chicago, October 22-25, 1907* (Chicago, 1908), p. 272.

[39] James J. Hill, *Address Before the Kansas City, Mo., Commercial Club, November 19, 1907* (n. p., n. d.), pp. 13-14. Also see Theodore P. Shonts, *Address Before the Appanoose Chautauqua, Centerville, Iowa, August 27, 1908* (n. p., 1908), pp. 6-11; Joseph Nimmo, Jr., *State and National Regulation of Railroads: Memorandum of December 10, 1908* (Washington, 1908), pp. 2-3, for attacks on state legislation at this time.

[40] Roosevelt, *Messages and Papers*, pp. 7202-7204; Theodore Roosevelt to Judson C. Clements, October 3, 1907, *Letters*, v, 815.

ager of an industry. The approach and point of view of the regulatory process begin to partake of those of business management. The commission becomes accepted as an essential part of the industrial system. . . . The commission becomes more concerned with the general health of the industry and tries to prevent changes which adversely affect it. Cut off from the mainstream of political life, the commission's standards of regulation are determined in the light of the industry affected."[41]

The Railroads and Uniform Classification

For all of its virtues, the Hepburn Act still failed to close all of the possibilities for rebating and arbitrary rate changes available to railroads interested in continuing such practices. The problem resulted from the failure of Congress to establish control over the freight classification system; no more enthusiastic advocates of their doing so could be found than among the railroads themselves. It was a relatively simple task for a railroad to grant a rebate by placing a commodity in a cheaper classification, or to raise rates by putting it in a higher category. Although a shipper might complain to the Commission in the latter case, most railroads were still unhappy with the potential power to destabilize rates and increase competition left in the hands of aggressive railroads. The growing underclassification of freight again became a common problem after 1906, and convictions by the Commission for rebating were still common in 1908.[42] Although some railroad men wanted the legalization of rate agreements as a solution—and Roosevelt sympathized with them—many also wanted strict government control of freight classifications.[43] In calling

[41] Marver H. Bernstein, *Regulating Business by Independent Commission* (Princeton, 1955), p. 87.
[42] Ripley, *Railroads: Rates and Regulation*, pp. 190, 209.
[43] See William C. Brown to Theodore Roosevelt, August 22, 1908,

for federal control of uniform classification, the railroads tried to bring the political power of the government to bear on their internal economic problems, and it is worth surveying the agitation for the reform as another example of the long and intimate dependence of the railroads on the federal government.

As early as 1882, the railroads attempted to create a single uniform freight classification on a voluntary basis and failed. When the Act of 1887 passed there were 138 classification systems in the United States. In 1888, the House passed a resolution authorizing Commission determination of classifications, but the Senate failed to concur because the Commission urged that voluntary efforts be attempted first. A voluntary agreement was worked out at railroad meetings during 1888 and 1889 that managed to reduce the classification areas to three major regions, with about a dozen minor ones remaining in various states.[44] The Western classification area covered all territory west of the Mississippi River, the Southern portion the traffic south of the Ohio and Potomac Rivers, and the "Official" area the remainder. While the new arrangement was certainly an improvement, it rapidly grew less satisfactory as the numbers of items to be classified increased (in the Official Classification, for example, from 2,500 in 1887 to about 6,000 in 1909), adding more leeway for misclassification.[45] The Interstate Commerce Commission, having learned its lesson during the early 1890's, repeatedly asked Congress to give the railroads one year to agree

in Charles J. Bonaparte Papers, Library of Congress, box 127, as an example of a railroad request for legalized rate associations.

44 U.S. Industrial Commission, *Report . . . of the Industrial Commission on Transportation* (Washington, 1901), IX, 860; Samuel O. Dunn, "Uniform Classification," *Railway Age Gazette*, XLVII (September 3, 1909), 413-416; Charles L. Langstroth and Wilson Stilz, *Railway Co-operation* (Philadelphia, 1899), p. 169.

45 Dunn, *Railway Age Gazette*, XLVII (September 17, 1909), 497.

on a classification voluntarily or otherwise to hand the power to accomplish the task over to the Commission, but shippers opposed the move.[46] In 1893, the railroads again tried to agree voluntarily on a system, but local shippers and state legislatures resisted all changes that threatened to raise rates. In 1896, a Senate resolution, which was eventually made into a related bill (S. 3205) by Senator Cullom, called for a final voluntary effort by the railroads, with Commission power to accomplish the task if necessary. Railroad men sympathized with the motion, as did a few shippers' associations, but Congress never acted upon it. "I do not believe that it is possible to reach uniformity except by an act of Congress," a railroad man pessimistic of its chances of passage wrote in 1895.[47] Congressional action "is our only hope of a uniform classification," a railroad attorney told Cullom in 1896, "as the railroads have themselves been trying to bring it about for a number of years without success. . . . The government is our only hope."[48] The Commission, with prompting from railroad men, continued requesting Congress for the power to fix a single classification system. The existing situation, they were told by a railroad traffic manager, is "a great promoter of misunderstandings, dissatisfaction and complaints, and in my belief it gives rise to many discriminations."[49] Railroad sentiment for a uniform system continued during the following years, but no effective action was taken after 1889.[50]

[46] I.C.C., *Seventh Annual Report, December 1, 1893* (Washington, 1893), pp. 50-55.
[47] A. C. Bird in *Proceedings of the Committee on Uniform Classification, Annual Convention of Railroad Commissioners,* New York, *October 23, 1895* (dittoed), p. 2, in Sen 54A-J 42.
[48] Franklin MacVeagh to Shelby M. Cullom, April 13, 1896, in Sen 54A-J 42.
[49] A. C. Bird to William R. Morrison, March 11, 1897, in I.C.C. Records, Virginia, file 37480; I.C.C., *Eleventh Annual Report,* p. 65.
[50] Industrial Commission, *Report . . . on Transportation,* IV, 17.

In 1906, during the debates on the Hepburn Bill, the Commission unsuccessfully let it be known that it would like a stipulation included in the law giving the railroads two years to agree voluntarily on a classification system or else hand the power over to the Commission.[51] In April 1907, the railroads, seeing no chance for federal action, again convened to try to work out the problem voluntarily. Local shipping interests opposed any changes, however, and the effort was viewed skeptically by railroad circles. "It is said that the Interstate Commerce Commission has threatened to take up the job unless the railroads soon come to an agreement," the *Railroad Gazette* wrote about the new move. "Why not let the Commission do it? Only by arbitrary action can the desired unification be accomplished, and arbitrary action will seem much more appropriate coming from that body . . . than from railroad officers who have to keep the peace with disgruntled shippers."[52] The railroads continued trying to solve the problem voluntarily until 1917, but shipper pressures blocked all progress. In this respect, federal rate regulation was welcomed by the railroads at this time and opposed by shippers with vested interests in existing inequities.[53]

The Rate Incident of 1908

One other phase of Roosevelt's relation to the railroads after the passage of the Hepburn Act until the end of his

[51] Edward Moseley to the Speaker of the House, April 9, 1906, in HR 59A-F 18.4.

[52] *Railroad Gazette*, XLII (April 26, 1907), 570.

[53] Ripley, *Railroads: Rates and Regulation*, p. 339; *Railway Age Gazette*, LII (February 2, 1912), 211-212; *ibid.*, February 9, 1912, pp. 224-225; Dunn, *ibid.*, XLVII (1909), 413-415. By 1914, however, no one, the railroads and I.C.C. included, wanted an immediate law for a single uniform classification. The Southern classification had 6,900 categories, the Official classification 12,700, and everyone feared the possible dislocations inherent in any effort to bring them together. See U.S. Senate, Committee on Interstate Commerce, *Uniform Classification of Freight, Hearings*, 63d Cong., 2d Sess., [March-May, 1914] (Washington, 1914), pp. 17, 39-40, 57ff., 78ff.

presidency bears testimony to his fundamentally solicitous attitude toward them. Freight revenue in 1908 and 1909 fell off from its 1907 high, and in 1908 railroad dividends began sliding; they fell sharply in 1909. Railroad executives correctly claimed that, unlike earlier years, overcapitalization was no longer a cause of railroad financial difficulties, and that bankruptcy, reorganizations, and the growth of property values had squeezed most of the water out of railroad stocks. Indeed, railroads now needed the infusion of new capital if they were to grow with the economy.[54] Most railroad leaders looked askance at the proposals of La Follette, who submitted several bills on the topic in 1906 and 1907, to make a "fair valuation" of railroads and use the findings as the basis of rates and capitalization. While railroads realized that some method of assuring investors of the soundness of railroad bonds and stock would be required if they were ever to win back a larger share of the securities market from industrial companies, they strongly opposed La Follette's scheme as *the* exclusive basis of capitalization and rates. The Interstate Commerce Commission agreed with them, and unequivocally opposed the La Follette proposal in a letter to the Senate Committee on Interstate Commerce in March 1908, and in public statements made by Prouty and others. The Commission also supported Roosevelt's call for a modification of the applicability of the anti-trust law to railroad rate associations.[55] At this time, the railroads, the

[54] Thayer, *Address Before the Buffalo Chamber of Commerce, April 18, 1907*, p. 20; Hultgren, *American Transportation*, pp. 336-338; *Letter of James J. Hill to Hon. John A. Johnson, Governor of Minnesota, January 14, 1907* (n. p., 1907), pp. 7-8. Evidence supports the railroad contention that they were not overcapitalized by 1910. Indeed, by 1913, the railroads were undercapitalized, and this trend continued over the decade. See Interstate Commerce Commission, *Statistics of Railways in the United States, 1930* (Washington, 1932), p. 117.

[55] Franklin K. Lane, "Railroad Capitalization and Federal Regulation," *Review of Reviews*, June, 1908, pp. 4-5 [pagination from the

President, and the Commission were on the best of terms. Martin A. Knapp, whose conservatism and pro-railroad sentiments never seemed to waver, in mid-1908 improved the Commission's good reputation with the harried railroads by announcing that "whatever may be our national or state policy in other respects, whatever regulations may be prescribed or obligations imposed, there must be the opportunity to charge rates which will give sufficient earnings to make the business fairly profitable and to attract the needful capital for its ample extension."[56]

By June 1908, the railroads were anxious for the opportunity to which Knapp referred. Profits were beginning to slip; they had just finished supporting the passage of the Employers' Liability Act in Congress and hoped that the business community would pay for the increased costs in the form of higher rates.[57] Despite the growing consolidation of shipper groups opposed to any rate increases, which was only to be expected, railroad interests were prepared to handle the ordinary opposition. George Perkins, in charge of the matter for Morgan, wrote his superior on July 21 that "I have had talks with a number of newspaper people and most of them have taken up the matter in a very friendly and helpful manner."[58] But the remaining hostile press, which even Perkins could not win over to a "helpful" attitude, got wind of the proposed increase and frightened Roosevelt

reprint]; W. H. Williams, *Address Before the Traffic Club of New York, November 24, 1908* (New York, 1908), pp. 4-5, 49, 56; Ivy L. Lee, "Railroad Valuation," *Bankers' Magazine*, July, 1907, p. 4 and *passim* [pagination from the reprint].

[56] Martin A. Knapp, "The Public and the Railways," *Annals of the American Academy of Political and Social Science*, XXXII (July, 1908), 98.

[57] William C. Brown of the New York Central, *Speech Before the Michigan Manufacturers' Association, Detroit, June 22, 1908* (n. p., 1908), pp. 9-11, maintains this.

[58] George W. Perkins to J. P. Morgan, July 21, 1908, George W. Perkins Papers, box 19.

into asking Perkins to have the railroads discuss the increase with the I.C.C. before acting on the matter. At the same time, Roosevelt wrote Bonaparte that the railroads should wait until December—after the elections—to raise their rates. "I have not much sympathy with most of the shippers, however, as the men who are making the most talk in this matter are those wealthy concerns, many of them by no means of impeccable character in their own private business."[59]

Perkins saw Roosevelt several times in July about the rate increase, and was frankly told that the Democrats would capitalize on it if the initiative came from the railroads. Roosevelt suggested that the large shippers and labor would be a better source for the agitation, and Perkins, the grand manipulator, told the President "you will gradually see their cooperation appear."[60] Bonaparte nevertheless warned Roosevelt that any rate increase would be politically dangerous irrespective of the source of the request. Moreover, a group of railroads collectively decided at the end of June to raise rates in Texas to test the government's intentions. Bonaparte admitted that the roads had a strong justification for a rate increase, and that the shippers were motivated by selfish ends, but the conspiracy to raise rates was technically illegal. The charge of conspiracy, however, was not brought against the railroad presidents, nor were rates increased. When faced with the alternative between accommodating Roosevelt and the Republican Party or facing William Jennings Bryan, who just the previous year ominously discussed the desirability of government ownership of the railroads, the railroads and Perkins opted

[59] Theodore Roosevelt to Charles J. Bonaparte, July 25, 1908, Charles J. Bonaparte Papers, box 133.
[60] George W. Perkins to Theodore Roosevelt, August 3, 1908; George W. Perkins to J. P. Morgan, July 31, 1908, George W. Perkins Papers, box 19.

for Roosevelt.[61] In economics, as in politics, one does not attack one's friends. Roosevelt had withstood the test of seven years. Taft, it was expected, would continue in his footsteps.

[61] Charles J. Bonaparte to Theodore Roosevelt, August 2, August 14, August 15, September 1, 1908, Charles J. Bonaparte Papers, box 184. Also see E. H. Gary to George W. Perkins, August 19, 1908, George W. Perkins Papers, box 19; Gary also advised delay.

CHAPTER IX

FREIGHT RATES,
POLITICS, AND THE PRESIDENT
1909-1912

THE railroads supported William Howard Taft in his campaign for the presidency because they regarded him as a man sympathetic to the problems of the industry.[1] Although the Republican platform of 1908 promised greater powers to the I.C.C. and a control of exorbitant rates and other sources of shipper grievances, few took the slightly anti-railroad rhetoric seriously during a campaign year. Taft himself, in his acceptance speech for the nomination, indicated his endorsement of rate agreements subject to Commission approval, diffusion of the Commission's responsibilities, and his support for physical valuation of the roads as one criterion for rates. But in December 1908, he hinted that the powers of the Commission were to be reduced, and even the docile Commission complained in the press somewhat irately.[2] The sanctity of the platform was violated, not for the first or last time in American history, even before the President was inaugurated.

Most historical accounts date the movement for railroad legislation during the Taft presidency from the fall of 1909.[3] But agitation for substantial changes began

[1] Theodore P. Shonts, *The Square Deal in Business and the Candidacy of William Howard Taft* [reprinted from *Chicago Tribune*, August 28, 1908] (n. p., 1908), is an example.

[2] *Baltimore News*, December 29, 1908.

[3] Kenneth W. Hechler, *Insurgency: Personalities and Politics of the Taft Era* (New York, 1940), chap. VIII; George E. Mowry, *Theodore Roosevelt and the Progressive Movement* (Madison, Wis., 1946), pp. 94ff.

(177)

much earlier. A Senate bill (S. 423) submitted by Senator Charles W. Fulton in 1908 called for radical revi-
sions of the existing law by allowing any upward change
of rates or classifications to be blocked by a protesting
shipper *before* going into effect. The railroads and their
friends strongly opposed the measure, but an uncomfort-
able number of important shipping groups either supported the bill or demanded Commission review of rate
changes before they went into effect.[4]

The resurgence of important shipper sentiment for
railroad regulation at this time was aided by the emer-
gence of Judson C. Clements as an articulate "public"
spokesman in the Interstate Commerce Commission, and
he gave voice to many of the shippers' grievances. Clements pointed out that since the passage of the Hepburn
Act until July 1908, the railroads had filed only one bill
in court against a Commission order, but that in the subsequent six months they had filed sixteen. He feared the
railroads would utilize the courts much more frequently
and might even nullify the Hepburn Act by such actions.
In addition, Clements urged a revision of the law to give
the Commission greater power to postpone the implementation of new rates until an investigation of their reasonableness could be made, and he called for extended
Commission power over capitalization and better valuations of railroad property.[5] Clements was the first major
break in the hegemony of the Commission, the first important figure not to identify with the railroads, as did
Knapp, or to regard them with sympathy, as did Prouty.

[4] HR 60A-H 16.17 contains letters and petitions to this effect from
Lumberman's Exchange of Philadelphia, Cattle Raisers' Association
of Texas, the St. Louis Merchants' Exchange, the San Francisco
Chamber of Commerce, and about twenty-five others. Sen 60A-J 62
also contains letters of support for S. 423, and a smaller amount of
opposition from railroads, etc. HR 60A-H 16.2 contains several pro-
railroad resolutions from the Merchants Association and the New
York Board of Trade and Transportation.

[5] Judson C. Clements, *Address Before the Atlanta Freight Bureau,
January 12, 1909* (n. p., n. d.), *passim.*

In early 1909, the railroad spokesmen in the Senate opposed any far-reaching new legislation. When submitting his negative report on the Fulton Bill in February 1909, Elkins asked that the Hepburn Act be given a chance to work before Congress embarked on new experiments.[6] Taft, too, gave the railroads little to worry about. He sent a confidential outline of his inaugural address to George Perkins, who told J. P. Morgan that it was "in all respects conciliatory and harmonizing in its tone."[7] Still, shipper .pressures mounted despite declining rates and railroad income. The Hepburn Act had not produced the desired results for many shippers, and the railroads were also interested in obtaining additional protection from the rising tide of state legislation, as well as the legalization of rate associations. In mid-April, 1909, Attorney General George Wickersham, Secretary of Commerce Charles Nagel, Knapp, Prouty, Representative Townsend, and other government officials met to discuss the anti-trust problem with special reference to the railroads.[8] This marks the beginning of the sequence of events that gradually led to the enactment of the Mann-Elkins Act. Subsequent developments until September were carried on quietly, and away from the eye of the general press, but the railroad journals watched every move carefully—and calmly. President Taft's railroad policies, the *Railway and Engineering Review* concluded in June, were not radical and would not be opposed. Business—and railroad—nerves had been quieted by the President, and for this they were grateful.[9] By July, the word was out that Taft was still planning to divide the judicial and administrative functions of the Commission

[6] U.S. Senate, Committee on Interstate Commerce, Senate Report No. 933, 60th Cong., 2d Sess., February 9, 1909 (Washington, 1909), p. 22.

[7] George W. Perkins to J. P. Morgan, February 25, 1909, George W. Perkins Papers, box 20.

[8] *Baltimore Sun*, April 15, 1909.

[9] *Railway and Engineering Review*, XLIX (June 12, 1909), 530.

by creating a commerce court, and if he succeeded, the *Railway World* commented, "he will have gained the unanimous approval of railway interests."[10] In early August, rumor had it that Taft might transform the Commission into a purely judicial body, investigation being left to the Bureau of Corporations and prosecution to the Department of Justice. At the same time, it was known that a committee consisting of Nagel, Prouty, Ballinger, Wickersham, and Townsend had been appointed by the President to report to him in the early fall on railroad legislation.[11] On September 3, this committee, including Knapp, met in New York and outlined a plan for a five-man commerce court, and although they were to hold subsequent meetings in order to present a complete bill, the commerce court remained the heart of their scheme.[12]

On September 20, Taft spoke at Des Moines and outlined the scope of what was to become his new legislation. The commerce court was the central theme of his message, and he proposed that the new court alone be allowed to nullify Commission decisions, short of the Supreme Court. Any one of the five judges, the President suggested, should have the power to put a 60-day stay on a Commission order, but the Commission should be given extra powers to initiate complaints and to annul or modify railroad regulations that impose burdens on shippers. The Commission, Taft recommended, should have the power to consider classifications, as well as control new stock issues. And although he called for a ban on acquiring stock in competing lines, Taft's proposal that railroads be allowed to enter rate agreements subject to Commission approval clearly pleased the railroads.[13] His statement, by any criterion, was pro-rail-

---

[10] *Railway World*, LIII (July 30, 1909), 633.

[11] *Ibid.*, August 13, 1909, p. 670.

[12] Minutes of Conference in New York, September 3, 1909, in William Howard Taft Papers, Library of Congress, series 2, file 100a.

[13] William Howard Taft, *Presidential Addresses and Speeches* (New York, 1910), I, chap. 25.

road. Even the *Railway and Engineering Review*, the most cautious and conservative of the railroad journals, decided, "The program of President Taft for further interstate commerce and anti-trust legislation as laid down by him in his speech at Des Moines, is not sufficiently radical to arouse much apprehension."[14] Although they preferred waiting until the Hepburn Act had a chance to operate fully, and positively opposed the proposal of Wickersham that the Commission be allowed to initiate complaints, the journal thought there would be no substantial opposition to Taft's proposals.

Not a few of the railroad journals regretted that Taft had not explicitly mentioned his earlier plan, dating back to July 1908, for dividing the functions of the Commission among other branches of the executive, but they praised the idea of a commerce court in strong terms.[15] Taft's subsequent assurances certainly did not hurt his good standing with the roads. Speaking at Galveston on October 22, he unequivocally admitted that "the only honest policy is a square deal to the railroads so as to give them the rates they ought to have and not allow popular prejudice to deprive them of reasonable profit for the investment, including the risk that they made when they went into the business."[16] Innocent enough in its generality, save perhaps as it suggested protection from "popular prejudice," the statement was regarded by the *Railway World* as a happy omen of things to come.[17]

In mid-November, William C. Brown, president of the New York Central and a friend of regulation, saw Taft about the widely rumored contents of the Wick-

[14] *Railway and Engineering Review*, XLIX (October 2, 1909), 881.
[15] *Railway Age Gazette*, XLVII (September 24, 1909), 329-330; *Railway World*, LIII (October 22, 1909), 873-874; *Railway Age Gazette*, XLVII (October 22, 1909), 740-741.
[16] Taft, *Addresses and Speeches*, I, 377.
[17] *Railway World*, LIII (October 29, 1909), 893.

ersham Committee's recommendations to the President.[18] From mid-November to mid-December, the railroad and financial community was extremely apprehensive and basically critical. The idea of a commerce court had always been pleasing, the legalization of rate agreements was desirable, and Commission regulation of securities issues at least had the virtue of reassuring investors as to their safety; but not a few railroads, according to the *Railway and Engineering Review*, disliked the prohibition on buying out competitors, the shipper's right to route his goods, and, most of all, Commission initiative in changing rates.[19] Early in December, Brown returned to see Taft, along with Frank Vanderlip of the National City Bank, W. W. Finley of the Southern Railroad, and F. A. Delano of the Wabash.[20] The Interstate Commerce Commission, in the meantime, had formally asked for power to prevent rate advances pending investigation, although it also indicated that even if granted the power, the fact that 184,000 tariff publications had been filed with the Commission over the past year would necessarily mean that shipper complaints would remain the heart of the rate-fixing system.[21] Railroad presidents continued seeing or writing Wickersham and Taft throughout December. Grenville M. Dodge wrote the President, "I am in no way opposed to the proper regulation of the roads. You know I was always a friend of the rate bill and there are many things in the bill that is now proposed that I have no objection to"; but he wished to eliminate the clause allowing a shipper to route his own shipments, and modify the stock issuance requirements

[18] *Ibid.*, November 19, 1909, p. 962.

[19] *Railway and Engineering Review*, XLIX (November 27, 1909), 1057. This account probably reflects the journal's conservatism. Also see *Railway World*, LIII (December 10, 1909), 1028-1029.

[20] *Financial World*, December 4, 1909, p. 3.

[21] Interstate Commerce Commission, *Twenty-Third Annual Report, December 21, 1909* (Washington, 1910), pp. 6-11.

preventing stocks and bonds from being issued at less than par.[22] On December 30, after a conference with Ripley of the Santa Fe, Finley of the Southern, George V. Massey of the Pennsylvania, E. G. Buckland of the New Haven, and A. H. Harris of the New York Central, Wickersham indicated that the section granting shippers the right to choose their routes was being sharply modified. What other changes were made to meet the objections of the railroad presidents is not known, but Wickersham sent a confidential draft of the bill to Dodge and solicited his comments.[23]

Between the end of December 1909 and January 7, 1910, when Taft delivered his special message to Congress on revision of the Interstate Commerce Law, an important series of conferences took place among Taft, Wickersham, and the presidents of six key railroads. On January 3, a meeting was held in the White House, and several days later Brown of the New York Central announced that the new railroad bill would be perfectly acceptable to any railroad willing to do business in "a straightforward and orderly manner." Although the detailed understanding reached between the President and the railroads is not available, the application of the Sherman Act to railroad combinations and the legalization of rate agreements were certainly paramount issues. In return for a clause in the new bill permitting rate agreements, a commerce court, and reasonable regulation of securities, the railroad men promised not to oppose the bill or to testify against it during the hearings before Congress.[24] Taft's January 7 message undoubtedly reflected this understanding.

[22] Grenville M. Dodge to William Howard Taft, December 22, 1909, William Howard Taft Papers, series 1, box 248.

[23] George Wickersham to Grenville M. Dodge, December 30, 1909, William Howard Taft Papers, series 1, box 248.

[24] Otto Gresham to William Howard Taft, January 4, 1910, William Howard Taft Papers, series 1, box 248; also clippings in

The first point in Taft's message of January 7, and the plank closest to the former judge, was a request for a commerce court of five circuit court judges, any one of whom could suspend a Commission order for 60 days. The commerce court would serve as the judicial court of review, subject only to the Supreme Court, and would not only expedite appeals of Commission decisions, but eliminate many of the Commission's judicial functions. Taft's second proposal was for the legalization of railroad rate agreements, subject to Commission approval. His third major proposal, designed to please shippers, was to allow the Commission to take the initiative in examining the fairness of an existing rate or classification, rather than waiting for a shipper to file a complaint. He also recommended that the Commission be empowered to stay a proposed rate for 60 days after its effective date. To mitigate the seemingly unhappy consequences of such a law for the railroads, Taft also pointed out that they had the right of appeal to the commerce court, and the fact that the enormous number of tariffs filed every year would of necessity mean a very limited use of this suspension power. While he granted the right of a shipper to choose an alternate route for his goods, Taft attached sufficient contingencies to the proposal to virtually nullify it—thereby meeting the objections of the railroads. He proposed, furthermore, that railroads be forbidden to acquire the stock of competitive roads—a regulation at least partially covered by the *Northern Securities* decision—or to issue stocks or bonds at less than par value. Commission regulation of the total amount of stocks and bonds issued would apply only to reorganizations. The President's final important

---

this box. Also see *Railway Age Gazette*, XLIX (July 1, 1910), 4; Elihu Root speech of April 1, 1910 in *Congressional Record*, XLV, 61:2, pp. 4101-4102; Mowry, *Roosevelt and the Progressive Movement*, p. 96.

proposal, inevitable in light of the fact that injuries among railroad employees had nearly doubled since 1895, was Commission power to prescribe safety appliances on railroads.[25]

Taft's message, and the Mann-Elkins Bill itself, were efforts to please a variety of diverse elements. Ultimately, in my opinion, the bill was weighted heavily, before amendments, to favor the railroads. But Taft, with his rather slow-moving political personality, was never able to bring all the railroads into line, much less the shippers, and in the process of the crossfire between the contending political interests within his own party, his political reputation as a progressive was to be smashed. "The message looks like an attempt to acquire all at once, and in a bulk, all the radical recommendations of the Republican platform, properly toned down and modified to suit the taste of the most conservative," the normally friendly *Railway World* commented.[26] The rate proposal, it thought, was "innocuous," the interlocking ownership proposal hazy, the rate agreement clause essentially good. On the whole, it wanted no action on the proposal at that time. The *Railway Age Gazette*, although it too had some mixed feelings about Taft's message, thought his suggestions "much less radical and objectionable than many of the proposals for additional federal railway legislation which are pending in Congress."[27]

The actual bill embodying the contents of Taft's speech was written by Wickersham, and submitted in the House by Townsend as H.R. 17536 and in the Senate by Elkins as S. 6737. Elkins was to supervise the passage of the bill through the Senate, where the strongest contest took place, and Taft's choice of Elkins

[25] [William Howard Taft], *Messages and Papers of the Presidents, March 4, 1909 to March 4, 1913* (New York, n. d.), pp. 7441-7448.
[26] *Railway World*, LIV (January 14, 1910), 27-28.
[27] *Railway Age Gazette*, XLVIII (January 14, 1910), 80.

and the conservative wing of the Republican Party as his allies in this crucial fight was to win much opposition from the Insurgents. In mid-January, when it was clear that Taft was going to work with the Cannon-Aldrich wing of the party, the President defended himself against his critics by praising Aldrich unequivocally and justifying the political necessity of working with Cannon, however much he personally desired to see Cannon's power as the Speaker of the House diminished. In terms strangely akin to those Roosevelt had addressed to Taft in 1903 when complaints of Roosevelt's alliances with conservatives were also circulating, the President declared that "to denounce him [Cannon] in unmeasured terms, or to denounce Aldrich, is to do great injustice to both of them, and I do not propose to be carried off my feet by a yelling by a lot of demagogues in respect to men who have done a great deal for the country."[28] Taft's unswerving loyalty to his friends was to win him the sort of Senate opposition that a more flexible Roosevelt managed to avoid in the struggle for the Hepburn Act. The original Elkins Bill, La Follette stated, was "the rankest, boldest betrayal of public interest ever proposed in any legislative body."[29] A significant number agreed with him.

Despite the fact that many of the key railroads pledged not to oppose the bill, and with other of the railroad interests lukewarm or indifferent, Taft was still to face difficult days. To allay the fears of some of the railroad men, Taft, on January 25, issued a statement that future anti-trust action would not be "indiscriminate." Railroads, Henry Fink of the Norfolk and Western declared, favored the commerce court and legalized rate associations

---

[28] William Howard Taft to Guy W. Mallon, January 17, 1910, in Henry F. Pringle's Notes, Theodore Roosevelt Collection, Harvard College Library, box 3.

[29] Robert M. La Follette, *La Follette's Autobiography* (Madison, Wis., 1913), p. 420.

in principle, but many were also apprehensive about the new rate proposal and securities regulation. Railroad men wanted faster Commission judgments, but were not sure the commerce court would fulfill the job. The confused reaction or indifference in railroad circles continued as the basic obstacle through January.[30]

The House held hearings on many railroad bills in January and February, but most of them were tangential, and only the Rock Island, of all the major railroads, appeared.[31] Senate hearings in February were more to the point. Although the National Board of Trade essentially had endorsed Taft's January proposals, save for the commerce court, and many shippers testifying before the House Committee on Interstate and Foreign Commerce called for the right to route their freight, the major organized shipper pressures came during the Senate hearings. The National Industrial Traffic League, a federation of Midwest commercial organizations, called for the passage of the Elkins Bill, as did the Chicago Association of Commerce. The National Live Stock Association, which was to ally itself with the Insurgents in Congress and help direct their campaign, demanded more extensive Commission control over rates and especially concentrated on the commerce court, calling it a pro-railroad measure.[32]

[30] *Railway World*, LIV (January 28, 1910), 61-62, 66-67.

[31] U.S. House of Representatives, Committee on Interstate and Foreign Commerce, *Hearings*, 61st Cong., 2d Sess. [January-February, 1910] (Washington, 1910), *passim*. The major topic of controversy in these hearings was the right of the shippers to route their freight, and shippers turned out in strength.

[32] U.S. Senate, Committee on Interstate Commerce, *Hearings . . . On S. 3776 and S. 5106*, 61st Cong., 2d Sess. [February, 1910] (Washington, 1910), pp. 28-70, 131ff., 147. S. H. Cowan was the leader of the Live Stock Association campaign, and Senator Cummins admitted he relied on him for aid in fighting the Elkins Bill. See *Congressional Record*, XLV, 61:2, p. 4515.

Subsequent shipper pressure was light, if the twenty or so petitions in Sen 61A-F 14 for Commission approval of proposed rate changes are an indication. The N.A.M. favored the Mann-Elkins

The Rock Island was also the only important railroad witness before the Senate Committee on Interstate Commerce. (It is clear that the other railroads were not going to oppose the Elkins Bill, and to support it publicly would have meant its inevitable defeat.) The Rock Island's criticisms were specific. It undoubtedly appeared at the hearings in order to block obstacles to its campaign of expansion by mergers, mergers that eventually led to its bankruptcy. It objected chiefly to the prohibition on stock ownership in competing companies, as well as government control of stock issues, but favored the legalization of rate agreements without filing them for Commission approval, and the commerce court. Despite the obvious opportunism motivating the line, the Rock Island's lawyer, E. B. Peirce, admitted "I am convinced from the last three or four years' experience that the interstate-commerce law has been one of the most valuable laws upon our statute books. . . . I think that the bill is of great advantage to the railroad companies. . . . I believe some such law is necessary to protect the railroads against the shippers, and the shippers against the railroads."[33]

Passing a New Bill

Taft's basic mistake in the subsequent legislative history of the Mann-Elkins Bill is that he supported the wrong caucus within Congress, and was unable or unwilling to switch sides when it was evident he needed additional legislative support. The political conflict between Midwestern Republican Insurgency, led by Albert B. Cummins, La Follette, and Joseph L. Bristow, and

Bill along with the legalization of rate association agreements. See National Association of Manufacturers, *Fifteenth Annual Convention, New York, May 16-18, 1910* (New York, 1910), pp. 8ff.

[33] U.S. Senate, *Hearings . . . On S. 3776*, 61:2, pp. 149-150; also see pp. 99-113, 165.

the conservative Republican forces of Elkins, Aldrich, Root, and Crane meant that political disputes were to subject the railroad bill to such extraneous issues as the powers of Speaker Cannon and the entire structure of legislative government. Much of the conflict between the opposing forces on railroad matters, I believe, was contrived; and although the consensus is that the forces of Insurgency won in the fight for railroad legislation in 1910, I would suggest rather that the differences between the two groups on this issue were not so great as has been commonly supposed, and that the conservatives were convinced they had won.[34] It is this writer's opinion that Taft attained his major demand—and through it the ultimate victory—and that on most other questions it was a draw between the contending political forces.

Early in the year Cummins, the leader of the Insurgents in the Senate, presented a bill (S. 3776) in opposition to the Elkins Bill. His measure, for the most part, was surprisingly mild. It included a restoration of the commodity clause, uniform classification, Commission power to allow a railroad to purchase the stock of competitors, and measures which many railroads would have preferred to those in the Elkins Bill. Its major distinction was a failure to include a commerce court, and it was on the court proposal that Cummins, under the tutelage of S. H. Cowan, attorney for the National Live Stock Association, turned his fire in March.[35] By making support for the railroad bill a test of party loyalty, and intruding the question of Republican solidarity into railroad legislation, Taft forced Cummins and his Senate allies into the opposition. Accepting the challenge, Cum-

---

[34] Mowry, *Roosevelt and the Progressive Movement*, pp. 96ff.; Hechler, *Insurgency*, chap. VIII, gives the standard version.

[35] His bill is in U.S. Senate, *Hearings . . . On S. 3776*, 61:2, pp. 11-24; Cowan's role is admitted in *Congressional Record*, XLV, 61:2, p. 4515.

mins forgot about his own bill and turned to the task of emasculating the Elkins Bill.

A coalition of Democrats and Republican Insurgents in the House was able, in mid-February, to destroy the legalization-of-rate-agreements proviso and to force Townsend to submit a new Administration bill in a revised form.[36] In a series of long speeches in early March, Cummins strongly concentrated his fire on the commerce court proposal and the system for approval of railroad rate agreements. The conservatives in the Senate thought it wise, under the circumstances, to formulate a number of technical concessions to the Insurgents that were, in fact, inconsequential. Wickersham, who was directing the campaign for the President, told Taft "I can see no possible objection to any of them."[37] The Insurgents considered the concessions a significant victory.[38] The conservatives, in reality, gave nothing and temporarily took some of the wind out of the sails of Insurgency.

Taft was also handicapped by Elkins' inept handling of the campaign for the bill in a delicate political situation, and Wickersham complained "it is unfortunate that somebody is not in charge of the bill who has a more exact mind."[39] Despite Cummins' willingness to allow rate association agreements so long as the Commission could review any increased rates they determined upon, the conservatives in the Senate decided to drop any type of rate association proposal from the Administration bill rather than lose face to the Insurgents.[40] The

[36] *Railway World*, LIV (February 25, 1910), 141; Mowry, *Roosevelt and the Progressive Movement*, p. 97.

[37] George Wickersham to William Howard Taft, March 19, 1910, in Henry F. Pringle Notes, box 3. Among other things, Elkins tried to suggest that, "So far as I know and hear, the railroads oppose the bill." *Congressional Record*, XLV, 61:2, p. 3464.

[38] Hechler, *Insurgency*, p. 168.

[39] George Wickersham to William Howard Taft, March 19, 1910, in Henry F. Pringle Notes, box 3.

[40] Cummins, by this time, was really opposed to traffic associa-

railroads would have been delighted to have rate associations even on Cummins' terms, which were implied by the review powers granted to the Commission anyway, but the intrusion of politics decimated the measure. The next major victory for the Insurgents came in early May, when the long-short haul clause was restored, presumably without any exceptions allowed. By this time the factions in the Senate were trying to play tit for tat. Aldrich, attempting to break up the Insurgent-Democratic alliance, was able to swing enough Democratic support to destroy Taft's mild proposal for Commission regulation of rates.[41] That there existed a significant railroad sentiment for this proposal, save among new or small railroads, made little difference. The motive behind the legislative changes in Taft's bill was political, and changes were made in many cases merely to score political points. Since both sides scored, the Senate vote for the Elkins Bill on June 3 was an overwhelming 50 to 12. Everyone thought they obtained what they wanted, and in fact they did.

Between the final discussions on the Mann-Elkins Bill in Congress and the vote on the combined bill, the railroads committed a tactical blunder of major proportions. The proposed railroad rate advance of 1908, which the Western railroads passed over as a political donation to the Taft campaign, had remained a dormant issue after the campaign because of rising railroad income and the return of prosperity. In May 1910, for some inexplicable reason, the Western railroads cooperatively raised their rates 8 to 20 per cent, to go

tions of any sort, but was willing to compromise. See his statement of April 21, *Congressional Record*, XLV, 61:2, pp. 5121ff.

[41] The political infighting is described by Mowry, *Roosevelt and the Progressive Movement*, pp. 99-102; Hechler, *Insurgency*, pp. 168-174. Also see *Railway World*, LIV (May 6, 1910), 358-359.

into effect June 1.[42] If any action was calculated to strengthen the hands of the Insurgents in Congress, this was it. Taft, caught off guard by their action and deeply embarrassed, was forced to issue an injunction on May 31 against 24 railroads. Perkins and key railroad men then initiated a campaign to convince major shippers to agree to a rate increase, and the Government to withdraw its injunction. On June 6, Taft, Wickersham, and representatives of the Western railroads met for four hours and worked out a compromise. Taft complained that their actions had strengthened the hands of the opponents of a reasonable bill, and the railroads agreed to withdraw their general rate advance until the Mann-Elkins Bill finally passed. The Government then withdrew its injunction and the threat of a suit. Taft told the railroad men that he felt they were entitled to a rate increase, but that they should refile their demand after the new law passed. Minor rate advances could still be made, and would not be opposed by the Commission unless there were complaints. Both the railroads and the President were satisfied with the new arrangement, and the matter was delayed for the time being, but the political damage could not be repaired. The Insurgents took advantage of the situation, and gave the Commission power to stay rate advances for as long as ten months.[43] "As the members of this Commission are fair-minded

[42] William Z. Ripley, *Railroads: Rates and Regulation* (New York, 1912), pp. 595-596, says the increase was due to rising costs of operation and especially to pressure for a wage increase. The timing of the railroads, however, was too irrational to support this view.

[43] George W. Perkins to J. P. Morgan, June 1, June 3, June 4, June 7, 1910, George W. Perkins Papers, box 21; Memorandum of Agreement, June 6, June 10, 1910, William Howard Taft Papers, series 2, file 925; George W. Perkins, Memorandum of June 11, 1910, George W. Perkins Papers, box 21; Martin A. Knapp to Charles D. Norton, July 13, 1910, William Howard Taft Papers, series 2, file 5.

men, it is generally believed that the railroads will be allowed to increase their freight-rates, though possibly, in some cases, not as much as they expected," Henry Seligman confidently reported on June 8.[44]

Despite the *faux pas* of the railroads, Taft and Wickersham still regarded the final Mann-Elkins Act, which passed the Senate by a vote of 50 to 11 on June 17, as a substantial victory for their side.[45] The act must be regarded essentially as the administrative consolidation of the principles of the Hepburn Act on rate matters, and not as a radical departure along new lines. The act's only fundamentally new innovation, the Commerce Court, allowed the more conservative railroads to seek protection via the judiciary. The Commerce Court, Taft's major goal, made the Mann-Elkins Act a substantial victory for the Administration even though its more comprehensive railroad program was either defeated or modified.

The Mann-Elkins Act failed, like the Hepburn Act, to give a workable standard for "just and reasonable" rates. It therefore left the matter with the Commission and the Commerce Court, to be decided according to the particular biases of the members of those bodies. The commodity clause was unamended, thereby leaving the Supreme Court's nullification of it standing and legalizing the opposition to the clause by the anthracite roads. Section 4, forbidding long-short haul discriminations, was reworded, but the railroads could apply to "be relieved from the operation of this section." (In the next eight months the Commission received over 5,000

[44] Henry Seligman to Isaac Seligman, June 8, 1910, Henry Seligman Papers, Letterbooks, vol. 2.
[45] George Wickersham to Charles D. Hilles, July 15, 1911, William Howard Taft Papers, series 2, file 100a; William Howard Taft to Wharton Barker, June 11, 1910, and William Howard Taft to John A. Sleicher, June 21, 1910, Henry F. Pringle Notes, box 4.

such applications and approved them all until they could be investigated.)[46] The major victory for the Insurgents was the right of the Commission to suspend a new rate, classification, or practice 120 days beyond the time it was to go into effect, with an additional maximum of six months if Commission hearings were not completed by that time. Although Taft had requested such a right of suspension for 60 days—and the older rule of 30 days' notice to the Commission and public before implementing a new rate remained—the Insurgents clearly won an anti-Administration victory on this point. The abortive rate advance strongly aided them. But since the Commerce Court could suspend or stay all Commission decisions, their victory was ultimately to be an illusory one. Under the new law, the Commission placed on the railroad the burden of proving that a rate was just, but this formal declaration did not change the actual nature of litigation before the Commission. And although shippers could choose between alternative routes under the new law, the Commission was empowered to make "reasonable exceptions." Taft's request to allow railroads to form rate agreements was dropped by Aldrich because of pique, but his request for Commission power to regulate stocks and bonds was at least partially satisfied in his authorization to appoint a special commission to investigate the matter.

The railroads reacted to the new bill calmly, and in early July they were further reassured by a joint statement by Taft and Knapp indicating that the power to suspend rates would be used sparingly, and that the rate advance proposed by the railroads seemed just and reasonable.[47] The railroads had confidence in Taft and Knapp, but they were not sure about the Insurgents.

[46] Interstate Commerce Commission, *Twenty-Fifth Annual Report, December 20, 1911* (Washington, 1912), p. 20.
[47] *Railway Age Gazette*, XLIX (July 8, 1910), 63.

Although rate regulation had the advantage of keeping rates up and maintaining them, a fact the railroad journals freely admitted, there was also apprehension that the new law might freeze rates at the point they were at its passage.[48] In the final analysis, the *Railway Age Gazette* concluded, "It does not necessarily follow that it will either hurt or help anyone. Like the previous laws to regulate interstate commerce, its effects will depend mainly on how it is administered and obeyed. . . . The present personnel and temper of the Interstate Commerce Commission encourage optimism."[49]

The Rate Case of 1910

From the summer of 1910 until the end of the year, the railroads optimistically turned their attention to the Commission in the hope of obtaining their much delayed rate increase. Though George Perkins attempted to mobilize friendly shippers behind an increase, mainly by using his International Harvester connections, or the petition campaign of the railroad unions, three factors were to thwart the railroads.[50] The most important obstacle was the rapid increase of railroad profits in 1910 as compared to 1909, and the patently false nature of the argument that railroads were not making enough money. The second was the rise of substantial shipper opposition, and the third was a feud within the Interstate Commerce Commission itself that eventually influenced its decision.

Despite the efforts of Perkins, the shipper organizations in the East and Midwest formed a temporary united front against the railroads for the first time in

[48] *Ibid.*, XLVIII (March 11, 1910), 511-512; *ibid.*, June 24, 1910, p. 1778; *ibid.*, XLIX (1910), 63-64.

[49] *Ibid.*, XLIX (July 1, 1910), 4.

[50] C. S. Funk to George W. Perkins, July 20, 1910, George W. Perkins Papers, box 21. Also see 5,000 to 7,000 railroad union petitions in Sen 61A-J 50.

many years. It was one thing for them to disagree, as they usually had, on abstract questions of legislation. But a rate increase was money out of the pocket, and that was quite concrete. The Eastern shipping groups, as their contribution to the campaign, donated a brilliant lawyer, in the person of Louis D. Brandeis, to defend their cause. Brandeis' briefs to the Commission are classic, and mark the first major national appearance of the relatively unknown Boston lawyer. With him came the doctrine of scientific management, and Brandeis did more in a few short months to popularize the concept and term "scientific management" than had its founders after years of labor.[51] Brandeis managed to overwhelm the Commission and the railroads, but especially the public press, with a seemingly irrefutable series of facts buttressed by the "scientific" doctrines of Taylor, Gantt, Emerson, and Gilbreth. Rates, the astute lawyer maintained, would be increased as much as 25 per cent over existing levels if the railroads' request was granted. Winning the press to his side, Brandeis maintained that by an application of scientific management to the railroad industry, railroad income could be substantially increased at the existing rates.[52]

The Commission, during the hearings on the rate increase, was split apart as a result of the appointment of Knapp to the chairmanship of the Commerce Court. Prouty, certainly no enemy of the railroads though an opponent of the 1910 rate advance, was anxious to

[51] Milton J. Nadworny, *Scientific Management and the Unions, 1900-1932* (Cambridge, 1955), chap. III, maintains this and discusses the entire affair.

[52] Louis D. Brandeis, *Brief on Behalf of Traffic Committee of Commercial Organizations of the Atlantic Seaboard, January 3, 1911, Docket No. 3400. . . .* (Boston, 1911); Interstate Commerce Commission, *Evidence Taken . . . In the Matter of Proposed Advances in Feight Rates by Carriers, August to December, 1910* (Washington, 1911), 10 vols. [also printed as Senate Doc. No. 725, 61:3].

obtain the vacated chairmanship of the Commission. During October, the *Journal of Commerce* rumored, the Commission was split on the rate increase question. At the same time, Prouty undertook to stop the appointment of a railroad traffic man to the Commission, a move Taft apparently seriously contemplated.[53] Prouty's chief opponent for the chairmanship within the Commission, Edgar E. Clark, was charged by his critics with having shown a blatantly pro-railroad attitude while serving as a judge. Taft defended Clark's honesty, and indicated "my relation with the Commission is not that of controlling their decisions," but the pressure on him was too great.[54] Prouty insisted that the seniority system for the chairmanship would be violated and that he also deserved the post. And, with an air of righteousness, Prouty insisted that Clark was pro-railroad.[55] Taft finally settled the matter by appointing Prouty chairman for one year, and providing for the annual rotation of the post in the future on a seniority basis.

Having won against the forces within the Commission that strongly favored a rate increase, Prouty was able to have the Commission rule against the rate increase in February 1911. Its reason, and it was not contrived for the occasion, was that the railroads were quite prosperous. Even Henry Seligman, whose railroad interests were substantial, admitted ". . . that the opinion of the commissioners is on very fair and broad lines, and the real truth of the matter is that the railroads were unable to make out a case."[56]

[53] Walter L. Fisher to Charles D. Norton, September 19, 1910; Charles A. Prouty to William Howard Taft, October 27, 1910, William Howard Taft Papers, series 2, file 5.
[54] William Howard Taft to James J. Hooker, November 11, 1910, in Henry F. Pringle Notes, box 4.
[55] Charles A. Prouty to William Howard Taft, December 20, 1910, William Howard Taft Papers, series 2, file 5.
[56] Henry Seligman to Isaac Seligman, February 27, 1911, Henry Seligman Papers, Letterbooks, vol. 2.

The Demise of the Commerce Court

The idea of a Commerce Court had been viewed with favor by the railroads since at least 1893, primarily as a means of protection against the Commission in the event it followed a policy inimical to their best interests. This did not mean that the commerce court idea and positive Commission regulation were exclusive—they were not—but such a court was regarded as a safety valve in the event of political pressure from undesirable directions. James Logan, the attorney for the Pennsylvania, drafted the original Elkins Bill of 1902 to include both a commerce court and greater powers for the Commission. To other railroad men, the idea of a court of specialized judges held out the possibility of a better informed judicial process that could save them much time and effort. Courts of appeal were always abundant, intelligent judges less so.[57]

It was generally thought in 1910 that the commerce court idea was Elkins' unique contribution, dating back to his unamended 1902 bill. As John B. Daish, a strong defender of the Court admitted in 1912, the Pennsylvania Railroad "practically dictated the language of the act."[58] In fact, however, the Pennsylvania merely approved the idea of a commerce court as Elkins gave it to them, and Elkins took the idea from Richard Olney, who, as I have indicated earlier, developed the idea in the form of the Sawyer Bill (S. 3805) of 1893. That Olney was the attorney of the Boston & Maine Railroad at the time he wrote the bill is not immaterial.[59] Olney

[57] For early railroad support for the idea, see Aldace F. Walker, "The Amendment of the Interstate Commerce Law," *Independent*, XLV (June 1, 1893), 735; for the railroad demand for a more efficient judiciary, see Edward D. Kenna to Stephen B. Elkins, April 25, 1903, Stephen B. Elkins Papers, box 8.

[58] John Daish to J. E. Hundley, July 11, 1912, copy in William Howard Taft Papers, series 2, file 100a.

[59] Elkins admitted his debt to Olney in Stephen B. Elkins to William H. Moody, December 12, 1904, William H. Moody Papers,

offered to help Elkins draft a bill in the frank hope of abridging the Commission's powers. Even Charles E. Perkins thought such a court would be perfectly safe. But Elkins tried instead to obtain a bill focused mainly on rebating. Although a commerce court was the heart of his subsequent proposals, it was not successful until 1910.[60]

The railroads were pleased with Taft's appointments to the Commerce Court in late 1910, and especially by his designation of Martin A. Knapp as chairman. Knapp, addressing the Railway Business Association in November 1910, took an unequivocal stand against state railroad regulation as "so illiberal and vexatious as to be little less than oppressive"; declared "the theory of competition as a working principle is unsuited to the condition of a public service"; and came out, amid "great applause and cheers," for "the legal sanction of associated action by railway systems" and higher railroad rates and earnings.[61] After such an overture, the Commerce Court proceeded to make itself the most unpopular judicial institution in a nation then in the process of attacking the sanctity of the courts. In 1911 alone, it decided thirty major cases, twenty-seven of them for the railroads—and this pattern was followed for the remainder of its career. It obstructed the Commission at every turn, and at least the Southern Railroad and the B. & O. argued for a transfer of rate-making powers to the Court without further legislation.[62] Until June

---

Letterbooks, vol. 13; Stephen B. Elkins to Richard Olney, January 22, 1902, Richard Olney Papers, vol. 93.

[60] Richard Olney to Stephen B. Elkins, January 25, 1902; Stephen B. Elkins to Richard Olney, February 6, 1902; Charles E. Perkins to Richard Olney, January 25, 1902, Richard Olney Papers, vol. 93.

[61] Martin A. Knapp, *Address Before the Railway Business Association, New York, November 22, 1910* (New York, 1910), pp. 6-7; *Railway Age Gazette*, XLIX (December 16, 1910), 1136-1137.

[62] See the briefs of Alfred P. Thom of the Southern, April 25, 1911, and Edward Barton of the B. & O., April 19, 1911, in U.S.

1912, when the Supreme Court sharply restricted its functions, the Court often ignored Commission findings to try a case over entirely. In addition to disputing Commission decisions without new facts of its own, the Court effectively set itself up as a parallel commission without challenging the right of the official Commission to act by statute.[63]

It was merely a matter of time before the Commerce Court was attacked by Congress. Even the Supreme Court, in the *Procter & Gamble* decision of June 1912, sharply condemned its effort to pass on the legality of the administrative features of the Act of 1887. From late 1911 until August 1912, when Taft's veto of a House and Senate bill to abolish the Commerce Court was nearly overridden, the Administration fought a rear guard effort to defend and save it. While Taft and Wickersham would not support a feeble effort in the House to strengthen the powers of the Court in the face of Supreme Court attacks on it, they nevertheless insisted on defending the Court as a desirable institution. (Though Wickersham proposed a bill allowing the Commerce Court to review only errors of law by the Commission.) The only support for strengthening the power of the Commerce Court came, ironically, from a pro-railroad Washington lawyer, John B. Daish, who had managed to obtain the permission of the National Hay Association, grain shippers, and various shipper organizations to represent them before Congressional hearings.[64] Pressure merely to save the Commerce Court,

---

Commerce Court Records, National Archives, Record Group 172, box 40.

[63] Frank Haigh Dixon, *Railroads and Government, 1910-1921* (New York, 1922), pp. 44-51; Ripley, *Railroads: Rates and Regulation*, chap. xviii; Robert E. Cushman, *The Independent Regulatory Commission* (New York, 1941), pp. 103-105, are good accounts of the Commerce Court's actions.

[64] U.S. House of Representatives, Committee on Interstate and Foreign Commerce, *Hearings*, 62d Cong., 2d Sess. [July-August, 1912] (Washington, 1912), pp. 3, 105ff., 231-232.

most of which also seems to have been organized by Daish, in addition came from a few shippers, and even the important *Commercial and Financial Chronicle* favored it.[65] Strangely enough, Prouty defended the Commerce Court's right of broad review and opposed its abolition. With true charity, some shippers and the Commission turned the other cheek.

The Commerce Court's days were numbered, nevertheless. In February 1912, Commissioner B. H. Meyer notified Taft of the questionable financial activities of Judge Robert W. Archbald of the Commerce Court, and Taft ordered Wickersham to investigate. In July, a special Congressional Committee initiated impeachment proceedings against Archbald, and it was soon discovered that he was freely using his office for a variety of business activities involving railroads, as well as to obtain railroad donations for pleasure trips and the like. On January 13, 1913, Archbald was charged on five counts.[66] Wilson, whose Attorney General favored a liberalization of the Commerce Court and not its destruction, took no initiative to destroy the Court. But in late 1913, Congress managed to abolish it.

[65] Many shipper telegrams and letters on the topic are on file in William Howard Taft Papers, series 2, file 100a. Also see *Commercial and Financial Chronicle*, LXXXXIV (June 22, 1912), 1657. Considerable shipper support for the Court appears to have extended into 1913 as well. In that year they supported a bill (H.R. 5902) to extend the right of appeal to the Court to the shippers. See U.S. House of Representatives, Committee on the Judiciary, *Jurisdiction of Commerce Court—Its Enlargement, Hearings,* 63d Cong., 1st Sess., June 21, 1913 (Washington, 1913). The Attorney General, the I.C.C., Daish, and the Merchants' Association of New York supported the bill. Some railroad leaders wished to preserve the Court, but they also maintained they had no special interest in it. See Frank Trumbull to Edward M. House, September 26, 1913, Edward M. House Papers, Yale University Library.

[66] U.S. House of Representatives, *Charges Filed Against Judge Robert W. Archbald,* House Doc. No. 730, 62d Cong., 2d Sess. [Letter from William H. Taft to House of Representatives, May 3, 1912] (Washington, 1912); *Proceedings of the United States Senate and the House of Representatives in the Trial of Impeachment of Robert W. Archbald,* Senate Doc. No. 1140, 62d Cong., 3d Sess. (Washington, 1913), I, 5-11.

The abolition of the Commerce Court would have been avoidable had it been run with a moderate amount of discretion, and it could have been most serviceable to the railroads had it been less enthusiastic in their behalf. Knapp, however, had always identified with the railroads, and the tensions between him and the Commission, which was hardly a radical organization, undoubtedly marred his judgments. The Archbald incident only compounded the Commerce Court's troubles and was more a logical symptom of its malaise than its cause. The railroads, or at least the interested railroads, seriously miscalculated with respect to the Commerce Court. There were other reliable alternatives open to them, such as the Commission, if they wanted protection or security.

The Consolidation of Railroad Support for Federal Regulation

The railroads, for the most part, maintained a favorable attitude toward the Commission during the last two years of the Taft Administration, despite the effort of a number of them to exploit the Commerce Court to the hilt. The reasons for their cordiality were twofold: the attacks of state regulatory agencies mounted in strength, and the Commission was still the best protection against them; and the Commission itself continued to be friendly to the interests of the railroads, despite the pressure of public sentiment on its 1911 rate decision. It continued settling the vast majority of shipper complaints informally, most of them centering on the issue of excessive charges. In 1910 alone it kept nearly 3,000 such complaints from becoming formal cases, and about an equal number were settled the same way in 1911.[67] Moreover, Charles Prouty became con-

[67] Interstate Commerce Commission, *Twenty-Fourth Annual Report, December 21, 1910* (Washington, 1911), pp. 193-354; I.C.C., *Twenty-Fifth Annual Report*, pp. 213-352.

cerned about the possibly unjust consequences of holding down rates, and gave the railroads confidence they might expect better from him in the future. "I think that today it is just as much the duty of the commission to see that the railroads are given reasonable rates which will yield them a fair return, as it is to see that no unreasonable rate is charged the shipper, and I believe this is in the highest interest of the shipper himself," Prouty was telling shipper organizations in 1912.[68] If a general advance in rates were needed, Prouty let it be known, the railroads would get it.

In June 1910, under authorization of the Mann-Elkins Act, Taft appointed a commission under the chairmanship of President Arthur Hadley of Yale to study the issuance of railroad stocks and bonds and to recommend legislation. Railroad men appearing before the commission strongly urged the extension of federal control over the railroads to exclude the states, and many endorsed the federal regulation of securities, as well as the physical valuation of railroads as *a* criterion of rates.[69] The Hadley Commission report, filed in December 1911, recommended greater profits for the railroads in order to raise capital to bring the system up to European safety and physical standards, and I.C.C. valuation of the physical property of railroads.[70]

Congress reported favorably on a valuation bill in 1912. In 1913, with La Follette as the prime mover and with Commission endorsement, Congress without opposition enacted a physical valuation law to investigate the original and replacement costs of the American railroad system. The study was placed under the charge of

[68] Prouty, *Address Before . . . National Hay Association, July 16, 1912*, p. 8.

[69] *Wall Street Journal*, December 23, 1910.

[70] U.S. House, *Report of the Railroads Securities Commission to the President*, House Doc. No. 256, 62d Cong., 2d Sess., December 11, 1911 (Washington, 1911), pp. 32-36.

Prouty, and was to last into the 1920's. Legislated in sympathy, and properly administered, the railroads could hardly oppose a measure they had themselves looked favorably upon for years. Besides, innumerable Western and Midwestern states had undertaken, or were beginning, their own physical valuations, and the railroads saw the national government as their only security.[71] Although it felt the money could be put to better use, the *Railway Age Gazette* thought a federal valuation of the railroads would at least stop the complaints of those who claimed the railroads were over-capitalized, and halt action based on such illusions. The *Railway World* regarded the matter favorably, and without equivocation.[72] Commission investigations of rates and railroad values had the function, Fairfax Harrison, president of the Chicago, Indianapolis, & Louisville declared, of certifying "to the world that under existing conditions the American railways are financially sound."[73]

With the notable exception of Howard Elliott, president of the Northern Pacific and a militant advocate of near laissez-faire in the railroad system, American railroad leaders strongly favored federal regulation at this time despite the setbacks administered by the Insurgents of Congress and the failure of the rate advance of 1910. They realized that, in the national political arena, public relations and political influence were indispensable for success, but they did not attempt to work in opposition to the framework of federal regulation, nor secretly pine for a restoration of the legislative conditions of the late

[71] Texas, Wisconsin, Minnesota, Washington, South Dakota, Nebraska, and New Jersey, among others, had already begun such valuations. William Z. Ripley, *Railroads: Finance and Organization* (New York, 1915), chap. XI.

[72] *Railway Age Gazette*, XLIX (September 30, 1910), 566-567; *Railway World*, LVIII (January, 1914), 1-3.

[73] Fairfax Harrison, *Speech Before the Transportation Club of Indianapolis, March 31, 1911* (n.p., 1911), p. 1.

nineteenth century. In brief, they not only accepted the existing system, but positively believed in it. Moreover, within the spectrum of approaches to the regulation of the railroads, the railroads aligned themselves with the extreme nationalist position. At the same time, by creating a Bureau of Railway Economics in 1910, the railroads began a campaign to educate the public on the railroad view of problems.[74]

In mid-October 1910, Theodore Roosevelt addressed the Traffic Club of St. Louis and called for an application of the "New Nationalism" to railroad regulation. "The railways would far rather trust themselves to the control of the nation than to be harried as they now are by many masters," the *Railway and Engineering Review* remarked on the former President's speech.[75] It was this threat of state legislative attacks that kept the railroads solidly behind the I.C.C. and federal regulation. In doing so they also admitted that federal controls were fair and desirable, although the rate case caused a few to forget that it was the railroads who were among the earliest advocates of federal regulation. "The railways must be controlled primarily and principally by the federal government," Walker D. Hines, chairman of the Santa Fe, told the Railway Business Association in late 1911.[76] "The supervision of the Interstate Commerce Commission, in its obnoxiousness," the conservative *Railway Record* of Chicago wrote, "is as nothing compared with what the state commissions have sought to enforce."[77] If the railroads did not like the continued threat of the

[74] See Howard Elliott, *Address Before the Publicity Club of Minneapolis, January 10, 1912* (St. Paul, 1912). In this statement Elliott, the most articulate conservative among key railroad men, attacked laws created by public opinion, and called for an educational campaign to control it.

[75] *Railway and Engineering Review*, L (October 15, 1910), 966.

[76] Walker D. Hines, *Speech Before the Railway Business Association, New York, November 22, 1911* (New York, 1911), p. 20.

[77] *Railway Record*, III (January 6, 1912), 2.

Sherman Act hanging over their heads, or the freezing of rates, they nevertheless strongly defended the basic institution of regulation. "As the operating company must exercise a monopoly of transportation over this highway," William W. Finley wrote in 1911, "it is a proper function of the government to prevent unreasonable or extortionate charges for the service performed."[78] "The principle of regulation we accept," William Sproule of the Southern Pacific told the San Francisco Chamber of Commerce in late 1912.[79] Seeing history somewhat hazily, H. U. Mudge, president of the Rock Island, announced, "I believe most railroad men now think that it would have been better for the railroads if the federal government had claimed the right to regulate all freight rates and that the railroads had conceded this from the start. . . ."[80]

"The day of the Manchester school and *laissez faire* is gone," Fairfax Harrison announced to a group of businessmen. The Commission assured the railroads that they would use the power of the law to "permit such advances of rates as may be necessary to maintain the sound financial condition which they certify now exists."[81] Could untrammeled competition assure the railroads that rates would go up when profits were low? Only the Commissioners, who "are increasingly willing to be fair, even when there are strong evidences of momentary popularity to be derived from doing the thing which

[78] William Wilson Finley, *The Railway as the Business Man's Partner* (New York, 1911), p. 16. Also see *Railway Age Gazette*, XLIX (July 22, 1910), 150, for a complaint on the Sherman Act.

[79] William Sproule, *Address Before the Annual Dinner of the Chamber of Commerce of San Francisco, December 9, 1912* (n.p., n.d.), p. 4.

[80] H. U. Mudge, *Address Before the Commercial Club of Topeka, Kansas, April 11, 1911* (n.p., n.d.), pp. 4-5. Also see Frank Trumbull, "The Evolution of Business Methods," *Railway Age Gazette*, LIII (November 29, 1912), 1046-1047, for a strong pro-regulation view.

[81] Harrison, *Speech Before the Transportation Club of Indianapolis*, p. 1.

is unfair," could provide such guarantees.[82] Railroad men reflected on the alternatives to national regulation, considered the cutthroat competition of the past and the less considerate state legislatures and commissions of the present, and concluded that the federal government was indeed a blessing. Harrison spoke for the larger part of the American railroad leadership when he admitted, "The day of the Manchester school and *laissez faire* is gone. . . . Personally, I do not repine at the change. . . ."[83]

[82] *Ibid.*, p. 7.   [83] *Ibid.*, p. 8.

CHAPTER X

WOODROW WILSON AND
THE TRIUMPH OF FEDERAL CONTROL
1913-1916

IT IS ironic that Woodrow Wilson, author of the New
Freedom, was to consolidate the domination of the
national government over railroad regulation, and to
provide the ultimate protection for the railroads that
they sought during the period of state railroad reforms
and Insurgency. If Roosevelt played the role of the self-
anointed and fundamentally conservative defender of
the best interests of the railroads, and Taft the role of
his politically inept but well-intentioned echo, Wilson
was to assume the part of the nationalistic advocate of
the railroads who allowed the railroads to define his
role for him. Such a function was possible because Wilson was not seriously interested in railroad problems,
and at least until 1916 these issues played a far lesser
role in his administration than in the preceding ones.
The unimportance of the railroad issue in comparison
to banking, trust, or tariff controversies permitted Wilson to rely on the initiatives of the railroad leaders.

If the railroads found Taft's failure to obtain some
of the desirable aspects of his original railroad bill
irritating, their commitment to federal regulation nevertheless remained firm. Wilson's aid to the railroads, both
in his support for their demands and in his appointments to the Interstate Commerce Commission, was to
strengthen their ties. In late 1913, the term of Judson
C. Clements on the I.C.C. expired. For a time there

was some question whether Wilson would reappoint the outstanding "public man" on the Commission.[1] Though Wilson did, in fact, reappoint Clements, in January 1914, he nominated Henry C. Hall and Winthrop M. Daniels as well. Although La Follette opposed Hall for the post because of his conservatism, his nomination passed without a fight. Daniels, however, was widely known as a "reactionary," but since he was an old Princeton friend of Wilson's, the President supported him despite the outspoken attacks of liberals and progressives. His nomination was confirmed only because of strong conservative Republican support.[2] Hall and Daniels were to move the not unsympathetic Commission even more firmly into the railroad camp.

The need of the railroads for the friendship of the President never seemed greater than in 1913 and 1914, for profits dropped sharply from 1911 through 1913, and it was obvious to the railroads that a general rate increase was imperative. Fortunately for them, the President was ready to lend a sympathetic ear, despite his preoccupation with other, more important, legislative matters. Although peripheral issues, such as the restoration of the Commerce Court or the legalization of rate agreements, were advocated now and again, the central aims of the railroads were higher rates and financial security.[3] In his January 20, 1914, message to Congress, Wilson announced: "The antagonism between business and government is over. . . . The Government and business men are ready to meet each other halfway in a common effort to square business methods with public opinion and the law." Although the message was

[1] *La Follette's Weekly*, v (December 6, 1913), 1.

[2] *Ibid.*, vi (April 18, 1914), 1; Belle Case La Follette and Fola La Follette, *Robert M. La Follette* (New York, 1953), i, 489; Arthur S. Link, *Wilson: The New Freedom* (Princeton, 1956), pp. 449-450.

[3] *Railway World*, lviii (1914), 1; Frederic A. Delano, *Address Before the Economic Club of New York, April 29, 1913* (n.p., n.d.), p. 6.

directed primarily toward business and industry, and not railroads, it signified a willingness on the part of the Administration to regard the problems of the railroad industry with tolerance and sympathy. Acknowledging that the straitened financial conditions of the railroads required ". . . a law which will confer upon the Interstate Commerce Commission the power to superintend and regulate the financial operations by which the railroads are henceforth to be supplied with the money they need for their proper development . . . ," Wilson also noted that ". . . those who are chiefly responsible for the actual management and operation of the railroads . . ." earnestly endorsed speedy action.[4] Business and the railroads responded to the speech with tremendous enthusiasm.

In mid-1913, thirty-five Eastern railroads applied for a general rate increase of 5 per cent, and hearings opened in November. Stressing that they had invested $600 million in three years but that their profits in 1913 were lower than in 1910, the Eastern lines, in hearings that were to last until May 1914, made by far their strongest case since 1908.[5] Wilson, during this interim period, was subjected to pressures from both the shippers and the railroads. Brandeis, in charge of the shippers' case, stressed the element of inefficiency in railroad practices, and was able to obtain Wilson's support for his efforts to open the books of railroad supply companies.[6] But shipper opposition this time was rela-

[4] *The Public Papers of Woodrow Wilson*, Ray Stannard Baker and William E. Dodd, eds. (New York, 1926), III, 82, 84-85.

[5] Daniel Willard and F. A. Delano, *The Case for Increased Rates* [brief to I.C.C., November 24, 1913], (n.p., 1913).

[6] Joseph Davies to Woodrow Wilson, February 3, 1914; Woodrow Wilson to Joseph Davies, February 4, 1914, Woodrow Wilson Papers, Library of Congress, series VI, box 11. Colonel House, who was personally friendly with Frank Trumbull, was also subjected to pressure on the rate question during 1913 and 1914, and was treated as a pipeline to Wilson. See, for example, Daniel Willard to Edward M. House, November 21, 1913; James Speyer to House, March 12,

tively feeble, and numerous business groups supported the railroads. Pressures, of course, were exerted from the pro-railroad side, and Congress, Wilson, and the Commission were deluged with petitions, editorials, and statements.[7] Indeed, railroad agitation was too great, and the Commission complained about it in their decision on the "Five Percent Case" in July 1914. But the Commission still granted the request of the railroads, and declared that the operating income in the Official Classification Territory east of the Mississippi and north of the Potomac and Ohio Rivers—with one-half the nation's freight volume—was smaller "than is demanded in the public interest"; investment was not large enough in the area. Rather than grant an across-the-board increase it allowed a 5 per cent rate advance only in Ohio, Illinois, Indiana, Michigan, and western Pennsylvania and suggested that all "unremunerative" rates be increased.[8] The "Five Percent" decision represented a major victory in the history of the railroads, not merely in that it significantly increased their 1914 profits in a year of declining business and gave them tacit authorization to inflate their rates. For the first time, the Commission made explicit its doctrine that the railroads had to receive a "living wage," in Commissioner James S. Harlan's phrase, if they were to attract investment and function profitably. The Commission—there was a minority that dissented—made clear that the only alternative to such a principle was government ownership, and although it should not surprise anyone that they

---

1914; Frank Trumbull to House, August 31, 1914, September 4, 1914, Edward M. House Papers, Yale University Library.

[7] James Speyer to Edward M. House, March 12, 1914, *The Intimate Papers of Colonel House*, Charles Seymour, ed. (Boston, 1926), I, 132-133; Frank Trumbull to Woodrow Wilson, February 17, 1914, Woodrow Wilson Papers, series II; *Congressional Record*, LI, 63:2, pp. 7727-8093, for complete documentation.

[8] *Interstate Commerce Commission Reports*, XXXI (Washington, 1915), pp. 351, 357, 403, 408.

were opposed to socialism, it made explicit what had been an operational reality for many years: the Interstate Commerce Commission was to protect the railroads in their function of making profits for individual capitalists so long as the railroads provided their services to the public on reasonably minimal standards of equality. It meant, in effect, the end of any ostensible commitments to the official economic ideology of the status quo, as vague, general, and variable as it was, and the creation of a political capitalism in which the federal government was to protect and aid private property in its attainment of profit, and to defend it against the possible onslaughts of other interests. As Commissioner Harlan expressed it:

"Many railroad investments in this country are exceedingly profitable to their owners. In common justice the investors in such properties are entitled to share in the general prosperity and to enjoy the just rewards of their foresight and wisdom so long as the rates exacted are reasonable. It is not only consistent with a national policy that invites the private ownership of railroads that there should be a liberal return on a particular railroad investment, when the property has been wisely planned and honestly constructed and is efficiently managed; but the full development of that policy, as well as justice, requires that such a return should be made. The public interest demands not only the adequate maintenance of existing railroads, but a constant increase of our transportation facilities to keep pace with the growth and requirements of our commerce. If, however, that development is to be accomplished with private capital, in conformity with our traditions, nothing can be more certain than that the facilities will not be provided except under such a system of regulation as will reasonably permit a fair return on the money invested."[9]

[9] Commissioner Harlan in *ibid.*, p. 359; also see p. 454.

It rapidly became obvious to the railroads that their efforts for even higher rates would have to obtain the active support of President Wilson if they were to get anywhere. Early in September 1914, Frank Trumbull, Rea, Willard, Fairfax Harrison, E. P. Ripley of the Santa Fe, and Hale Holden of the C. B. & Q. visited Wilson with a prepared statement. They complained that their credit had been impaired by state attacks and regulations, the abrupt disappearance of the European capital market, and declining earnings. The recent 5 per cent increase was insufficient to meet these problems, some of which were a result of the war. What was needed from the federal government was greater sympathy and cooperation. The following day Wilson wrote to Trumbull, and his September 10 letter was to the railroads what his January 20, 1914, message to Congress was to industry and business. Your assertion, Wilson wrote Trumbull, "is a lucid statement of plain truth. . . . You ask me to call the attention of the country to the imperative need that railway credits be sustained and the railroads helped in every possible way, whether by private co-operative effort or by the action, wherever feasible, of governmental agencies, and I am glad to do so, because I think the need very real."[10] The text of the correspondence was immediately released, and all the irritations of the past decade caused by delays in rate increases and inept or flamboyant Presidents disappeared. Wilson's September 1914 letter marks the beginning of what was probably one of the closest unions between the railroads and the federal government since the inception of the Interstate Commerce Commission. Moreover, the railroads wanted to make it even closer.

President Wilson's letter to Trumbull, the *Railway World* reported, "has met with the universal approval of business men throughout the country."[11] The Railway

[10] *Railway Age Gazette*, LVII (September 11, September 18, 1914), 462, 506.

[11] *Railway World*, LVIII (September, 1914), 703.

Business Association passed a resolution commending the President. "It seems to me," J. P. Morgan, Jr., wrote Wilson, "that the whole country has great cause to be thankful to you for the expressions in your letter to Mr. Trumbull upon railway matters. Such expressions are of great assistance in the present anxious situation."[12] The railroads, Benjamin F. Bush of the Missouri Pacific announced, are going through "the greatest crisis in the history of American railroads," but Wilson appreciated the situation and would help save them.[13]

Wilson's letter to Trumbull was sincere, and reflected a serious commitment on his part. In September, the Eastern railroads petitioned the I.C.C. for a 5 per cent rate increase in the territory not covered by the July advance. Although Wilson was warmly encouraged by Henry Lee Higginson and Charles Francis Adams, Jr., to approve the advance, he needed little prodding.[14] On October 29, Wilson wrote a pointed letter to the man whose confirmation he had fought to obtain—Commissioner Winthrop M. Daniels. "I am awaiting the decision of the Commission in the newly opened rate case with deep and serious anxiety. I believe that a concession to the railroads is absolutely necessary to steady and relieve the present extraordinary difficulties of the financial situation."[15] On November 17, to strengthen the confidence of business in his Administration, Wilson sent W. G. McAdoo a letter that, according to Arthur S. Link, could very well have been the "funeral oration for the New Freedom."[16] The letter, which was immediately

[12] J. P. Morgan, Jr., to Woodrow Wilson, September 18, 1914, Woodrow Wilson Papers, series II.

[13] Benjamin F. Bush, *Address Before the Missouri Press Association, September 17, 1914* (n.p., n.d.), pp. 7-9.

[14] Henry Lee Higginson to Woodrow Wilson, October 22, 1914, October 26, 1914; Charles Francis Adams, Jr., to Woodrow Wilson, October 29, 1914, Woodrow Wilson Papers, series II.

[15] Woodrow Wilson to Winthrop M. Daniels, October 29, 1914, Woodrow Wilson Papers, series II.

[16] Link, *Wilson: The New Freedom*, p. 470.

given to the press, suggested that all of the major social problems that Wilson had inherited were "righted." What was necessary, the President urged, was a spirit of cooperation among all men and between business and government.[17] "The spirit of co-operation which your letter breathes is an example to all of us and will help solve other problems," Trumbull wrote Wilson immediately.[18] The McAdoo and Trumbull letters, the president of the Lehigh Valley Railroad wrote Tumulty, "will put a damper on railroad 'baiting' throughout the country."[19]

The significance of the spate of statements and decisions from the various branches of the federal government defending and aiding the railroads, as well as the attacks of the states, was not lost on the railroads. The responsibility of the government, according to Democratic House leader Oscar W. Underwood, was to maintain the general welfare of the railroads, for the good of the public as well as the railroads, in order to stimulate business conditions and to prevent demands for government ownership. What was necessary, E. P. Ripley, president of the Santa Fe, presciently suggested, was a partnership between the federal government and the railroads. Let the railroad system be organized into regional boards, as were the banks, and let the government send representatives to those boards. In return for a veto power over any proposed action, the government would guarantee the railroads net earnings not less than the average of those over the past five years, and 6 per cent on improvements. Such a system, Ripley declared, "would do away with the enormous wastes of

[17] The letter is printed in *Public Papers of Woodrow Wilson*, III, 210-214.
[18] Frank Trumbull to Woodrow Wilson, November 18, 1914, Woodrow Wilson Papers, series II.
[19] Walter Fahy to Joseph P. Tumulty, November 19, 1914, Woodrow Wilson Papers, series II.

the competitive system and permit business to follow the line of least resistance."[20] Carping criticisms were to continue to appear in railroad journals or to be expressed by railroad leaders, but their basic devotion to the system of federal regulation should not be confused with their criticism of the details of it, especially since they strongly disagreed among themselves on those details. The *Railway Age Gazette* was proud of the fact that it had advocated the Hepburn Act, the federal regulation of securities, and the extension of federal control over the states.[21] Samuel Rea wanted shorter waiting time before a challenged rate went into effect, a larger Commission with longer tenure, and higher rates; but after all this was said, he made it known "I believe in regulation by Commission, and I urge, therefore, that we do not encourage destruction of such regulation, but rather its conservation, by adapting it, as we have banking regulation and other laws, to suit the needs of the Country as they change from time to time."[22]

In December 1914, the I.C.C. allowed the 5 per cent rate increase to be extended to the entire Eastern classification territory. Railroad men appreciated the importance of the principles laid down by the Commission in the case, and that the I.C.C. had now formally become a guarantee of relative security and profits. The rate advance was important, "but what I consider of even more importance is its recognition of the needs of the railroads for increased revenues and the reiteration of its former statement as to its duty and purpose to aid, so far as it legally may, in the solution of the problem as to what course the carriers may pursue to meet the

[20] *Traffic World*, XIV (October 31, 1914), 798; Oscar W. Underwood, Speech Before the Sphinx Club, New York, March 9, 1915, in *Congressional Record*, LII, 63:3, Appendix, pp. 851-852.

[21] *Railway Age Gazette*, LVII (December 11, 1914), 1073-1074.

[22] Samuel Rea, *Address Before the New York Chamber of Commerce, December 3, 1914* (n.p., n.d.), p. 10.

situation," wrote Daniel Willard immediately after the decision.[23] Several months later he more correctly declared that "The two decisions of the Interstate Commerce Commission in the so-called Five Per Cent. Rate Case contain the essentials of a Bill of Rights for the roads."[24] The Commission, only a few months later, refused a 5 per cent rate increase to the Western roads. What is important in the "Five Percent" decision is the principle enunciated as a guide to action, not each particular application of that principle. The railroads had indeed come a long way from the days of cutthroat competition, bankruptcies, and rate wars.

National vs. State Regulation

The continuing aggravation of the state regulatory problem merely strengthened the commitment of the railroads to federal regulation under Wilson's presidency. Wilson was sympathetic to the railroads' problems with the states, even though it was in the realm of rates and the administration of the Interstate Commerce Commission that he was able to take a more active role in helping the railroads. The Supreme Court, especially in the *Minnesota Rate* decision of 1913 and the *Shreveport* decision of 1914, extended the power of the Interstate Commerce Commission to regulate intrastate rates in order to remove interstate discriminations. In other decisions, the Court tried to establish the supremacy of federal authority.[25] But the volume of state legislation the railroads considered cumbersome far exceeded the Supreme Court's ability to keep up with it,

[23] Daniel Willard, "Effect of the Rate Advance Decision," *Railway Age Gazette*, LVIII (January 1, 1915), 8.

[24] Daniel Willard, *Address at Dartmouth College, March 22, 1915* (n.p., 1915), p. 10. Also see Frank Trumbull, *Address Before the National Hay Association, Cedar Point, Ohio, July 12, 1916* (New York, 1916), p. 4, for more praise of the Five Percent decision.

[25] George G. Reynolds, *The Distribution of Power to Regulate Interstate Carriers Between the Nation and the States* (New York, 1928), pp. 137ff., for a discussion of Supreme Court actions.

and since many of the laws were contradictory and burdensome in their differences, railroad agitation for federal supremacy increased. In 1913 alone, forty-two state legislatures passed 230 railroad laws affecting the railroads in such areas as extra crews, hours of labor, grade crossings, signal blocks, and electric headlights—and many of the laws were expensively contradictory. In 1914, the railroads claimed, 166 railroads were forced to spend $28 million to meet the requirements of state laws. State taxes per mile of railroad increased 140 per cent between 1900 and 1916. Nineteen different states regulated security issues, fourteen had dissimilar safety appliance acts, and twenty-eight had headlight laws. From 1902 through 1910, railroad spokesmen complained, nearly 1,300 state laws regulating railroads were passed, and 442 were enacted during the next five years. Federal railroad laws in 1909 filled 175 pages, those of New York and Pennsylvania alone nearly 1,500. Many states ignored federal rulings, and Alabama had a law that any railroad appealing its procedures to a federal court would forfeit its license to operate in the state.[26] The National Association of Railway Commissioners, founded in 1888 to work for uniform state legislation, virtually admitted in 1913 that it still had a long way to go before it achieved its goal.[27] "The distinguishing fact about the system of rail-

[26] Ivy L. Lee, *Address*, February 9, 1914 (St. Louis, 1914); Delano, *Address Before the Economic Club of New York*, pp. 8-9; Francis H. Sisson, "Regional Railroad Control Proposed on Same Plan as a Reserve Bank System," *Journal of the American Bankers Association*, IX (August, 1916), 112; testimony of Julius Kruttschnitt, in U.S. Congress, Joint Committee on Interstate and Foreign Commerce, *Interstate and Foreign Transportation, Hearings*, 64th Cong., 1st Sess. [November, 1916-November, 1917] (Washington, 1917), pp. 893-894; Interstate Commerce Commission, *Statistics of Railways in the United States, 1900* (Washington, 1901), p. 97; Interstate Commerce Commission, *Statistics of Railways in the United States, 1916* (Washington, 1918), p. 98.

[27] National Association of Railway Commissioners, *Proceedings of the Twenty-Fifth Annual Convention, October 28-31, 1913* (New York, 1914), p. 78.

road regulation which has so far developed in this country is that it is indefinite, inconsistent and not yet established on recognized principles," concluded Ivy Lee, the Pennsylvania Railroad's public relations man, in presenting the railroad view in 1915.[28] His president, Samuel Rea, had demanded earlier that "the regulatory power of the Interstate Commerce Commission should be clearly extended to the supervision and control of all rates and practices which directly, or remotely, affect interstate transportation or commerce."[29]

The Railroad Executives' Advisory Committee, formed in 1914 and representing the large majority of the railroads, moved to present a unified program of reform. Frank Trumbull, chairman of the advisory committee and a personal friend of Colonel House, made it apparent from the start that the railroads would urge comprehensive federal control of the railroad system. "The time has arrived for blood remedies instead of court plasters" was a fair summary of his philosophy.[30] In August 1914, the advisory committee presented a comprehensive plan for federal regulation modeled on the lines of the Federal Reserve System; its central theme was control over state regulation. "It is impossible for a State commission to interfere in the affairs of any railroad without having at least an indirect effect on interstate commerce," Alfred P. Thom, the chief lawyer of the committee, told the press. "Therefore, the functions exercised by State commissions conflict with the functions properly belonging to Congress, and thus are unconstitutional."[31] The committee

[28] Ivy L. Lee, *Address Before the American Association for the Advancement of Science, Columbus, Ohio, December 30, 1915* (n.p., 1915), p. 4.

[29] Rea, *Address Before Chamber of Commerce, December 3, 1914*, p. 7.

[30] Quoted in *Loco*, VII (1916), 141. He also advocated federal regulation of railroad securities. See *Railway Age Gazette*, LX (March 31, 1916), 748.

[31] *New York Times*, August 12, 1916.

called for the enlargement of the I.C.C. to about twenty-five commissioners, distributed in about eight regions to take care of local cases. The commission in each zone could decide whether a decision might be appealed to a central board in Washington. In addition, the committee called for elimination of the Commission's power to suspend a rate for as long as ten months, and sought the testing of the reasonableness of a rate after it had been put into practice. The preparation and prosecution of cases before the Commission, it was suggested, should be handed over to the Department of Justice or a special bureau.[32] At no point was the necessity of federal regulation as such challenged. Quite the contrary, the advisory committee called for its extension.

The *Shreveport* decision by the Supreme Court, in the opinion of state railroad commissioners, did not cancel the state rate-making powers.[33] This attitude at times placed the railroads in the midst of conflicts between state commissions and the Interstate Commerce Commission. In 1915, a battle between the Texas Railroad Commission and the I.C.C. as to whose orders were to be obeyed left the railroads facing a possible injunction from one of the commissions if they took any action at all. Similar conflicts arose in other states.[34] "The regulating done by the federal government is in intelligence and fairness as far above that done by the states as the heavens are above the earth," the *Railway Age Gazette* wrote in September 1915. "State regulation ought to be either eliminated or brought into harmony with and subjection

[32] *Ibid.*; Sisson, *Journal of the American Bankers Association*, IX (1916), 112.

[33] Robert R. Prentis, "The Relation Between National and State Railway Regulation," *Railway Age Gazette*, LIX (December 31, 1915), 1229, for an important expression of this opinion.

[34] *Railway Age Gazette*, LIX (August 20, 1915), 309-310; *New York Times*, September 14, 1916.

to federal regulation."[35] Regulation, Frank Trumbull of the C. & O. advocated, had to be made as comprehensive as the new federal banking system, superseding the state laws. But in criticizing state regulation, Trumbull and other railroad executives went to pains to indicate "it is not to criticize the principle or to seek relaxation in the stringency. . . ."[36] Again and again they reiterated, in the words of L. E. Johnson of the Norfolk & Western, that "They are in favor of effective regulation because they know that this is the only alternative to government ownership. . . . They would be in favor of it even in the absence of the danger of government ownership, because they recognize the fact that effective regulation, if it be also wise and fair, will promote the interests and protect the rights not only of the general public but also of the owners, the officers and employees of the railways themselves."[37] "The greatest hope of the railways and the public in the future lies in intelligent regulation," Frederic A. Delano of the Wabash agreed with a vague truism.[38]

By 1916, the railroads finally began gaining the up-

[35] *Railway Age Gazette*, LIX (September 3, 1915), 415. Also see *ibid.*, LVII (December 11, 1914), 1074; and the *Gazette's* editor, Samuel O. Dunn, "The Interstate Commerce Commission and the Railroads," *Annals of the American Academy of Political and Social Science*, LXIII (January, 1916), 155-172.

[36] Frank Trumbull, *Address Delivered at a Dinner to E. P. Ripley, Chicago, October 30, 1915* (n.p., 1915), p. 10.

[37] L. E. Johnson, *Address Before the Western Society of Engineers, Chicago, November 2, 1915* (n.p., n.d.), p. 5; also pp. 9-14, 21-23.

[38] Delano, *Address Before Economic Club of New York*, p. 10. Such a response was evoked by railroad men to meet every problem, including the relationship of the railroads to finance. During 1914 the House passed a bill to regulate railroad securities (H.R. 15657), and the concept was endorsed by B. F. Yoakum on the grounds that, "If the Government should approve a railroad security, it would in effect, morally speaking, indorse it, and this high approval of the issue should make such a bond sell at the lowest rate of interest current for gilt-edge securities. . . ." *Congressional Record*, LI, 63:2, p. 9801; also see Walker D. Hines, "The Conflict Between State and Federal Regulation of Railroads," *Annals of the American Academy of Political and Social Science*, LXIII (January, 1916) 191-198.

per hand in their fight against the state regulatory systems. Victory did not come immediately, but a strong current of sympathy for the position of the railroads eventually brought more concrete results in the form of rate advances and legislation. In early 1916, for example, Taft came out strongly for federal imposition of uniform railroad legislation on the states, and in March the Philadelphia Bourse, an alliance of ten major business organizations, announced a much publicized plan for undisputed federal control of regulation, splitting the Commission into district commissions to speed cases, and creating a central railroad court of appeals.[39] The Federal Reserve System and the Federal Trade Commission were held by railroad men as models to be duplicated. Daniel Willard of the B. & O. told the American Newspaper Publishers Association in April of 1916, ". . . as we have gradually grown and become transformed from a loose confederacy of States into one great Nation, the necessity for Federal instead of State control has become more and more apparent concerning many matters of nation-wide importance—such necessity has been reflected in . . . the Federal Reserve Act, Federal Trade Commission, etc. Gradually, consistently and naturally, as I view it, the change in railroad regulation from State to Federal is also taking place, and the thing most desired is that the complete change shall be accomplished in as brief a time as practicable. . . ."[40]

[39] William Howard Taft, *Address Before the Annual Dinner of the Traffic Club of New York, February 21, 1916* (New York, 1916), pp. 7, 10; [Philadelphia Bourse], *A Report Submitted by a Sub-Committee to the Joint Committee on Reasonable Regulation of Railroads, March 14, 1916* (Philadelphia, 1916), pp. 6, 22-23; *Commercial and Financial Chronicle*, cii (March 25, 1916), 1122.

[40] Daniel Willard, *Address Before the American Newspaper Publishers' Association, April 27, 1916* (n.p., 1916), p. 3. Also see Edward J. White, *State and Federal Control of Carriers* [a paper to the Kansas State Bar Association], January 27, 1916 (n.p., 1916); Railway Business Association, *Defects in Railroad Regulation* [Bulletin No. 18], *April 10, 1916* (New York, 1916); *Traffic World*, xvii (June 24, 1916), 1325-1326; Frank Trumbull, *Address Before the*

Support of the railroad position increased, and the 1916 Republican platform called for complete federal control of railroad regulation, even if a Constitutional amendment were required. The Democrats, though passing over the topic in their platform, were committed to the comprehensive Congressional inquiry into the railroad problem that Wilson had called for in his December 1915 message to Congress at the request of Frank Trumbull, chairman of the C. & O. The railroads looked forward to such an investigation with high hopes. "It is a fine beginning of another piece of constructive work by your administration," Trumbull enthusiastically telegraphed the President, "and I am confident that you will do for the railroads of this country as much as you have already done for the banks."[41]

The fact that the Supreme Court had affirmed the Interstate Commerce Commission's supremacy over state laws did not eliminate the desirability of formal laws, according to railroad spokesmen.[42] Their position, moreover, was strongly supported by important shippers, including the Massachusetts Board of Trade, National Association of Manufacturers, and Philadelphia Bourse. Even the *New York Times* was sympathetic. But most important of all was Wilson's cooperation in endorsing the type of systematic inquiry the railroads demanded as a prelude to more far-reaching legislation. In a public letter to Oscar W. Underwood on March 28, 1916, Wilson underscored his sympathy for the plight of the railroads:

"The railways of the country are becoming more and

National Hay Association, passim; Loco, VII (August, 1916), 137-143, for railroad attacks on state regulation and their demands for comprehensive federal controls.

[41] Frank Trumbull to Woodrow Wilson, December 7, 1915, copy in Edward M. House Papers.

[42] *Railway Review,* LIX (August 26, 1916), 281; *Traffic World,* XVIII (August 19, October 7, October 14, 1916), 125-126, 721-722, 774.

more the key to its successful industry, and it seems to me of capital importance that we should lay a new groundwork of actual facts for the necessary future regulation.

"I know that we all want to be absolutely fair to the railroads, and it seems to me that the proposed investigation is the first step toward the fulfilment of that desire."[43]

The Railroad Executives' Advisory Committee's plan for regional offices for the I.C.C. did not remain exclusively a railroad proposal, since it was one of the major topics considered in the hearings of the Joint Committee on Interstate and Foreign Commerce from November 1916 through 1917. Created as a result of Wilson's 1915 message to Congress and his subsequent aid for implementing legislation, the Congressional committee was authorized by Congress in July 1916, with Senator Francis G. Newlands as chairman. At the hearings, Alfred P. Thom, the counsel of the Executives' Advisory Committee, delivered the major railroad statement. Although the hearings covered a wide range of topics, from rates to government ownership, Thom stressed that "The railroads believe that the first step is for the Federal Government to take exclusive control of these instrumentalities of interstate commerce," not merely to regulate the railroads but to protect them.[44] Using the new banking system as the ideal model, Thom urged the creation of a series of regional commissions, the compulsory federal incorporation of all railroads, Commission control of minimum as well as maximum rates, and exclusive federal supervision of stock and bond issues as a means of protecting them from the vicious state regulatory sys-

[43] *Ibid.*; *Resolution of the Massachusetts Board of Trade*, December 28, 1916 (multilithed); *New York Times*, September 14, 1916; Wilson to Underwood, March 28, 1916, as quoted in *New York Sun*, March 30, 1916.

[44] U.S. Congress, Joint Committee on Interstate Commerce, *Hearings*, 64:1, p. 48. Also see Arthur B. Darling, ed., *The Public Papers of Francis G. Newlands* (Boston, 1932), II, 373-393.

tem.[45] This theme of attacking "generally dangerous and possibly disastrous" state regulation was stressed by railroad men in subsequent testimony.[46] Relief could come only from the national government.

The increasing railroad success in winning important new public and political support during the presidency of Wilson was due to two factors. One was their growing sophistication in the area of public relations and their conscious development of skills in this field; another, and more important, was the sympathetic attitude of Woodrow Wilson.

The public relations program of the railroads was aided by an increasingly friendly contact between railroad executives and business and merchant groups—the major source of potential opposition—and by the development of formal public relations departments. Ivy Lee, perhaps the most famous publicist of the period, was hired by the Pennsylvania Railroad to cultivate the proper "corporate image," and Howard Elliott of the Northern Pacific carried on a very extensive program throughout his territory. The B. & O. hired J. Hampton Baumgartner, whose simple philosophy was "this is the age in which publicity accomplishes things," to administer their program. Baumgartner, who warned the Railway Executives' Advisory Committee that "It is injudicious to make heavy inroads into advertising expense in the interest of economy," carried on a major campaign, with continuous releases and stories, to reach the 685 papers in the area served by the B. & O.[47] The B. & O., Baumgartner told the Virginia Press Association in mid-1913, wants "to bring about a friendly understanding of the problems of

[45] *Ibid.*, pp. 76-81, 89-91, 98-100, 104.
[46] *Ibid.*, pp. 658, 893-895.
[47] J. Hampton Baumgartner, *Address Before the Conference of Railway Executives' Advisory Committee, Washington, May 27, 1916* (n.p., n.d.), pp. 5-6; J. Hampton Baumgartner, *Address Before the Virginia Press Association, June 13, 1913* (n.p., 1913), p. 2.

business through your cooperation."[48] And it was through their subsequent success in obtaining such cooperation in all areas of the country that the railroads began neutralizing shipper and newspaper opposition.

The World War

The First World War was to endow the federal government with the wide-reaching powers capable of solving the railroad problem from the point of view of the railroads. But were there no desire on the part of the Administration and the President to utilize those powers, the subsequent extension of federal control over the railroad system, and its particular form, would undoubtedly have been different. In August 1916, with the threatened strike of railroad employees, Wilson called for the enlargement and reorganization of the I.C.C. along the essential lines laid down at the time by the Railroad Executives' Committee, as well as a rate advance to cover the cost of higher wages.[49] Despite these concessions, from August 1916 to March 1917 there was a disagreement between the railroads and Wilson over the Adamson Act, providing for an eight-hour day for railroad workers; this was the major blemish on their amicable relations during the Wilson presidency. But this obstacle was quickly overcome, to the benefit of the railroads, if only because Wilson wished to mend his political fences before the impending presidential election. On September 23, he emphatically proclaimed his neutrality in the conflict between rail workers and employers, and counseled mutual love. Wilson delighted railroad executives by appointing General George W. Goethals and two equally acceptable members to the three-man commmis-

---

[48] Baumgartner, *Address Before the Virginia Press Association*, p. 3. Also see Willard, *Address Before the American Newspapers Publishers Association*, p. 2.

[49] Woodrow Wilson, *Messages and Papers of the Presidents, March 4, 1913, to March 4, 1917* (New York, 1917), pp. 8147-8148.

sion to study the effects of the eight-hour law—and recommend changes to the President and Congress—authorized by the Adamson Act. Frank Trumbull had brought to Colonel House's attention General Goethals, who had managed to turn an eight-hour railroad law in the Panama Canal Zone into a conservative measure fully acceptable to the railroad leaders.

Wilson repeated his demand for a stronger I.C.C. in his December message to Congress, and asked for the power to take over the railroads in the event of war.[50] At the same time, the I.C.C. requested that all existing rates and regulations be legalized as "just and reasonable" so that they could proceed in the future with a clean slate—a unique assumption that Congress failed to act upon. But Congress did authorize, in August 1917, an enlargement of the Commission from seven to nine men, and granted the Commission the power to split itself into as many regional groups as might be necessary, with a minimum of three members in each; their decisions were to be subject to review only by the full Commission. In April and May 1917, the railroad system was organized into the Railroads' War Board, and, in December, McAdoo was appointed Director General of the railroads. The anti-trust and anti-pooling laws were effectively suspended in order to bring the railroad system into a state of maximum coordination. The Railroad Administration created seven major regions, and appointed a railroad man to head each region. Although each railroad was assigned a federal officer to work alongside the private executives, the large majority of these "federal men" were from the railroads themselves. Even McAdoo's successor, Walker D. Hines, was an old rail-

[50] *Ibid.*, pp. 8183-8184; *Public Papers of Woodrow Wilson*, IV, 301-307; Frank Trumbull to Edward M. House, September 1, 1916, Edward M. House Papers; *Railway Age Gazette*, LXI (October 13, 1916), 649-650.

road president.[51] And the federal government guaranteed the railroads a return as great as the average profit they had received between June 1914 and June 1917, plus a sufficient allowance for maintenance and depreciation. The direct cost of the operation to the government was well over one billion dollars invested in railroad securities.[52]

The Federal Railroad Control Act of March 1918, passed at the request of President Wilson, granted a virtually absolute rate-making power to the new federal Railroad Administration, with review limited only to the I.C.C. Although the Commission had refused to grant an across-the-board 15 per cent rate increase to the railroads in the spring of 1917, it did allow a considerable number of rates to be raised in various regions over the course of the year. But in May 1918, without prolonged hearings, the Railroad Administration announced a general 25 per cent freight rate increase, with substantial additional increases for passenger fares—an undebated move that evoked much admiration from the railroads for its efficiency. Freight revenue per ton mile increased from .72 cents in 1916, around which point it had hovered for nearly two decades, to 1.07 cents in 1920. Freight revenue per ton increased from $1.96 in 1916 to $3.24 in 1920, and operating revenues from $3,691 million to $6,310 million.

On February 28, 1920, the day before the railroads were returned to private control, they obtained the fa-

[51] Interstate Commerce Commission, *Thirtieth Annual Report, December 1, 1916* (Washington, 1916), p. 92; *Thirty-First Annual Report, December 1, 1917* (Washington, 1917), pp. 59-61; Walker, D. Hines, *War History of American Railroads* (New Haven, 1928), chap. III, gives much detail on railroad control of the Railroad Administration.

[52] William J. Cunningham, *American Railroads: Government Control and Reconstruction Policies* (Chicago, 1922), pp. 34-35; Frank H. Dixon, *Railroads and Government, 1910-1921* (New York, 1922), p. 206, says the cost was nearly $2 billion; "Making the Railroads a Single Wartime System," *Analist*, x (December 3, 1917), 707-708.

mous Transportation Act of 1920. A six-month profit guaranty agreement poured an additional $530 million of federal funds into railroad coffers.[53] The Transportation Act represents the final victory of the railroads under the Wilson Administration, and was the logical culmination of their more than forty years of agitation and education for comprehensive federal railroad regulation designed to provide rationalization and stability to the industry. Moreover, the Interstate Commerce Commission embarked even more unequivocally on a course that was to win increasingly for it the reputation of being the shield of the railroads against the public in the 1920's.[54] The act of 1920 embodied many of the specific proposals advocated by the Railway Executives' Advisory Committee and most of the major general regulatory goals of railroads since the inception of the first federal law. Albert Fink would have been very gratified. The act permitted pooling, exempted railroads from the Clayton Act, and positively ordered the Commission "to prepare and adopt a plan for the consolidation of the railway properties . . . into a limited number of systems." It extended the control of the Commission, whose membership was enlarged to eleven, over railroad security issues. The Commission formally recognized the principle of the Five Percent Case as its guide to rate policy, and took the responsibility of assuring the railroads of returns on their investments neither in excess nor below fair standards determined primarily by property valuations. It was given the power to establish minimum rates and to assure, by a complex revolving fund scheme, that a return of 5 1/2 to 6 per cent would become the standard of railroad prosperity. The power of the federal government

[53] Hines, *War History of American Railroads*, p. 223.
[54] E. Pendleton Herring, *Public Administration and the Public Interest* (New York, 1936), chap. XII; see *Railway Review*, LXVI (April 10, 1920), 611-612, for Prouty's militant defense of this principle and the concept of the Five Percent decision.

over state regulatory commissions and rulings was made comprehensive and absolute if questions of discrimination or preferences were involved. The rate-making powers of the states were left in a shambles.[55]

The automobile and trucking industries, and not shippers or radical state legislatures, were to nullify the benefits to the railroads of the Transportation Act. Nothing could save the railroads from the impact of the revolution in American transportation that was beginning to roll off the assembly lines of Detroit.

[55] Dixon, *Railroads and Government*, chaps. XV-XXIII, is the best analysis. Also see I. L. Sharfman, *The Interstate Commerce Commission* (New York, 1931-1937), I, 183ff.; Robert E. Cushman, *The Independent Regulatory Commissions* (New York, 1941), pp. 115-129; U.S. Attorney General's National Committee to Study the Antitrust Laws, *Report, March 31, 1955* (Washington, 1955), p. 263.

CONCLUSION

THE conventional interpretation of federal railroad regulation warrants a radical reappraisal, for the motives and consequences of regulation have been misunderstood. Historians have overlooked all-too-many crucial factors. The railroad industry continued to remain operationally competitive despite the merger and consolidation movement of the 1890's led by J. P. Morgan. Rates were not affected by mergers, because at the very time that vast railroad systems were being tied together there were many smaller, successfully run companies remaining, and new entries meant that the absolute number of operating railroads was actually to increase until 1907. Despite the vast capital resources available to him, Morgan was never able to fulfill his ambition of consolidating regional railroad systems to the extent necessary to control the rates of the area, in large part because the managerial abilities of Morgan's assistants proved to be inadequate and often incompetent. Pooling efforts, although technically illegal, failed not because of the law but because of the inability of dozens of important railroads in the major regions to act in a concerted, cooperative manner for sustained periods.

The railroads realized that they needed the protection of the federal government, and they became the leading advocates of federal regulation on their own terms. The principle of federal railroad regulation per se was accepted by an important segment of the railroad community by 1880, and the relative importance of this group increased gradually over the period until, by 1916, it included the vast majority of railroad men interested enough to leave some record of their views. The first

major incident stimulating railroad support for federal
regulation of railroads was the Great Strike of 1877,
which came on the heels of the failure of the first efforts
to create a voluntary pool structure. The strike of 1877
pointed to the danger of attacks on the railroads, not
merely from the workers—whose threats were greatly
exaggerated by the railroads at the time—but from the
states and the Granger movement. The hostility of workers and farmers, many of whom controlled state politics,
pointed to the possibility of local attacks which threatened to dislocate railroad systems that were regional, if
not national, in their scope. Federal railroad regulation
appeared to many railroad leaders as a safe shield behind which to hide from the consequences of local democracy, as well as a means of solving their own internal
problems. In the spectrum of viewpoints on regulation,
the railroads, especially after 1900, took their stand with
the extreme nationalists, and were the leading advocates
of this position. If the public could be led in a direction
compatible with their interests, many railroad men realized, much more serious attacks could be avoided in the
future.

The federal regulation of railroads from 1887 until
1916 did not disappoint the American railroad industry.
If railroad leaders often disagreed on the details—disagreements that extended into their own ranks on any
specific issue—the railroads nevertheless supported the
basic principle and institution of federal regulation. And,
as we have seen, they enthusiastically worked for its extension and for the supremacy of federal regulation over
the states. Rate regulation was guided by the premise
that the railroads were to receive a reasonable profit and,
in effect, were to be protected from the risks and mis-
fortunes inherent in the official ideology and economic
value system of the status quo. Under the benevolent
supervision of the Interstate Commerce Commission, the

conditions of the industry improved sharply, as internecine competition was replaced by rate maintenance and
the elimination of rebates, and as the railroad system
received protection from the attacks of both the states
and powerful shippers. The percentage of railroad stock
paying dividends increased from 39 per cent in 1888 to
67 per cent in 1910, and the average rate of dividends
on all stock rose from 2.1 per cent to 5 per cent over the
same period.[1] If the federal regulation of railroads was
only partially responsible for this improved performance,
the Five Percent decision of 1914 formalized the federal
government's responsibility to maintain private profit,
and the Transportation Act of 1920 determined a level
of profit which had been the cherished and usually un-
attained goal of the railroads since the 1870's.

From its inception, the Interstate Commerce Commission entered into a condition of dependency on the railroads, and the railroads quickly began relying on the
Commission as a means of attaining their own ends.
Given the shortcomings of the existing law until 1903,
this mutual reliance was both natural and inevitable.
Railroad efforts to circumvent the inadequacies of the
existing law and solve internal, competitive problems by
voluntary means involved the Interstate Commerce Commission to a major extent. The rise of the Interstate
Commerce Law Association in 1889 was merely an attempt to create voluntary means of enforcing the basic
aims of the law—or at least so the railroads claimed. In
1899, the Commission also was drawn into a similar
effort. Well before the end of the century the I.C.C. had
reached that stage, described in the writings of political
scientists dealing with regulatory commissions in later
periods, in which its primary function was to minister to
the needs of the industry which it was ostensibly to regu-

---

[1] Interstate Commerce Commission, *Statistics of Railways in the
United States, 1916* (Washington, 1918), p. 35.

late on behalf of an amorphous, implicitly classless, public interest.[2]

That the Commission regarded the voluntary projects of the railroads with solicitude, or sympathized with them when the Supreme Court in 1897 and 1898 undercut the basis of any future projects, was the logical outcome of the key personnel running the Commission during its early years. Indeed, it is not unreasonable to assert that the primary commitment of the major directors of Commission policy was essentially pro-railroad. Certainly Thomas Cooley can be said to qualify fully for this appellation, and Martin Knapp was only slightly more restrained in his advocacy of positions identical to those of the majority of the railroads. The free interpretation of the law, the creation of informal procedures which prejudiced the rights of shippers or were administered in favor of the railroads, the outspoken public defense of pooling and legislative measures identical or nearly identical to those called for by the railroads, all suggest that the Interstate Commerce Commission was a failure from the shipper's viewpoint, and that much of the seemingly ineffective role of the Commission until 1903 was a matter of self-choice. The development after 1900 of a minority of articulate spokesmen who did not always advocate the railroad position within the Commission, was a relatively short-lived phenomenon. Wilson, in any event, turned the tide in 1914 decisively against the possibility of a genuinely neutral Commission. Ultimately, however, the very nature of the Commission concept was not conducive to the protection of the small shipper or the general consumer. Large shippers were protected by rebates

2 See Samuel P. Huntington, *Clientalism: A Study in Administrative Politics* (Unpublished Ph.D. thesis, Harvard University, 1950), chap. 5; Marver H. Bernstein, *Regulating Business by Independent Commission* (Princeton, 1955), *passim*; James M. Landis, *Report on Regulatory Agencies to the President-Elect.* December, 1960 [published by U.S. Senate, Committee on the Judiciary, 86th Cong., 2d Sess., 1960], pp. 71-72.

or their ability to pass increased freight costs on to the consumer in the form of higher prices. The small shipper could not afford to file a formal complaint against the railroad, and was discouraged by the Commission's mediation offices from doing so. The consumer, for the most part, was left entirely helpless by the existing structure, and the Commission was ultimately an affair of consequence only to businessmen. From this viewpoint, its major function was to determine the division of business profits, not to redress the basic distribution of income, much less correct the economic imbalance that was created by the rise of a privately controlled industrial structure. Within its assumption that its basic responsibility was to the existing economic order—no one should be surprised that there was no desire by anyone to replace the fundamental system—the I.C.C. was aligned, for the most part, with the railroads.

The direction of federal regulation was not the responsibility merely of a sympathetic Commission, however. Theodore Roosevelt, whose presidency witnessed more major railroad legislation than any other, was deeply committed to the obligation of the national government to protect the railroads, not merely from the public but from themselves. He reiterated the proposition that, if modest and reasonable railroad legislation were not forthcoming, government ownership or more extreme legislation would be called for by the public. But in assigning himself the role of protector of the railroads from radicalism, he acted not merely because he was conservative but because he also accepted a theory of the general welfare that assumed, as he stated in his 1905 message to Congress, that the health of the railroad industry in the hands of its present owners would also maximize the general prosperity of the entire nation. Again and again Roosevelt repeated the assurance that he had no desire to attack the vital interests of the honest railroad men, and he frequently attacked the strongly anti-railroad actions of the states and the muckrakers. Illustrating the concept of social justice described by Anatole France's tale of the equal right of the poor man and rich man in a democracy to sleep under a bridge at night, Roosevelt called for "as much a square deal for the rich man as for the poor man." In the final analysis, Roosevelt was not interested in redressing the balance of economic power within the existing society, but in imposing vague codes of moralistic conduct on railroad men which, in their concrete implications, hardly affected the large majority of railroads in any tangible manner. Quite the contrary, insofar as his railroad program was specific, and those specifics were often formulated by Knox, Cassatt, Lodge, and other conservatives, Roosevelt advocated measures close to the hearts of many important railroad men. And insofar as Roosevelt proposed the domination of the federal government over the regulatory apparatus, which later bloomed into the New Nationalism, it can also be said that he incidentally supported, for his own reasons, the desire of the railroads for centralized federal regulation.

Of greater importance, Roosevelt failed to attack the vital interests of the railroads on any significant count, and in large part this failure was an inevitable consequence of his theory of economic development and his fundamental acceptance of the proposition that the general welfare would be best served by aiding the interests of honest, decent railroads. Roosevelt, in brief, remained a conservative on railroad legislation at least insofar as the basic status of the railroads was concerned, and never damaged, and never sought to damage, their vital interests as he or the railroads interpreted them. Centralized federal regulation was the program of conservatism, and the means of protecting the railroads from the less controllable states. And it is for this reason that the railroads, for the most part, supported Roosevelt and found they could work with him to their mutual satisfaction.

Neither Roosevelt, Taft, nor Wilson ever used regulation to attack the essential interests of the railroads, and they never failed to be solicitous of the good will of the railroads. This continuity of executive policy from 1900 to 1916 is the pervasive reality in federal railroad regulation. In this respect, there was no fundamental difference on any important particulars between the New Freedom and the New Nationalism. Both left the Commission under conservative domination, and both Roosevelt and Wilson repeatedly consulted with railroad men when considering action or legislation affecting their vital welfare. In most instances the railroad men were allowed to define the boundaries, and even many of the details of proposed legislation.

It is especially ironic, however, that the New Freedom became the logical culmination of the centralist theory of the New Nationalism. Wilson, more than any other President, responded sympathetically to the call of railroad leaders for comprehensive federal domination of railroad regulation, and it was under the New Freedom that the ultimate consolidation of federal control took place. Operationally, then, the continuity between the Square Deal or New Nationalism and the New Freedom is direct. The ideological intonations in election speeches, much exaggerated by historians, must be forgotten. Wilson was an advocate of the same centralized federal control of the railroads as were the leading railroad executives. The President was influenced directly by the railroads, and responded to their efforts generously; he never allowed his allegedly Jeffersonian sympathies on states' rights to influence his actions.

The basic similarity of the New Nationalism, the New Freedom, and the program of the railroads for federal control and domination points to what this writer feels to be the major significance of railroad regulation for an understanding of progressivism. Government control, per se, is not a sufficient criterion of progressivism, if by that term we mean an effort to redress the balance of economic power existing in society and to make the dominant economic forces susceptible to the control and welfare of the large majority of the people. This definition, quite properly, is the one assumed by most historians to describe progressivism. But the phenomenon described in this study was not an effort to democratize the economy via political means, but a movement to establish stability and control within the railroad industry so that railroads could prosper without the fearful consequences of cutthroat competition. It was, in fact, an effort to use political means to solve economic problems while maintaining the essential theory of social priorities and values of a capitalist economy. National regulation of the railroads, from 1887 until 1916, was an attempt to create a political capitalism for the sake of the railroads, and the railroads supported it for precisely this reason. Indeed, they were the most crucial factor behind the federal regulation of the railroads. And although it was necessary to pay lip service in political rhetoric to the desire to enhance and protect the general public welfare, at least Roosevelt explicitly made it clear that the public welfare would be served by the government concerning itself first with the welfare of the honest railroads. As in all other areas of the economy, the public welfare would be served by the automatic workings of the economy. In this respect, the value system and distribution theory of laissez-faire were accepted by Roosevelt, Taft, and Wilson, but important exceptions were made that allowed the mechanics of the economic machinery to be tampered with in such a way as to prevent its negative consequences to special industries— the railroads in this case—while preserving the existing social and economic relationships inherent in a capitalist economy.

If one removes the traditionally positive and democratic implications from the historians' usual definition of progressivism, progressivism in operational reality becomes a political capitalism whereby important economic interests utilize the power of the federal government to solve internal economic problems which could not otherwise be solved by voluntary or non-political means. In effect, the economy was brought to a rationalized status by achieving through political means those economic ends once thought to be attainable by automatic economic mechanisms. This, in fact, is the central implication of the federal regulation of railroads, a movement supported and given dynamism by an increasingly important sector of the railroads. In this respect, federal railroad regulation was the first of many successful efforts to create rationalization and stability in the economy by political means. The goal of these efforts was not progressivism in the traditional sense, as historians have commonly interpreted that term, but a political capitalism which solved the internal problems of an industry and protected it from the attacks of a potentially democratic society.

BIBLIOGRAPHY

THE following bibliography consists exclusively of materials cited in the footnotes, and does not include a considerable body of additional related materials on railroads, business, and politics examined during the course of research. A number of items cited in the footnotes are not cited here. These consist of newspaper clippings gathered from a wide variety of newspapers during the period 1901-1908, and conveniently centralized in a massive collection of scrapbooks in the Theodore Roosevelt Room, Harvard College Library. Also excluded are unsigned editorial statements and news items from such railroad journals as the *Railway World*, *Railroad Gazette*, *Railway Review*, *Railway and Engineering Review*, and other railroad and general periodicals, as well as the *Congressional Record*.

The collections of printed railroad materials in the libraries of Harvard University, the Bureau of Railway Economics in Washington, and the Interstate Commerce Commission in Washington were of primary importance. Many of these bulletins, pamphlets, and proceedings are the last remaining copies in existence.

Manuscript Collections

Charles Francis Adams, Jr., Papers, Massachusetts Historical Society

Nelson Aldrich Papers, Library of Congress

Charles J. Bonaparte Papers, Library of Congress

Bureau of Railway Economics Library

Andrew Carnegie Papers, Library of Congress

U.S. Commerce Court Records (Record Group 172), National Archives

Stephen B. Elkins Papers, West Virginia Collection, West Virginia University Library

James R. Garfield Papers, Library of Congress

Henry Lee Higginson Papers, Baker Library, Harvard Business School

Edward M. House Papers, Yale University Library

U.S. House of Representatives Records (Record Group 233), National Archives

U.S. Interstate Commerce Commission General Records, 1887-1900, General Services Administration Depot, Springfield, Virginia

U.S. Interstate Commerce Commission Files, I.C.C. Building, Washington

U.S. Interstate Commerce Commission Library, I.C.C. Building, Washington

Philander Knox Papers, Library of Congress

John D. Long Papers, Massachusetts Historical Society

James R. Mann Papers, Library of Congress

William H. Moody Papers, Library of Congress

Richard Olney Papers, Library of Congress

George W. Perkins Papers, Columbia University Library

Henry Pringle Notes on William Howard Taft, Theodore Roosevelt Room, Harvard College Library

Henry Seligman Papers, Baker Library, Harvard Business School

U.S. Senate Records (Record Group 46), National Archives

William Howard Taft Papers, Library of Congress

Henry Villard Papers, Houghton Library, Harvard University

Woodrow Wilson Papers, Library of Congress

Books

Beard, Charles A. and Mary, *The Rise of American Civilization.* 2 v. New York, 1934.

Benson, Lee, *Merchants, Farmers, and Railroads: Railroad Regulation and New York Politics, 1850-1887*. Cambridge, 1955.

Bernstein, Marver H., *Regulating Business by Independent Commission*. Princeton, 1955.

Blum, John Morton, *The Republican Roosevelt*. Cambridge, 1954.

Brandeis, Louis, *Other People's Money—And How the Bankers Use It*. 2nd edn. New York, 1932.

Bruce, Robert V., *1877: Year of Violence*. Indianapolis, 1959.

Buck, Solon Justus, *The Granger Movement, 1870-1880*. Cambridge, 1913.

Burgess, George H., and Miles C. Kennedy, *Centennial History of the Pennsylvania Railroad Company, 1846-1946*. Philadelphia, 1949.

Campbell, E. G., *The Reorganization of the American Railroad System, 1893-1900*. New York, 1938.

Cleveland, Grover, *Letters of Grover Cleveland, 1850-1908*. Allan Nevins, ed. Boston, 1933.

Cochran, Thomas C., *Railroad Leaders, 1845-1890*. Cambridge, 1953.

Coolidge, Louis A., *Orville H. Platt*. New York, 1910.

Cullom, Shelby M., *Fifty Years of Public Service*. Chicago, 1911.

Cunningham, William J., *American Railroads: Government Control and Reconstruction Policies*. Chicago, 1922.

Cushman, Robert E., *The Independent Regulatory Commissions*. New York, 1941.

Daggett, Stuart, *Railroad Reorganization*. Boston, 1908.

Depew, Chauncey M., *My Memories of Eighty Years*. New York, 1922.

Dixon, Frank Haigh, *Railroads and Government: Their Relations in the United States, 1910-1921*. New York, 1922.

Faulkner, Harold U., *The Decline of Laissez Faire, 1897-1917*. New York, 1951.

———, *The Quest for Social Justice, 1898-1914*. New York, 1931.

Fink, Henry, *Regulation of Railway Rates on Interstate Freight Traffic*. New York, 1905.

Foord, John, *The Life and Public Services of Simon Sterne*. London, 1903.

Foraker, Joseph Benson, *Notes of a Busy Life*. 2 v. Cincinnati, 1917.

Garraty, John A., *Henry Cabot Lodge*. New York, 1953.

Goodrich, Carter, *Government Promotion of American Canals and Railroads, 1800-1890*. New York, 1960.

Grodinsky, Julius, *The Iowa Pool: A Study in Railroad Competition, 1870-84*. Chicago, 1950.

———, *Jay Gould: His Business Career, 1867-92*. Philadelphia, 1957.

———, *Transcontinental Railway Strategy, 1869-1893*. Philadelphia, 1962.

Hammond, M. B., *Railway Rate Theories of the Interstate Commerce Commission*. Cambridge, 1911.

Hechler, Kenneth W., *Insurgency: Personalities and Politics of the Taft Era*. New York, 1940.

Hedges, James Blaine, *Henry Villard and the Railways of the Northwest*. New Haven, 1930.

Hendrick, Burton J., *The Life of Andrew Carnegie*. 2 v. Garden City, N.Y., 1932.

Herring, E. Pendleton, *Public Administration and the Public Interest*. New York, 1936.

Hines, Walker D., *War History of American Railroads*. New Haven, 1928.

Hofstadter, Richard, *The Age of Reform: From Bryan to F. D. R.* New York, 1955.

House, Edward M., *The Intimate Papers of Colonel House*. Charles Seymour, ed. v. i. Boston, 1926.

Hultgren, Thor, *American Transportation in Prosperity and Depression*. New York, 1948.

Jones, Eliot, *The Anthracite Coal Combination in the United States*. Cambridge, 1914.

Kennan, George, *E. H. Harriman*. 2 v. Boston, 1922.

Kirkland, Edward Chase, *Men, Cities, and Transportation: A Study in New England History, 1820-1900*. 2 v. Cambridge, 1948.

La Follette, Belle Case, and Fola La Follette, *Robert M. La Follette*. 2 v. New York, 1953.

La Follette, Robert M., *La Follette's Autobiography*. Madison, Wis., 1913.

Lambert, Oscar Doane, *Stephen Benton Elkins*. Pittsburgh, 1955.

Landis, James M., *Report on Regulatory Agencies to the President-Elect*. December, 1960. Washington, 1960.

Langstroth, Charles S., and Wilson Stilz, *Railway Co-operation*. Philadelphia, 1899.

Link, Arthur S., *Wilson: The New Freedom*. Princeton, 1956.

Meyer, Balthasar Henry, *Railway Legislation in the United States*. New York, 1903.

Mowry, George E., *The Era of Theodore Roosevelt, 1900-1912*. New York, 1958.

———, *Theodore Roosevelt and the Progressive Movement*. Madison, Wis., 1946.

Myers, Gustavus, *History of the Great American Fortunes*. New York, 1937 [?].

Nadworny, Milton J., *Scientific Management and the Unions, 1900-1932*. Cambridge, 1955.

Nevins, Allan, *John D. Rockefeller: The Heroic Age of American Enterprise*. 2 v. New York, 1940.

Newlands, Francis G., *The Public Papers of Francis G. Newlands*. Arthur B. Darling, ed. 2 v. Boston, 1932.

Paul, Arnold M., *Conservative Crisis and the Rule of*

Law: Attitudes of Bar and Bench, 1887-1895. Ithaca, N.Y., 1960.

Peirce, E. B., *Digest of Decisions of the Courts and Interstate Commerce Commission, 1887 to 1908.* Chicago, 1908.

Reynolds, George G., *The Distribution of Power to Regulate Interstate Carriers Between the Nation and the States.* New York, 1928.

Rhodes, James Ford, *History of the United States, 1850-1896.* New York, 1920.

Ripley, William Z., *Railroads: Finance and Organization.* New York, 1915.

———, *Railroads: Rates and Regulation.* New York, 1912.

Roosevelt, Theodore, *The Letters of Theodore Roosevelt.* Elting E. Morison, ed. 8 v. Cambridge, 1951-54.

———, *Messages and Papers of the Presidents, September 14, 1901, to March 4, 1909.* New York, n.d.

Satterlee, Herbert L., *J. Pierpont Morgan: An Intimate Portrait.* New York, 1939.

Schiff, Jacob H., *Jacob H. Schiff: His Life and Letters.* Cyrus Adler, ed. 2 v. Garden City, N.Y., 1928.

Sharfman, I. L., *The Interstate Commerce Commission.* 4 v. New York, 1931-37.

Steffens, Lincoln, *Autobiography.* New York, 1931.

Stephenson, Nathaniel, *Nelson W. Aldrich: A Leader in American Politics.* New York, 1930.

Sterne, Simon, *Railways in the United States.* Preface by "M. S. S." New York, 1912.

Stickney, A. B., *The Railway Problem.* St. Paul, 1891.

Taft, William Howard, *Messages and Papers of the Presidents, March 4, 1909 to March 4, 1913.* New York, n.d.

———, *Presidential Addresses and Speeches.* v. 1. New York, 1910.

Tarbell, Ida M., *The History of the Standard Oil Company*. 2 v. New York, 1904.

———, *The Nationalizing of Business, 1878-1898*. New York, 1936.

Taylor, George Rogers, and Irene D. Neu, *The American Railroad Network, 1861-1890*. Cambridge, 1956.

Walters, Everett, *Joseph Benson Foraker: An Uncompromising Republican*. Columbus, 1948.

Wiebe, Robert H., *Businessmen and Reform: A Study of the Progressive Movement*. Cambridge, 1962.

Wilson, Woodrow, *Messages and Papers of the Presidents, March 4, 1913, to March 4, 1917*. New York, 1917.

———, *The Public Papers of Woodrow Wilson*. Ray Stannard Baker and William E. Dodd, eds. v. iii. New York, 1926.

Public Documents

Pennsylvania Senate and House of Representatives, *Report of the Committee Appointed to Investigate the Railroad Riots of July, 1877, May 23, 1878*. Harrisburg, 1878.

U.S. Attorney General's National Committee to Study the Anti-trust Laws, *Report, March 31, 1955*. Washington, 1955.

U.S. Bureau of the Census, *Historical Statistics of the United States, Colonial Times to 1957*. Washington, 1960.

U.S. v. The New York, New Haven & Hartford RR Co., Original Petition [July, 1914] in the District Court of the United States, Southern District of New York. Washington, 1914.

U.S. Industrial Commission, *Report of the Industrial Commission on Transportation*. v. iv. Washington, 1900.

———, *Report of the Industrial Commission on Transportation.* v. IX. Washington, 1901.

———, *Final Report.* House Doc. No. 380, 57th Cong., 2d Sess. v. XIX. Washington, 1902.

U.S. Interstate Commerce Commission, *Conference Rulings of the Commission, April 1, 1911.* Washington, 1911.

———, *Evidence Taken . . . In the Matter of Proposed Advances in Freight Rates by Carriers, August to December, 1910.* 10 v. Washington, 1911. Also printed as Senate Doc. No. 725, 61:3.

———, *Intercorporate Relationships of Railways in the United States as of June 30, 1906.* Washington, 1908.

———, *New York, New Haven & Hartford Railroad Co., Evidence . . . Relative to . . . Financial Transactions. . . .* 2 v. Washington, 1914. Also printed as Senate Doc. No. 543, 63:2.

———, *Railways in the United States in 1902: A Forty-Year Review of Changes in Freight Tariffs.* Washington, 1903.

———, *First Annual Report, December 1, 1887.* Washington, 1887.

———, *Fourth Annual Report, December 1, 1890.* Washington, 1890.

———, *Sixth Annual Report, December 1, 1892.* Washington, 1892.

———, *Seventh Annual Report, December 1, 1893.* Washington, 1893.

———, *Eighth Annual Report, December 1, 1894.* Washington, 1894.

———, *Ninth Annual Report, December 1, 1895.* Washington, 1896.

———, *Eleventh Annual Report, December 6, 1897.* Washington, 1897.

———, *Twelfth Annual Report, January 11, 1899.* Washington, 1899.

———, *Thirteenth Annual Report, January 15, 1900.* Washington, 1900.

———, *Eighteenth Annual Report, December 19, 1904.* Washington, 1904.

———, *Twenty-First Annual Report, December 27, 1907.* Washington, 1907.

———, *Twenty-Third Annual Report, December 21, 1909.* Washington, 1910.

———, *Twenty-Fourth Annual Report, December 21, 1910.* Washington, 1911.

———, *Twenty-Fifth Annual Report, December 30, 1911.* Washington, 1912.

———, *Thirtieth Annual Report, December 1, 1916.* Washington, 1916.

———, *Thirty-First Annual Report, December 1, 1917.* Washington, 1917.

———, *Statistics of Railways in the United States, 1900.* Washington, 1901.

———, *Statistics of Railways in the United States, 1916.* Washington, 1918.

———, *Statistics of Railways in the United States, 1930.* Washington, 1932.

U.S. Congress, Joint Committee on Interstate and Foreign Commerce, *Interstate and Foreign Transportation, Hearings,* 64th Cong., 1st Sess. [November, 1916-November, 1917] Washington, 1917.

U.S. House of Representatives, *Charges Filed Against Judge Robert W. Archbald.* 62d Cong., 2d Sess. [Letter from William H. Taft to House of Representatives, May 3, 1912] Washington, 1912.

———, *Report of the Railroads Securities Commission to the President.* House Doc. No. 256, 62d Cong., 2d Sess., December 11, 1911. Washington, 1911.

U.S. House of Representatives, Committee on Commerce, *Arguments and Statements*. House Misc. Doc. No. 55, 47th Cong., 1st Sess., February 21-March 28, 1882. Washington, 1882.

———, *Arguments and Statements*. 48th Cong., 1st Sess., January, 1884. Washington, 1884.

U.S. House of Representatives, Committee on Interstate and Foreign Commerce, *Hearings on . . . H.R. 146, 273. . . .* 57th Cong., 1st Sess., April, 1902. Washington, 1902.

———, *Hearings*, House Doc. No. 422, 58th Cong., 3d Sess. [December, 1904-January, 1905] Washington, 1905.

———, *Hearings*, 61st Cong., 2d Sess. [January-February, 1910] Washington, 1910.

———, *Hearings*, 62d Cong., 2d Sess. [July-August, 1912] Washington, 1912.

U.S. House of Representatives, Committee on the Judiciary, *Jurisdiction of Commerce Court—Its Enlargement, Hearings*. 63d Cong., 1st Sess., June 21, 1913. Washington, 1913.

U.S. Senate, Senate Doc. No. 39, 54th Cong., 1st Sess., December 24, 1895. Washington, 1895.

———, Senate Doc. No. 287, 54th Cong., 1st Sess., May 25, 1896. Washington, 1896.

———, *Railway Rates and Charges, Etc*. Senate Doc. No. 259, 55th Cong., 2d Sess., May 6, 1898. Washington, 1898.

———, Senate Doc. No. 180, 59th Cong., 1st Sess. Washington, 1905.

———, *Rate Legislation*. Senate Doc. No. 249, 59th Cong., 1st Sess., March 5, 1906. Washington, 1906.

———, Senate Doc. No. 292, 59th Cong., 1st Sess., March 28, 1906. Washington, 1906.

———, Senate Doc. No. 394, 59th Cong., 1st Sess., April 21, 1906. Washington, 1906.

———, *Railroad Rate Legislation: Views of the Mi-*

nority. Senate Report 1242, Part 2, 59th Cong., 1st Sess., June 28, 1906. Washington, 1906.

———, *Proceedings of the United States Senate and the House of Representatives in the Trial of Impeachment of Robert W. Archbald.* Senate Doc. No. 1140, 62d Cong., 3d Sess. Washington, 1913.

U.S. Senate, Committee on Interstate Commerce, *Hearings . . . Re S. 892.* 52d Cong., 1st Sess. [February, 1892] Washington, 1892.

———, *Hearings on S. 3577.* Senate Misc. Doc. No. 126, 53d Cong., 3d Sess., December 14, 1892. Washington, 1892.

———, *Hearings . . . On S. 1534.* February-March, 1894, in Senate Doc. No. 39, 55th Cong., 1st Sess., April 15, 1897. Washington, 1897.

———, *Hearings . . . On Senate Bill No. 3354.* 55th Cong., 2d Sess., March, 1898. Washington, 1898.

———, *Hearings on S. 1439.* 56th Cong., 1st Sess., January, 1900. Washington, 1900.

———, *Hearings, Railway Freight Rates and Pooling.* 57th Cong., 1st Sess. [February-March, 1902] Washington, 1902.

———, *Hearings, Regulation of Railway Rates.* Senate Doc. No. 243, 59th Cong., 1st Sess. [December, 1904-May, 1905] Washington, 1906.

———, Senate Report No. 933, 60th Cong., 2d Sess., February 9, 1909. Washington, 1909.

———, *Hearings . . . On S. 3776 and S. 5106.* 61st Cong., 2d Sess. [February, 1910] Washington, 1910.

———, *Uniform Classification of Freight, Hearings.* 63d Cong., 2d Sess. [March-May, 1914] Washington, 1914.

U.S. Senate, Select Committee on Interstate Commerce, *Report.* Senate Report No. 46, 49th Cong., 1st Sess., January 18, 1886. Washington, 1886.

——, *Testimony*. 49th Cong., 1st Sess. [May 20-November 18, 1885] Washington, 1886.

U.S. Treasury Department, *Report on the Internal Commerce of the United States, December 1, 1879*. Washington, 1879.

Reports and Proceedings

Advisory Commission, *Report of Messrs. Thurman, Washburne & Cooley, Constituting an Advisory Commission on Differential Rates by Railroads*. New York, 1882.

Board of Arbitration, *Argument Regarding the Division of East Bound Freight from Chicago between the Terminal Roads, Submitted to the Board of Arbitration, August, 1879*. New York, 1879.

Bureau of Railway Economics, *The Conflict Between Federal and State Regulation of the Railroads*. Bulletin No. 15. Washington, 1911.

Chamber of Commerce of State of New York, *On the Proposed Increase of Power to the Interstate Commerce Commission*. New York, 1905.

Interstate Commerce Law Association, *Proceedings of Conferences between Presidents of Railroad Lines West of Chicago and St. Louis and Representatives of Banking Houses, January 8th and 10th, 1889*. New York, 1889.

Joint Executive Committee, *Proceedings, 1877-1880*. New York, 1878-80.

——, *Proceedings of the Joint Executive Committee*. September 16, 1880. New York, 1880.

——, *Proceedings and Circulars, 1882*. New York, 1882.

——, *Proceedings and Circulars, 1883*. New York, 1883-84.

Joint Executive Committee, Passenger Department, *Proceedings*. June 12-14, 1883. New York, 1883.

Joint Rate Association, *Proceedings and Circulars of the Joint Rate Committee of the Trunk Line, Central Traffic and Western Freight Associations, 1889 and 1890*. Chicago, 1891.

Joint Traffic Association, *Proceedings of the Board of Managers of the Joint Traffic Association, December 13, 1895, to June 30, 1896*. New York [?], 1896 [?].

National Association of Manufacturers, *Proceedings of the Ninth Annual Convention—1904, May 17-19, 1904, Pittsburg, Penna*. New York, 1904.

———, *Proceedings of the Tenth Annual Convention, Atlanta, Ga., May 16-18, 1905*. New York, 1905.

———, *Proceedings of the Eleventh Annual Convention, New York, May 14-16, 1906*. New York, 1906.

———, *Fifteenth Annual Convention, New York, May 16-18, 1910*. New York, 1910.

National Association of Railway Commissioners, *Proceedings of the Committee on Uniform Classification, Annual Convention of Railroad Commissioners, New York, October 23, 1895*. Dittoed.

———, *Proceedings of the Twenty-Fifth Annual Convention, October 28-31, 1913*. New York, 1914.

National Board of Trade, *Proceedings of the Eleventh Annual Meeting, Washington, December, 1880*. Boston, 1881.

———, *Proceedings of the Fourteenth Annual Meeting, Washington, January, 1884*. Boston, 1884.

———, *Proceedings of the Fifteenth Annual Meeting, Washington, January, 1885*. Boston, 1885.

———, *Proceedings of the Sixteenth Annual Meeting, Washington, January, 1886*. Boston, 1886.

———, *Proceedings of the Twenty-First Annual Meeting, New Orleans, December, 1890*. Boston, 1891.

National Civic Federation, *Proceedings of the National Conference on Trusts and Combinations, Chicago, October 22-25, 1907*. Chicago, 1908.

National Convention of Railroad Commissioners, *Report of Committee on Pooling of Freight, etc.* April, 1894. N.p., 1894.

New York Board of Trade and Transportation, *Report of the Special Committee on Railway Freight Grievances.* New York, 1883.

Official Stenographer's Report of the Testimony of Charles S. Mellen and Edward D. Robbins Before the Hon. Charles A. Prouty at Boston, Mass., May 2, 1913. Boston, 1913.

Philadelphia Bourse, *A Report Submitted by a Sub-Committee to the Joint Committee on Reasonable Regulation of Railroads, March 14, 1916.* Philadelphia, 1916.

Railway Business Association, *Defects in Railroad Regulation.* Bulletin No. 18, April 10, 1916. New York, 1916.

Southern Railway and Steamship Association, *Agreement and Rules Adopted in Convention at Atlanta, Ga.* Atlanta, 1875.

———, *Proceedings of the Convention.* Atlanta, 1875-76.

Trans-Mississippi Commercial Congress, *16th Session of Trans-Mississippi Commercial Congress, Proceedings, Portland, Ore., August 16-19, 1905.* St. Louis [?], 1905.

Trunk Line Association, *Articles of Association of the Trunk Lines—Copy of Trunk Line Contract of February 20th, 1889.* Philadelphia, 1894.

Articles, Speeches, and Pamphlets

Adams, Charles Francis, Jr., *The Federation of the Railroad System.* Boston, 1880.

———, "The Interstate Commerce Law," [December, 1888] *Compendium of Transportation Theories,* C. C. McCain, ed. Washington, 1893. Pp. 178-184.

Ashley, Ossian D., *Railroad Corporations and the People*. New York, 1893.

Baker, Ray Stannard, "Railroads and Popular Unrest," *Collier's*, xxxvii (June 9, 1906), 19-22.

———, "Railroads on Trial: How Railroads Make Public Opinion," *McClure's Magazine*, xxvi (March, 1906), 535-549.

Baumgartner, J. Hampton, *Address Before the Virginia Press Association, June 13, 1913*. N.p., 1913.

———, *Address Before the Conference of Railway Executives' Advisory Committee, Washington, May 27, 1916*. N.p., n.d.

Benton, John E., "The State Commissions and the Interstate Commerce Commission," in Interstate Commerce Commission, *Exercises Commemorating the Fifty Years' Service of the Interstate Commerce Commission* (Washington, 1937). Pp. 22-36.

Blanchard, G. R., *Argument Before the Committee of the United States Senate on Interstate Commerce, March 2, 1894*. N.p., 1894.

———, *Reply to S. M. Cullom*. [Reprint of an article in *Railway Age and Northwestern Railroader*, April 14, 1893] Chicago, 1893.

———, "Shall Railway Pooling Be Permitted," *The Forum*, v (August, 1888), 652-665.

———, *Traffic Unity, popularly called "Railway Pools."* New York, 1884.

———, *Why Pooling Should Be Legalized: A Letter to the Hon. Shelby M. Cullom, June 9, 1890*. N.p., 1890.

Blum, John M., "Theodore Roosevelt and the Hepburn Act: Toward an Orderly System of Control," in *The Letters of Theodore Roosevelt*. Elting E. Morison, ed. v. vi. Cambridge, 1952. Pp. 1558-1571.

———, "Theodore Roosevelt and the Legislative Process: Tariff Revision and Railroad Regulation, 1904-

1906," *The Letters of Theodore Roosevelt.* Elting E. Morison, ed. v. iv. Cambridge, 1951. Pp. 1333-1342.

Brandeis, Louis D., *Brief on Behalf of the Traffic Committee of Commercial Organizations of the Atlantic Seaboard, January 3, 1911, Docket No. 3400. . . .* Boston, 1911.

Brown, William C., *Address Before the Buffalo Chamber of Commerce, April 18, 1907.* N.p., 1907.

———, *Speech Before the Michigan Manufacturers' Association, Detroit, June 22, 1908.* N.p., 1908.

Bush, Benjamin F., *Address Before the Missouri Press Association, September 17, 1914.* N.p., n.d.

Carnegie, Andrew, "My Experience with Railway Rates and Rebates," *The Century Magazine,* lxxv (March, 1908), 722-728.

Clements, Judson C., *Address Before the Atlanta Freight Bureau, January 12, 1909.* N.p., n.d.

Cooley, Thomas M., *Address Before the Boston Merchant's Association, January 8, 1889.* N.p., 1889.

———, "The Interstate Commerce Act—Pooling and Combinations Which Affect Its Operation," [January, 1889] *Compendium of Transportation Theories,* C. C. McCain, ed. Washington, 1893. Pp. 242-250.

———, "Popular and Legal Views of Traffic Pooling," *The Railway Review,* xxvii (January 8, 1887), 15-17.

———, "Railroad Commissions," *The Railway Review,* xxiii (February 10, 1883), 71-72.

———, "The Railway Problem Defined," [March, 1891] *Compendium of Transportation Theories,* C. C. McCain, ed. Washington, 1893. Pp. 7-19.

———, *Speech Before the 3rd Annual Meeting of National Association of Railway Commissioners, 1891.* N.p., 1891 [?].

Crandall, Ruth, "American Railroad Presidents in the 1870's: Their Backgrounds and Careers," *Explora-*

tions in Entrepreneurial History, II (July 15, 1950), 282-296.

Creelman, James, "All is Not Damned," *Pearson's Magazine*, XV (June, 1906), 543-554.

Delano, Frederic A., *Address Before the Economic Club of New York, April 29, 1913*. N.p., n.d.

Destler, Chester McArthur, "The Opposition of American Businessmen to Social Control During the 'Gilded Age,'" *Mississippi Valley Historical Review*, XXXIX (March, 1953), 641-672.

Doster, James F., "The Conflict Over Railroad Regulation in Alabama," *Business History Review,* XXVIII (December, 1954), 329-342.

Dunn, Samuel O., "Uniform Classification," *The Railway Age Gazette*, XLVII (September 3, 1909), 413-414.

———, "The Interstate Commerce Commission and the Railroads," *Annals of the American Academy of Political and Social Science*, LXIII (January, 1916), 155-172.

Elliott, Howard, *Address Before the Publicity Club of Minneapolis, January 10, 1912*. St. Paul, 1912.

Evan, J. D., "Federal vs. State Regulation," *Van Norden Magazine*, II (August, 1907), 53-56.

Fink, Albert, "The Legislative Regulation of Railroads," *The Engineering Magazine*, IX (July, 1895), 623-634.

———, *Relative Cost of Carload and Less than Carload Shipments and Its Bearing Upon Freight Classification*. Chicago, 1889.

Finley, William Wilson, *The Railway as the Business Man's Partner*. New York, 1911.

Gilchrist, D. T., "Albert Fink and the Pooling System," *Business History Review*, XXXIV (Spring, 1960), 24-49.

Graser, Ferdinand H., "Purpose and Work of the Interstate Commission," *The Railway World*, L (May 11, 1906), 389-391.

Grosvenor, W. M., "The Communist and the Railway," *The International Review*, IV (September, 1877), 585-599.

Harrison, Fairfax, *Speech Before the Transportation Club of Indianapolis, March 31, 1911*. N.p., 1911.

Hill, James J., *Address Before the Kansas City, Mo., Commercial Club, November 19, 1907*. N.p., n.d.

———, *Letter of James J. Hill to Hon. John A. Johnson, Governor of Minnesota, January 14, 1907*. N.p., 1907.

Hines, Walker D., *Speech Before Railway Business Association, New York, November 22, 1911*. New York, 1911.

———, "The Conflict Between State and Federal Regulation of Railroads," *Annals of the American Academy of Political and Social Science*, LXIII (January, 1916), 191-198.

Hudson, Henry, "The Southern Railway & Steamship Association," *The Quarterly Journal of Economics*, V (October, 1890), 70-94.

Huntington, Collis P., "A Plea for Railway Consolidation," [September, 1891] *Compendium of Transportation Theories*, C. C. McCain, ed. Washington, 1893. Pp. 251-259.

Johnson, L. E., *Address Before the Western Society of Engineers, Chicago, November 2, 1915*. N.p., n.d.

Kirkman, Marshall M., *The Relation of the Railroads of the United States to the People and the Commercial and Financial Interests of the Country*. Chicago, 1885.

Knapp, Martin A., *Address Before the Railway Business Association, New York, November 22, 1910*. New York, 1910.

———, "National Regulation of Railroads," *The Annals*

of the *American Academy of Political and Social Science*, XXVI (November, 1905), 613-628.

———, "The Public and the Railways," *The Annals of the American Academy of Political and Social Science*, XXXII (July, 1908), 97-101.

———, *Speech Before Railway Congress at Columbian Exposition, June 23, 1893.* Chicago, 1893.

———, and Paul Morton, *Speeches Before the National Association of Merchants and Travelers, August 7, 1899.* N.p., 1899.

Lane, Franklin K., "Railroad Capitalization and Federal Regulation," *Review of Reviews* (June, 1908).

Lee, Ivy L., *Address, February 9, 1914.* St. Louis, 1914.

———, *Address Before the American Association for the Advancement of Science, Columbus, Ohio, December 30, 1915.* N.p., 1915.

———, "Railroad Valuation," *The Bankers' Magazine* (July, 1907).

Meyer, Ernest C., "Judge Cooley's Contribution to the Interstate Commerce Commission," *Detroit Law Review*, VII (March, 1937).

Midgley, J. W., "Why Private Car Lines Were Overlooked in the Esch-Townsend Bill," *The Railroad Gazette*, XXXVIII (April 14, 1905), 357-358.

Miller, George H., "Origins of the Iowa Granger Law," *Mississippi Valley Historical Review*, XL (March, 1954), 657-680.

Moseley, Edward A., *Speech Before the Pennsylvania Millers' State Association, September, 1900.* Washington, 1900.

Mudge, H. U., *Address Before the Commercial Club of Topeka, Kansas, April 11, 1911.* N.p., n.d.

Nash, Gerald D., "Origins of the Interstate Commerce Act of 1887," *Pennsylvania History*, XXIV (July, 1957), 181-190.

Nimmo, Joseph, Jr., *A Commercial and Political Danger*. Washington, 1902.

———, *Criticism of the Eleventh Annual Report of the Interstate Commerce Commission*. N.p., 1898.

———, *Form of Bill to Secure the Just and Orderly Conduct of the American Railroad System, July 17, 1893*. N.p., 1893.

———, *Joseph Nimmo, Jr., to Aldace Walker, May 26, 1890*. N.p., 1890.

———, *Pooling and Governmental Control of the Railroads*. Washington, 1888.

———, *The Railroad Problem*. [reprinted from U.S. Treasury, *Annual Report on the Internal Commerce of the United States*, October 1881] Washington, 1881.

———, *State and National Regulation of Railroads: Memorandum of December 10, 1908*. Washington, 1908.

Peabody, James, "The Necessity of Railway Compacts Under Governmental Regulation," *The Independent*, XLV (June 1, 1893), 737-738.

Petroleum Producers' Union, *A Brief History of the Standard Oil Company*. [Penna.?] ca. 1880.

———, *A History of the Organization, Purposes and Transactions of the General Council of the Petroleum Producers' Unions . . . From 1878 to 1880*. Titusville, Penna., 1880.

Prentis, Robert R., "The Relation Between National and State Railway Regulation," *The Railway Age Gazette*, LIX (December 31, 1915), 1229.

Prouty, Charles A., *Address Before the Economics Club of Boston, March 9, 1905*. N.p., 1905.

———, *Address Before Nineteenth Annual Convention of the National Hay Association, Kansas City, Mo., July 16, 1912*. N.p., 1912.

———, "Competition and Railway Rates," *Illinois Manu-*

facturers' Association Bulletin, May, 1902, pp. 3-9.

———, "National Regulation of Railways," *Publications of the American Economic Association* (Third Series) IV (February, 1903), 71-83.

———, "The President and the Railroads," *The Century Magazine*, LXXI (February, 1906), 644-653.

———, "Railway Pooling—From the People's Point of View," *The Forum*, XXIV (December, 1897), 454-460.

———, "The Rate Bill: What It Is and What It Will Do," *The American Monthly Review of Reviews*, XXXIV (July, 1906), 65-70.

Rea, Samuel, *Address Before the New York Chamber of Commerce, December 3, 1914*. N.p., n.d.

Rice, W. W., speech in the House of Representatives on December 8, 1884, reprinted as *Interstate Commerce*. Washington, 1885.

Rich, Edgar J., *Address Before the Massachusetts Board of Trade, February 7, 1906*. Boston, 1906.

Schoonmaker, Augustus, "The Interstate Commerce Commission and Its Work," *The Railroad Gazette*, XXIII (October 16, 1891), 725-726.

———, "Unity of Railways and Railway Interests," *Compendium of Transportation Theories*. C. C. McCain, ed. Washington, 1893. Pp. 57-66.

Scott, Thomas A., "The Recent Strikes," *The North American Review*, CXXIV (September, 1877), 351-362.

Shinn, William P., "The Relations of Railways to the State," *The Railway Review*, XXVI (March 6, 13, 1886), 109-110, 121-122.

Shonts, Theodore P., *Address Before the Appanoose Chautauqua, Centerville, Iowa, August 27, 1908*. N.p., 1908.

———, *The Square Deal in Business and the Candidacy*

of William Howard Taft. [reprinted from *Chicago Tribune*, August 28, 1908] N.p., 1908.

Sisson, Francis H., "Regional Railroad Control Proposed on Same Plan as a Reserve Bank System," *Journal of the American Bankers Association*, IX (August, 1916), 110-112.

Spencer, Samuel, *Address Before the Traffic Club of Pittsburg, April 7, 1905.* N.p., n.d.

———, *An Address Delivered Before the Board of Trade of the City of Newark, October 11, 1905.* N.p., n.d.

———, "Railway Rates and Industrial Progress," *The Century Magazine*, LXXI (January, 1906), 380-387.

Sproule, William, *Address Before the Annual Dinner of the Chamber of Commerce of San Francisco, December 9, 1912.* N.p., n.d.

Stetson, Francis Lynde, *Address Before the Economic Club of New York, June 5, 1907.* N.p., n.d.

Stickney, A. B., "Legislative Regulation of Railroad Rates," *Political Science Quarterly*, XXI (March, 1906), 28-37.

Taft, William Howard, *Address Before the Annual Dinner of the Traffic Club of New York, February 21, 1916.* New York, 1916.

Thayer, John B., *Speech Before the Buffalo Chamber of Commerce, April 18, 1907.* N.p., 1907.

Thurber, F. B., *The Relations of Railroads to the Public.* Washington, 1879 [?].

Trumbull, Frank, *Address Delivered at a Dinner to E. P. Ripley, Chicago, October 30, 1915.* N.p., 1915.

———, *Address Before the National Hay Association, Cedar Point, Ohio, July 12, 1916.* New York, 1916.

———, "The Evolution of Business Methods," *The Railway Age Gazette*, LIII (November 29, 1912), 1046-1047.

Unsigned, "Tainted News," *Colliers*, XXXIX (May 4, 1907), 13-15.

Veazey, W. G., *Address Before the Railway Congress, Columbian Exposition, June 21, 1893.* Chicago, 1893.

Walker, Aldace F., *Aldace F. Walker to E. P. Bacon, April 23, 1900.* N.p., 1900.

———, "The Amendment of the Interstate Commerce Law," *The Independent*, XLV (June 1, 1893), 733-735.

———, *Argument Before Senate Committee on Interstate Commerce, June 4, 1890.* Washington, 1890.

———, "Has the Interstate Commerce Law Been Beneficial?" *The Forum*, XVII (April, 1894), 207-216.

———, "The Pooling of Railway Earnings," *The Railway Magazine*, II (February, 1897), 122-123.

———, *Railway Associations.* Chicago, 1890.

———, *Speech Before the National Transportation Association, November, 1892.* Chicago, 1892.

———, *Speech Before the Sunset Club, Chicago, April 2, 1891.* Chicago, 1891.

———, "Unregulated Competition Self-Destructive," *The Forum*, XII (December, 1891), 505-518.

Welliver, Judson C., *Catching Up With Roosevelt.* [reprint from *Munsey's Magazine*, March, 1912] New York, 1912.

White, Edward J., *State and Federal Control of Carriers*, [a paper to the Kansas State Bar Association] January 27, 1916. N.p., 1916.

Wiebe, Robert H., "Business Disunity and the Progressive Movement, 1901-1914," *Mississippi Valley Historical Review*, XLIV (March, 1958), 664-685.

Willard, Daniel, *Address at Dartmouth College, March 22, 1915.* N.p., 1915.

———, *Address Before the American Newspaper Publishers' Association, April 27, 1916.* N.p., 1916.

———, "Effect of the Rate Advance Decision," *The Railway Age Gazette*, LVIII (January 1, 1915), 8-9.

———, and F. A. Delano, *The Case for Increased Rates*. [brief to I.C.C., November 24, 1913] N.p., 1913.

Willcox, David, "Governmental Rate Making is Unnecessary and Would be Very Dangerous," *North American Review*, CLXXX (March, 1905), 410-429.

———, "Proposed Interstate Commerce Legislation," *The Railway World*, XLIX (February 3, 1905), 87-90.

Williams, W. H., *Address Before the Traffic Club of New York, November 24, 1908*. New York, 1908.

Wright, John A., "Control of Railways by the General Government," *The Railway World*, XXI (August 17, 1877), 771-775.

INDEX

Act of 1887, *see* Interstate Commerce Act of 1887

Adams, Charles Francis, Jr., 16, 28, 47; and I.C.C., 57, 59-61; on pooling, 29, 58; on railroad commissions, 36-37, 43, 46; and Woodrow Wilson, 214

Adamson Act of 1916, 226-27

Addyston Pipe and Steel Co. decision, 83n

Alabama Midland Ry decision, 81, 85

Aldrich, Nelson W., 108, 131, 137, 139, 140, 143-44, 151, 159, 186, 191, 194

Allison, William B., 108, 135, 139, 143

antitrust law and railroads, 179. *See also* pools, railroads, Sherman Act

Archbald, Robert W., 201-02

Bacon, Edward P., 93-94, 98-99, 102-05

Bailey, Joseph W., 140-41, 144

Baker, Ray Stannard, 94, 113, 118n-19n

bankruptcies, 7-8, 67, 173

Baumgartner, J. Hampton, 225

Benson, Lee, 16n, 21, 23-24

Bernstein, Marver, 168-69

Bird, A. C., 119

Blanchard, George R., 29, 38, 71, 73, 79

Bliss, William, 45

Blum, John M., 127, 139, 143

Bonaparte, Charles J., 113, 162

Bragg, Walter L., 49, 68

Brandeis, Louis D., 156, 160-61, 196, 210

Bristow, Joseph L., 188

Brown, William C., 167, 181-82

Bryan, William Jennings, 56, 175

Buck, Solon J., 20

Bureau of Corporations, 160

Bureau of Railway Economics, 205

Caldwell, B. D., 120

Calhoun, William J., 85n

Camden, J. N., 44n

Campbell, E. G., 65

Cannon, Joseph, 108, 136, 186

Carnegie, Andrew, 96, 138

Cassatt, Alexander J.; background, 96-97; efforts to rationalize industry, 97, 99; and Hepburn Bill, 130, 134, 139-40, 146, 153; and railroad legislation, 111n, 117, 236

Chandler, William E., 72

Chicago Inter-Ocean, 41

Chicago Railway Review, 38

Clapp, Moses E., 139

Clark, Edgar E., 197

Clayton Act of 1914, 229

Clements, Judson C., 79, 178, 208-09

Cleveland, Grover, 46-48

Cochran, Thomas C., 29n

Commerce Court; background of, 103, 198; demise of, 198-202; and I.C.C., 116; Insurgents and, 190; railroad support, 181-82, 186-87, 198; Taft and, 180, 184

Commercial and Financial Chronicle, 201

commodity clause, 163-64

competition, 3-4, 17, 20, 30n,

(265)

AMERICAN HISTORY TITLES IN THE NORTON LIBRARY